SSS: Social Skill Strategies (Book B)

A CURRICULUM FOR ADOLESCENTS

by

Nancy Gajewski

Patty Mayo

THINKING PUBLICATIONS® Eau Claire, WI

A Division of McKinley Companies, Inc.

© 1989 Thinking Publications®
A Division of McKinley Companies, Inc.

Thinking Publications grants limited rights to individual professionals to reproduce and distribute pages that indicate duplication is permissible. Pages can be used for student instruction only and must include Thinking Publications' copyright notice. All rights are reserved for pages without the permission-to-reprint notice. No part of these pages may be reproduced in any form, electronic or mechanical, including photocopy, recording, or any information storage and retrieval system without permission in writing from the publisher.

00   99   98   97   96   95   94   10   9   8   7   6   5

ISBN   0-930599-52-7

Illustrations: Brad Krause and Linda Lofgren
Cover: James Christoffersen
Cover Design: Robert T. Baker

Printed in the United States of America

A Division of McKinley Companies, Inc.

P.O. Box 163
Eau Claire, WI 54702-0163
-2488
FAX 1-715-832-9082

DEDICATION

To our parents Gerald and Henrietta Wildman
and Everett and Barbara White for their love and
guidance, and to our husbands Luke and Mike
for their encouragement and support

ACKNOWLEDGEMENTS

The authors would like to express their appreciation to all those who have helped in the completion of this curriculum. We thank Barb Bialzik, Wendy Drew, Suzanne Gallagher, Arlene Craker, Mary Knapstein, and Kathie Martino for generously devoting their time in field testing units from **SSS** with their students, and Al Wheeler for his critique of Chapter Two. A very special thank you to Vicki Lord Larson, Sue Gruber, Walter Harris, Polly Hirn, Pattii Waldo, and Jill Wheeler for their many, many hours in reviewing **SSS** in its entirety. An additional thank you to Pattii Waldo, who allowed some of the activity pages she created to be included in **SSS**. We are grateful to Nancy McKinley for her technical and editorial advice and for making it possible for us to share this curriculum with you. Finally, we thank our husbands, Luke Gajewski and Mike Mayo, for their encouragement, support, and patience.

PREFACE

Social skill competence is critical for a person to function productively in the home, school, and community. Yet, many of the students in our educational systems, both in and out of special education programs, remain socially incompetent. The purpose of **SSS: Social Skill Strategies** is to provide a comprehensive curriculum which can be used with pre-adolescents and adolescents (grades 5-12). Adults with social skill deficits might also benefit from specific **SSS** activities if the activities are carefully chosen by professionals.

Special education teachers, speech-language clinicians, guidance counselors, school psychologists, reading specialists, and alternative or regular education teachers will find **SSS** to be an invaluable source for promoting social communication skill gains with their students.

Chapter One reviews the current literature in social skill training. Chapter Two describes 1) how to identify students with social skill needs; 2) how to structure a social skills class; 3) how to teach a social skill unit using a seven-step approach; and 4) how to promote transfer and generalization of social skills taught. The major portion of **SSS** offers social skill units which include several activity pages to be used with students to improve their comprehension and use of each social skill. The activity pages have been written at a third grade reading level according to the Fry (1977) readability formula and at a fifth grade reading level according to the Dale-Chall (1948) readability formula.

We feel that the social skills addressed within this program are universal across cultural and socio-economic groups, with the exception of a few skills (e.g., the rules for eye contact and proximity are different in the Oriental and Italian cultures.) The user of this curriculum, however, may choose to adapt some of the specific names or situations described within the units, to meet the needs of the students being taught.

This curriculum is a framework and does not take the place of a teacher's individual creativity or need for flexibility. We sincerely hope you find **SSS: Social Skill Strategies** to be a useful resource for improving the social communication skills within your students.

Nancy Gajewski
Teacher of the Emotionally Disturbed
D.C. Everest Jr. High School

Patty Mayo
Speech-Language Clinician
D.C. Everest Jr. High School

TABLE OF CONTENTS

INTRODUCTORY SKILLS (BOOK A)

    Skill A-1.   Eye Contact
    Skill A-2.   Manners
    Skill A-3.   Volume
    Skill A-4.   Time And Place
    Skill A-5.   Tone Of Voice
    Skill A-6.   Getting To The Point
    Skill A-7.   Staying On Topic And Switching Topics
    Skill A-8.   Listening
    Skill A-9.   Starting, Maintaining, And Ending A Conversation
    Skill A-10.   Proximity
    Skill A-11.   Body Language
    Skill A-12.   Making A Good Impression
    Skill A-13.   Formal/Informal Language

GENERAL INTERACTION SKILLS (BOOK A)

    Skill A-14.   Giving Reasons
    Skill A-15.   Planning What To Say
    Skill A-16.   Interrupting
    Skill A-17.   Giving A Compliment
    Skill A-18.   Accepting A Compliment
    Skill A-19.   Saying Thank You
    Skill A-20.   Introducing Yourself
    Skill A-21.   Introducing Two People To Each Other
    Skill A-22.   Making A Request
    Skill A-23.   Offering Help
    Skill A-24.   Asking For Help
    Skill A-25.   Asking Permission
    Skill A-26.   Accepting NO
    Skill A-27.   Making An Apology
    Skill A-28.   Stating An Opinion
    Skill A-29.   Agreeing/Disagreeing
    Skill A-30.   Convincing Others
    Skill A-31.   Giving Information
    Skill A-32.   Dealing With Contradictions
    Skill A-33.   Being Honest
    Skill A-34.   Being Optimistic

CREDITS

The cognitive planning strategy (Figure 1. The MBC Poster) on page 17 is from Walter J. Harris, Ph.D. ***Making Better Choices: A Curriculum for Teaching Cognitive Planning and Social Skills to Improve Social and Academic Behavior.*** Orono, ME: MBC Publications, 1987. Reprinted with permission.

The cooperative learning and traditional learning groups chart on page 5 and the 18 aspects of a cooperative learning lesson on pages 24, 349-350 are from David W. Johnson and Roger T. Johnson. ***Cooperation in the Classroom.*** Edina, MN: Interaction Book Company, 1984. Reprinted with permission.

Chapter One

A RESEARCH FOUNDATION

SOCIAL COMMUNICATION SKILLS: THE NEW WAVE

During the past decade, awareness of the need for teaching social skills to exceptional children has intensified. This heightened concern about the social competence of individuals with behavioral/emotional disturbances, learning disabilities, mental retardation, and speech/language disorders results from a plethora of research documenting the limited acceptance of handicapped students by their non-handicapped peers (Perlmutter, Crocker, Cordray, and Garstecki, 1983; Schloss, Schloss, Wood, and Kiehl, 1986; Schumaker and Hazel, 1984a).

Individuals With Emotional Disturbances/Behavioral Disorders

Schloss et al. (1986) state that "The main distinguishing characteristic of behaviorally disordered persons is deficits in social skill performance" (p. 1). Kauffman (1977) characterizes behaviorally disordered children as ". . . those who chronically and markedly respond to their environment in socially unacceptable and/or personally unsatisfying ways" (p. 23). Numerous studies have documented the correlation between social skill deficits and problems later in life: Juvenile delinquency (Roff, Sells, and Golden, 1972), psychiatric hospitalization (Goldsmith and McFall, 1975), bad conduct discharges from the military (Roff, 1961), and other problems have been associated with social skill deficits. Thus, it is essential for individuals with emotional/behavioral disorders to receive social skill instruction and to improve their social competence if they are to function adequately in society.

Individuals With Learning Disabilities

In an extensive review of research in the area of learning disabilities, Schumaker and Hazel (1984a) summarized empirical evidence indicating that learning disabled students have numerous problems with social skills. For example, learning disabled children are less liked than their non-learning disabled peers (Perlmutter et al., 1983), they perform similarly to juvenile delinquents on a role play test of social skills (Schumaker, Hazel, Sherman, and Sheldon, 1982), they participate with the lowest frequency among groups of low participators in school activities (Deshler and Schumaker, 1983), and their social problems continue into adulthood (Vetter, 1983). According to Schumaker and Hazel (1984b), the following weaknesses in interpersonal interactions were found in learning disabled children: 1) They tend to choose less socially acceptable behaviors in different situations; 2) They are inept at predicting consequences for behaviors; 3) They misunderstand different social cues; 4) They are less likely to adapt their behavior to meet the needs of their listener; 5) They exhibit a lower occurrence of appropriate verbal/nonverbal skills than their non-handicapped peers, and 6) They perform certain inappropriate skills at a significantly higher level of occurrence. Traditionally, learning disability programs have addressed academic weaknesses such as reading and spelling; however, weaknesses in social communication skill competence should also be remediated.

Individuals With Mental Retardation

Greenspan and Shoultz (1981) report that mentally retarded workers are significantly more likely to be terminated from employment for social skill deficits than for non-social reasons. If handicapped individuals are unable to compensate for their academic deficits through social competence, they are more likely to be underemployed and less likely to be satisfied than their non-handicapped peers (White, Schumaker, Warner, Alley, and Deshler, 1980). A comprehensive vocational training program for mentally retarded individuals must include a social communication skills component.

Individuals With Speech/Language Disorders

According to Wiig (1982a), social skill development is delayed in many exceptional students and has been found to develop as late as adolescence. Shames and Wiig (1982) document a need for social skill instruction with adolescents who have language disorders, developmental delays, severe hearing impairments, or who have been raised in a non-English speaking culture. Wiig (1982a) indicates additional needs for adults with acquired aphasia, for congenitally blind adolescents, and for shy children in regular classrooms. It is evident that social communication skills should be assessed and remediated within students who have speech/language disorders.

SOCIAL COMMUNICATION SKILLS: HOW ARE THESE SKILLS DEFINED?

Despite the recent upsurge in interest to improve social skills, confusion exists because of a lack of consensus among researchers regarding the specificity of definitions for social skills (Gresham, 1981a; Schumaker and Hazel, 1984a). According to Schloss et al. (1986), "Two approaches to the conceptualization of social skills are present in current literature. The first provides a general reference to the broad domain of social adjustment. The second identifies discrete behaviors recognized as contributing to social adjustment" (p. 2). Foster and Ritchey (1979) propose that social skills may be considered a part of a broader construct known as social competence. Hazel, Sherman, Schumaker, and Sheldon (1985) believe that social competence may be seen as a composite of skills:

1. Determining which social behaviors are appropriate in situations.
2. Determining which verbal and nonverbal social skills are appropriate.
3. Performing social skills fluently and in correct combinations.
4. Correctly perceiving verbal and nonverbal cues from another person(s).
5. Flexibly adjusting to feedback from another person(s).

The authors of this resource support the view proposed by Hazel et al. (1985), that being a socially appropriate individual requires more than correct execution of isolated social skills.

SOCIAL COMMUNICATION SKILLS: WHAT TYPES OF DEFICITS EXIST?

Gresham (1981b) has conceptualized social skill deficits along three dimensions: skill deficits, performance deficits, and self-control deficits. A *skill deficit* would indicate that the person has not acquired the necessary social skills (e.g., a child who accepts a compliment poorly because he was never taught to say "thank you"). This type of deficit would also include people with language disorders who have word-finding difficulties, or problems sequencing what they want to say.

2

A **performance deficit** describes the person who has the skills but does not perform them because of response-inhibiting anxiety or low motivation. For example, learning disabled individuals' feelings of incompetence might cause them not to use social skills even though the skills are present in their repertoires (Pearl, Donahue, and Bryan, 1983).

A **self-control deficit** labels the person who lacks adequate behavior controls to inhibit impulsive, disruptive, or aggressive social behavior (e.g., a child may possess the social skill of negotiating and may even use the skill at various times; however, his lack of self-control may sometimes get in the way of his performance of the skill). Schumaker and Hazel (1984a) suggest that any single child's deficits may be a combination of the three deficits (e.g., the absence of eye contact may represent a performance deficit, while the same child's inability to start a conversation may represent a skill deficit). Social skill instruction must address each of the three deficit types when they exist.

SOCIAL COMMUNICATION SKILLS: ASSESSMENT

Handicapped students are a heterogeneous group with respect to their social skill abilities, and an assessment system is needed to determine the individual needs for each student. Unfortunately, few acceptable assessment procedures have been developed (Arkowitz, 1981).

Gresham (1982) shares the concern that few, if any, well-standardized instruments have been developed to assess the social skill competence of handicapped children. He states that, "Generally speaking, advancements in the assessment of social skills have not kept pace with the advancements in social skill training techniques" (p. 128). Gresham also maintains that our lack of assessment procedures creates problems for our understanding of the "nature" of social skills, for our planning, and for our evaluation of training success (Gresham, 1981a).

Arkowitz (1981) suggests the following criteria for adequately measuring social skills:

1. Measure a person's behaviors as well as the consequences of those behaviors.
2. Identify overt behaviors and cognitive behaviors.
3. Look at quality and quantity of behaviors.
4. Determine if social skills are a part of the person's repertoire.
5. Look at the use of social skills in situations of interest.

Gresham (1981b) reminds us that a social skills assessment device should be psychometrically acceptable (i.e., have good reliability and validity, be sensitive to changes in the student, and give specific diagnostic information for instructional programming). Schumaker and Hazel (1984a) assert that in order to be useful to educators, a social skills assessment device should be quick and easy to administer and not require additional resources. While a number of social skill assessment devices exist (Goldstein, Sprafkin, Gershaw, and Klein, 1980; Jackson, Jackson, and Monroe, 1983; Wiig, 1982a; Wiig, 1982b), no single device meets all of the above criteria.

Social skill assessment devices can be categorized into six general types: 1) Naturalistic behavioral observation; 2) Analogue observation, which involves direct observation in contrived rather than naturalistic settings; 3) Behavioral rating scales; 4) Behavioral checklists; 5) Sociometric devices, which involve peer assessment; and 6) Assessments using hypothetical situations (Gresham, 1981b; Schumaker and Hazel, 1984a). After reviewing the advantages and disadvantages of the aforementioned assessment types, Schumaker and Hazel (1984a) recommend the use of behavioral rating scales for screening older individuals. They also state that "Behavioral checklists seem to be the most practical instruments for teachers to use for pinpointing target behaviors; preferably, they should be used in conjunction with contrived situations in the natural environment" (p. 429). **SSS: Social Skill Strategies** provides behavioral rating scales and checklists for the social skills taught within the curriculum. (See Appendices A, B, C, and D.)

SOCIAL COMMUNICATION SKILLS: HOW TO TEACH THESE SKILLS

Several procedures have been used to improve social skill competence, but procedures should be chosen according to which type of deficit the individual is thought to exhibit. For a skill deficit, procedures should focus on teaching the student how to perform different skills (Schumaker and Hazel, 1984b). Stephens (1978) presents evidence that for skill deficits, modeling and coaching are best used to teach new skills. Schumaker and Hazel (1984b) advocate the use of description, modeling, rehearsal, and feedback for teaching new skills.

Performance deficits are best remediated through manipulation of antecedents or consequences of behaviors (Gresham, 1981b). Schumaker and Hazel (1984b) recommend that for a performance deficit, procedures should focus on motivating individuals to increase their use of appropriate social skills.

For self-control deficits, procedures should focus on teaching strategies that decrease the use of inappropriate behaviors and that promote the use of more appropriate behaviors. Reports show that self-control deficits have been remediated through a variety of cognitive behavior modification techniques such as self-control training, self instruction, verbal mediation, relaxation, and self reinforcement (O'Leary and Dubey, 1979). **SSS: Social Skill Strategies** includes techniques and activities appropriate for the three social skill deficit types.

In addition, the educator should promote social skill acquisition and use through group interaction rather than through teacher-directed activities. The use of cooperative learning techniques is an effective way to encourage group interaction. When educators plan a lesson, they choose between structuring that lesson in these ways: 1) A competitive manner in which students participate in an activity to determine who is best; 2) An individual manner where students work alone and at their own pace, or 3) A cooperative manner where small groups of individuals work together to achieve an academic goal. Each of these three techniques has merit. Unfortunately, our current educational system utilizes competitive and individual methods the vast majority of the time.

The theory of cooperative learning is not new; however, it has been revived in the 1970s and 1980s by professionals such as David Johnson and Roger Johnson (1984), Robert Slavin (1974), and Elliot Aronson (1978). Currently, the research is filled with information about the academic and social benefits of cooperative learning. According to Johnson and Johnson (1986), there is ". . . a considerable difference between putting students physically into groups (merely re-arranging desks) and structuring groups for cooperative learning (promoting positive inter-dependence and collaborative skills)" (p. 31). In order for a group experience to be truly cooperative, Johnson, Johnson, Holubec, and Roy (1984) state that the experience must incorporate the following four basic elements:

1) Positive Interdependence - Students must be dependent upon one another for task completion.

2) Face-to-Face Interaction - There must be verbal exchange among students.

3) Individual Accountability - Each student must be held accountable for learning the material so students can provide support and assistance to each other.

4) Appropriate Use of Interpersonal and Small Group Skills - Students must be taught the social skills needed for cooperative learning, and teachers must observe the groups to see that the skills are being used.

Johnson and Johnson (1984) outline the differences between cooperative learning groups and traditional learning groups in the following way:

Cooperative Learning Groups	Traditional Learning Groups
Positive interdependence	No interdependence
Individual accountability	No individual accountability
Heterogeneous	Homogeneous
Shared leadership	One appointed leader
Shared responsibility for each other	Responsibility only for self
Task and maintenance emphasized	Only task emphasized
Social skills directly taught	Social skills assumed and ignored
Teacher observes and intervenes	Teacher ignores group functioning
Groups process their effectiveness	No group processing

Reprinted with permission

Bohlmeyer and Burke (1987) cite the following benefits of cooperative learning: improved interpersonal relationships, improved cross-ethnic relationships, improved cross-sex relationships, increased self-esteem, improved role-taking abilities, and greater achievement. An effective social skills curriculum should incorporate cooperative learning techniques.

Current literature also addresses the importance of using "whole brain" learning strategies. Research indicates that both sides of the brain have different functions (Clark, 1986; Hatcher, 1983; McCarthy, 1983). The left brain is more responsible for linear, sequential, analytic, rational thinking while the right brain is more metaphoric, spatial, and holistic in nature (Clark, 1986; Gorovitz, 1982). It is important to be aware of the differences between the left and right brain and the way in which each person learns best. However, current research emphasizes the importance of teaching students to use both sides of the brain rather than relying solely on the dominant side. Learners who use both sides of the brain do best academically and socially (Webb, 1983) **SSS: Social Skill Strategies** provides a variety of "whole brain" learning activities.

SOCIAL COMMUNICATION SKILLS: GETTING THESE SKILLS TO TRANSFER AND GENERALIZE

Currently, discussion on social skills training is focused on whether the skills learned in the classroom are transferring to other settings and if the social skills are maintained over time. Previously, the assumption was made that use of skills would transfer to different settings automatically. An increasing body of research disproves this assumption (Stokes and Baer, 1977; Wahler, Berland, and Coe, 1979; Wehman, Abramson, and Norman, 1977). Stokes and Baer (1977) describe those training efforts which do not specifically plan for generalization as the "train and hope" type. Research on skill generalization (particularly in the area of social skill instruction) is limited.

"A behavioral change is generalized when it proves durable over time, when it appears in a wide variety of possible environments, or when it spreads to a wide variety of related behaviors" (Baer, Wolf, and Risley, 1968, p. 96). Educators have not developed a ". . . systematic, data-based technology for promoting transfer across . . . settings" (Anderson-Inman, 1986, p. 563).

Numerous variables have been identified that increase the probability that transfer will occur. Goldstein et al. (1980) describe the following:

1. Use of general principles which apply to training and real-life settings.
2. Overlearning (the higher the degree of original learning, the greater the probability for transfer).
3. Identical elements (the greater the number of identical elements in both the training and application settings, the greater the chance for transfer).

Current social skill research has gone beyond the fundamentals of teaching social skills and is emphasizing procedures for skill transfer. Teaching social skills is a relatively simple task. The challenge involves teaching the skills in a manner that will encourage students to use them in other settings. Teaching for transfer needs to be purposefully planned (Mayo and Gajewski, 1987). Schumaker and Hazel (1984b) urge that instructional strategies should enable instructors to teach skills and promote generalization and maintenance of those skills in natural settings. Walker (1979) summarized the problem in the following way: "The rule to remember is what you teach is what you get and where you teach it is where you get it" (p. 298).

Schumaker and Hazel (1984a) reported several studies which indicated that instructional procedures such as modeling, rehearsal, and feedback are not sufficient for producing generalized use of newly learned social skills. They conclude: 1) Criterion performance in role playing does not indicate how a child will do in the natural environment; 2) The final measure of the success of a social skill program must be taken in the natural environment, and 3) Students need generalization training in addition to traditional social skill instruction to promote transfer of skills. In addition, Adelman and Taylor (1982) propose that the lack of generalization of social skills may be caused by a lack of emphasis in social skill programs on the motivational aspect of social skill usage.

Self-regulated learning is a promising technique for promoting the transfer of social skills. Self-regulated learning encourages individuals to manage their cognitive abilities and motivational level, and thus attempt to improve their learning (Paris and Oka, 1986). A similar term, *metacognition,* is defined as having the student decide which strategy to use, decide when to use it, and finally, to monitor how effective the strategy was. For example, a student uses metacognition when he independently decides that apologizing is the appropriate skill to use, decides on the best time to make the apology, carries out his plan, and evaluates whether or not he made the apology correctly. Schumaker and Hazel (1984b) state that students must be prepared for problems that will arise, even when the student is using the social skill appropriately. Students must understand that there are people they will deal with who may be unreasonable because they are not socially skilled and, therefore, the students must be able to identify situations when the use of various skills is not feasible (e.g., when to negotiate and when it's useless to negotiate).

One curricular program which incorporates the idea of self-regulated learning in conjunction with social skill instruction is the **Making Better Choices Program** (Harris, 1984). The program includes two components for social skills instruction: 1) A metacognitive section, and 2) A social skill instruction section. In the first section, Harris teaches "cognitive planning strategies" which the students use for each social skill. Cognitive planning strategies teach students to go beyond simple usage of social skills. The strategies help students: 1) To control impulsiveness so they can make intelligent choices about social skills; 2) To decide on a plan (the skill steps); 3) To put the plan into action, and 4) To evaluate the results of using the social skill.

When teaching metacognitive strategies to students, it is essential that educators initially model the cognitive planning strategies for their students. "A characteristic of successful metacognition strategy instruction is the gradual transfer of control of the strategy from the teacher to the students" (Palincsar, 1986, pg. 122). In addition, the number of skill steps should be kept to a minimum and written as simply as possible. In a recent study, Gelzheiser, Shepherd, and Wozniak (1986) report that ". . . students, who have fewer rules (skill steps) to learn are better able to attain proficiency and to generalize" (pg. 127). **SSS: Social Skill Strategies** provides a list of specific transfer/generalization ideas (refer to page 21). In addition, this program incorporates ideas for transfer in every unit.

SOCIAL COMMUNICATION SKILLS: SUMMARY

Research documents a need for social skill education. Exceptional education professionals should be concerned with the social competence of the individuals they serve. Not only do many individuals with learning disabilities, mental retardation, behavioral/emotional disturbances, and speech/language disorders demonstrate social skill incompetence, but they can possess this weakness for different reasons. They may have skill deficits, performance deficits, and/or self-control deficits. A comprehensive social skills curriculum should be tailored for students with any or all of these three deficit types. Although a standardized social skill assessment device is long overdue, research indicates that the use of behavioral rating scales is currently the most effective for older students. Educators should work towards identifying which students need instruction and the priority skills for each student identified. Research documents acquisition of social skills after direct instruction, but it does not document generalization of those skills. Therefore, a professional interested in improving a student's social competence must directly plan for the transfer and generalization of each social skill taught. An effective way to do this is by pairing cognitive strategy training with social skill instruction so that students are able 1) To control impulsiveness so they can make intelligent choices about social skills; 2) To decide on a plan; 3) To execute the plan, and 4) To evaluate results of using the social skill.

SSS: Social Skill Strategies provides a seven-step approach for improving social communication skills that will be described in the next chapter. The seven-step approach incorporates the various techniques which were discussed within this chapter.

Chapter Two

RESOURCE GUIDELINES AND PROCEDURES

SSS: SOMETHING FOR EVERYBODY

The **SSS: Social Skill Strategies** program has been divided into two books: Book A and Book B include the same beginning chapters and the same appendices, but they include different social skill units. Book A includes social skill units A-1 to A-34 and Book B includes the social skill units B-1 to B-29. The titles of each unit are listed in the Table of Contents. The skills have been put into the five categories of: Introductory Skills (Book A), General Interaction Skills (Book A), Peer Interaction Skills (Book B), Management Skills (Book B), and Emotional Expression Skills (Book B). The books provide curriculum for a two-year social skills course when taught daily for a forty-five minute period.

SSS: Social Skill Strategies includes materials and a description of how to identify which students have social communication skill deficits and, therefore, need social skill instruction. The books explain the procedure for assessing and developing a hierarchical list of the social skills in need of instruction. This resource describes the procedure for establishing a social skills course, and a format for structuring a class period. It supplies a comprehensive description of a seven-step procedure for teaching each of the social communication skill units. This program provides suggestions for promoting transfer and generalization of the social skills mastered in a classroom situation.

Each unit in **SSS: Social Skill Strategies** focuses on a different social skill and includes structured activities which teach students about the skill and provide opportunities for practice. The number of activity pages within each unit varies depending on the complexity of the specific social skill. The units incorporate a wide variety of instructional techniques (e.g., group discussion, games, role plays, visualizations, cartoons, group projects, and guided practice pages).

Some of the activity pages within units are objective in nature; however, an answer key has *not* been generated. Numerous correct responses exist for many of the objective items and an answer key might stymie creative thought and discussion. Educators using this resource should focus on a student's rationales for answers as much as they do on the student's responses. As long as the student has a logical justification for a given response, it should be accepted as correct.

SSS: Social Skill Strategies is appropriate for students in grades five through twelve. Professionals (e.g., educators, counselors, psychologists) involved with special education students will find this resource invaluable for providing social skill instruction. In addition, **SSS** can be used when dealing with regular education students who may also be experiencing social skill difficulties. This resource includes materials and ideas that will be effective for teaching students with social skill deficits, performance deficits, and self-control deficits as described on pages 2-3 of Chapter One.

SSS contains letters which can be sent to parents and professionals who have contact with the students receiving social skill instruction (See Appendix E). The letters explain the rationale

8

for teaching social skills and give suggestions to parents and professionals for promoting transfer of appropriate social skill use.

SSS: IDENTIFYING STUDENTS WITH SOCIAL SKILL DEFICITS

Schumaker and Hazel (1984a) advocate the use of behavioral rating scales and checklists for identifying older individuals with social skill deficits and for pinpointing target behaviors for those who do demonstrate weaknesses. Kazdin and Matson (1981) suggest using the strategy of subjective evaluation by obtaining information and feedback from "informed others" to establish training targets. Textbooks for educators emphasize the need for input from clients and their significant others as to which social skills to address. However, client interviews, self-monitoring, and self-ratings are seldom employed to identify training priorities (Schloss et al., 1986). The **SSS** program includes two rating scales: one which is a self-rating scale and one which is to be completed by significant others. The **SSS** program also advocates the use of client interviews, and self-monitoring by students.

Rating Scale - Adult Form

SSS: Social Skill Strategies provides a social communication skills rating scale to be completed by a parent, case manager, and any other adult who has observed the student's use of social skills in a natural setting (See Appendix A). The estimated readability for this rating scale is seventh grade, according to the Fry Readability Scale (Fry, 1977). The Social Communication Skills Rating Scale (Adult Form) asks the adult to rate the student on each of the 63 social skills contained in **SSS** based on his/her observation of the student. Each social skill is described on the rating scale to make it as explicit as possible. The rating scale has been broken into the five categories of: Introductory Skills, General Interaction Skills, Peer Interaction Skills, Management Skills, and Emotional Expression Skills. The adult may complete the entire rating scale or only certain sections, depending on the information desired. Use of this rating scale may be more effective if a knowledgeable educator is present when the adult completes it to explain items the adult does not understand.

Rating Scale - Summary Form

When the rating scales have been completed and returned to the educator, the scores may be compiled on the Student Social Skill Summary Form, which is partially shown below and is included in Appendix B.

STUDENT'S NAME:	Identified as Being Problematic	Demonstrated Comprehension of Skill in Class	Demonstrated Correct Use of Skill in Class	Reported/Observed Correct Use of Skill Outside of Class	GRADE: _____ YEAR: _____	Identified as Being Problematic	Demonstrated Comprehension of Skill in Class	Demonstrated Correct Use of Skill in Class	Reported/Observed Correct Use of Skill Outside of Class
A-1. Eye Contact					B-1. Reputation				
A-2. Manners					B-2. Starting A Friendship				
A-3. Volume					B-3. Maintaining a Friendship				
A-4. Time And Place					B-4. Giving Emotional Support				
A-5. Tone Of Voice					B-5. Giving Advice				
A-6. Getting To The Point					B-6. Ignoring				
A-7. Staying On Topic And Switching Topics					B-7. Responding To Teasing				

STUDENT SOCIAL SKILL SUMMARY FORM

This summary form lists all of the 63 social skills rated, with a place to indicate which skills were rated as being problematic. There are different ways for educators to record the data. One alternative is to place a checkmark next to the social skills which were rated as being either a *one* (never) or a *two* (seldom) and not to mark anything next to the social skills which were rated as being either a *three* (sometimes), a *four* (often), or a *five* (always). Another alternative is to place a checkmark next to only those rated as *one, two,* or *three.* A third alternative would be to write down the number assigned by the adult, instead of using a checkmark. The authors suggest using this form in a way that works best for the educator.

There are several possible uses of the Student Social Skill Summary Form once it has been completed. One use is for the student to include a copy of it in his journal so the student has an overview of the 63 social skills and a listing of those skills which are problematic for him (See *SSS:* JOURNAL DESCRIPTION, page 15). Another use is for a copy of it to be included with the student's IEP to record when social skill objectives have been met. This can be done by placing a checkmark next to those social skills for which the student demonstrated comprehension and use in the classroom, and another checkmark next to those social skills reported or observed used outside of the classroom.

Rating Scale - Student Form

SSS: Social Skill Strategies includes a social communication skills rating scale, to be completed by the students themselves, on all 63 social skills (See Appendix C). This form is written at a fourth grade reading level, according to the Fry Readability Scale (Fry, 1977). This form is similar to the adult form, except that it is written in first person, (e.g., EYE CONTACT - I am good at looking at a person during a conversation). Educators may have students who are referred for special education programs complete the scale during the evaluation process. If there are students in the social skills class who have not had the opportunity to complete the rating scale, they may complete it during the first two class sessions. Although a brief description of each social skill is included on the student rating scale, the authors advocate reading the rating scale aloud, while the students rate themselves, to provide explanation as needed and to avoid erroneous responses by disabled readers.

Student Conference

A conference should be held with each student individually, shortly after completion of the rating scales. During the conference, the educator and student should review the student's self assessment and the educator should ask the student to identify the skills which he/she feels are most problematic. By allowing the students to comment, they may be more motivated to improve their social skill deficits. The authors realize that some students will deny having any social skill problems and will complete the rating scale in an unrealistic manner.

Independent Activities

While the educator is conferencing with an individual student, the other students can be completing one of the ten independent activity pages included in **SSS** (See Appendix F). The independent activities discuss social communication skills in a general manner and may be completed with minimum supervision. Each activity page takes approximately one 45-minute class period for most students to complete. The authors realize that some of the independent activities (e.g., word searches) do not have the same educational value as the activities within the units; however, they were purposely designed so the students could complete them independently.

Class Summary Form

After completing the conferences and rating social skills for instruction, the educator may compile each student's data on the Class Summary Form, which is shown here (for Book B) and is included in Appendix D.

CLASS SUMMARY FORM
BOOK B (Mark the social skills which are problematic for each student.)

STUDENTS' NAMES / SOCIAL SKILLS	B-1. Reputation	B-2. Starting A Friendship	B-3. Maintaining A Friendship	B-4. Giving Emotional Support	B-5. Giving Advice	B-6. Ignoring	B-7. Responding To Teasing	B-8. Peer Pressure	B-9. Joining In	B-10. Being Left Out	B-11. Tattling	B-12. Being Assertive	B-13. Making A Complaint	B-14. Receiving A Complaint	B-15. Giving Constructive Criticism	B-16. Accepting Constructive Criticism	B-17. Making An Accusation	B-18. Dealing With A False Accusation	B-19. Compromising/Negotiating	B-20. Accepting Consequences	B-21. Expressing Feelings	B-22. Dealing With Anger	B-23. Dealing With Embarrassment	B-24. Coping With Fear	B-25. Dealing With Humor	B-26. Dealing With Failure	B-27. Expressing Affection	B-28. Dealing With Disappointment	B-29. Understanding The Feelings Of Others	SSS: SOCIAL SKILL STRATEGIES (Book A)
																														282

To complete the form, the name of each student who was identified as having a social skills need should be written down the left-hand column. Then, mark the social skills found to be problematic for each student. By doing this, you will have a profile of each of your student's needs. The Class Summary Form can help you identify the priority social skills and the sequence in which you will want to teach them in the class. It can also be useful for determining who should be grouped together for social skill instruction. If a certain social skill, for example - accepting a compliment, was not found to be problematic for any of the students, no instructional time should be spent developing that social skill. Suppose, conversely, a social skill is a problem for several of your students, but not for all. When you teach that social skill in class, the students who are not deficient in that area can be given the choice of participating with the class or working alone on one of the ten independent activity pages. Although some skills are prerequisites for others, there is no clear-cut hierarchy of skills. Therefore, the educator should teach the skills in order of need and not necessarily in the order presented in **SSS**. It is highly recommended, however, that the Introductory Skills be addressed first because they are prerequisites to other skills taught in the program.

SSS: PRE-GROUP SKILLS

Before instruction in social skills can begin, the educator must identify which students are capable of learning in a group and which are not. Many educators, because of the nature of their students (e.g., aggressive, acting-out) will find it impossible to hold any type of "group" instruction. A criterion for **SSS: Social Skill Strategies** is that the students be able to function in a group without causing major disruptions. Some students are not yet at this level. One excellent behavioral program, **Dubuque Management System** (Keystone Area Education Agency,

1990), provides a structured approach which enables students to work in a group. Inquiries can be directed to **Dubuque Management System**, Keystone Area Education Agency, 1473 Central Avenue, Dubuque, Iowa 52001.

SSS: STRUCTURING A SOCIAL SKILLS CLASS

Based on a review of current research and experience in teaching social skills to students, the authors feel it is ideal if educators can conduct a social skills class daily. In addition, they advocate a specific structure for each social skill class as depicted below.

Reinforcement Time:	Pair Practice	
	Visualization	5 min.
	Question Review	
Instruction Time:	Instruction of Social Skills	35 min. (approximately)
Personal Time:	Personal Page	5 min.

Reinforcement Time

The purpose of the reinforcement activities (i.e., pair practice, visualization, and/or question review) is to reinforce past social skills that students have learned. These activities should be completed during the first five minutes of every class period. The educator may wish to do only one or two of the activities each day, depending on how long the activities take with the particular students in the class.

Pair Practice

The first activity in the reinforcement section is pair practice. This activity involves having pairs of students do short, specified role plays. The pair practice activity should not be initiated until after a few social skills have been taught so students have more than one skill to practice. In addition, this activity should not be implemented until the students feel comfortable in role playing situations. When introducing the pair practice activity, the educator should explain that the students will be practicing the use of various social skills they have already learned. It is important for the educator to give the following rationale to their students:

Educator: Each of you will be role playing over and over again the skills that you need to work on. You will do this at the beginning of the class period. The reason you will practice them over and over is the more you do something, the easier it becomes for you. For example, the more you give speeches to audiences, the easier it becomes to give them.

Early in the year, when the students have learned a limited number of social skills, all the students will be role playing the same social skills during this activity. As soon as possible, the educator should individualize the social skills to be role played for each student by referring to the Class

Summary Form (See Appendix D). The priority social skills chosen for each student should be recorded on the Pair Practice Record sheet, which is shown below and included in Appendix G.

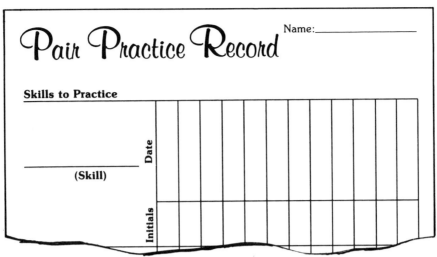

The Pair Practice Record sheet should be given to students to include in their journals. To complete this activity, have the students work in pairs. After both students have role played a social skill, they should initial each other's sheet to indicate which social skill was practiced. Eventually, the students should be able to complete this activity without receiving help from the educator.

Visualization

The second activity during the reinforcement section is visualization. This activity involves having students form a mental image of themselves. The students should imagine themselves performing one of their priority social skills. For example, a student who has difficulty with eye contact should form a mental image of himself using good eye contact. Explain to the students that many successful people use this strategy (e.g., athletes, salesclerks, actors). Remember that some students may not have much experience in forming mental images. Other students may be in the habit of forming only negative images in their minds. Therefore, initially the educator must verbally guide the students through this activity. The use of simple social skills (e.g., accepting a compliment) is suggested when first doing this. The following example illustrates how an educator could guide the students through a visualization activity:

Educator: It's time for visualization. You may close your eyes if you'd like. Today, I'd like to have you receive a compliment in the correct way. When someone gives you a compliment, you say "Thank you." Picture this in your mind: Your teacher walks over to you and gives you a compliment about how well you did on your assignment. Picture yourself looking at your teacher, smiling, and saying, "Thank you."

After guiding several visualizations, the educator should fade the amount of verbal instructions provided until the students begin to do the visualization activities independently. After completion of the activity, the educator may want to ask individual students to describe the images they formed.

Question Review

The last activity during the reinforcement time is the question review. This activity involves the educator asking a few questions about previously taught social skills. A list is provided for the educator which includes several review questions for each social skill unit (See Appendix H). Question #1 for each unit always asks for the definition of the social skill. Question #2 asks for the skill steps or important tips to remember. The remaining questions pertain to application of the skill. The educator should ask the class a few questions from any previously taught social skill unit. The compiled list of questions makes it easy for the educator to choose questions quickly for the day. The purpose of this activity is to remind students continually of important aspects from past social skill units.

Instruction Time

This is the main portion of the class period during which direct instruction of social skills takes place. This portion of the class will be described later. (See SSS: TEACHING A SOCIAL SKILL UNIT on page 15).

Personal Time

The personal time should take place during the last five minutes of each class period. The purpose of this activity is to increase the students' positive feeling about their use of social skills. This activity was adapted from a self-concept curriculum entitled **Affective Skill Development for Adolescents** (Dembrowsky, 1983). The personal time activity involves having the students say the following statement aloud and in unison: "I am a good person. I am a friendly person. When I use my social skills, I get along better with people." This statement can be found on the top of the Personal Page, which follows and is included in Appendix I.

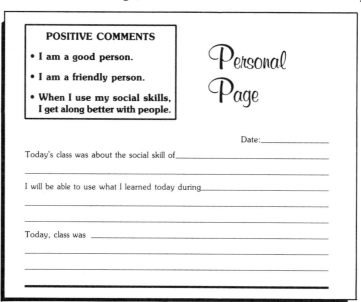

The purpose for the personal time activity should be explained to the students. The rationale is that the more often you say or think positive things about yourself, the more likely you are to incorporate those positive thoughts into your belief system (Dembrowsky, 1983). Educators must say the statement along with the students to acknowledge their belief in the benefits of the activity. Next, the students should complete the bottom of the Personal Page immediately after saying the positive statement aloud. The rationale for this activity is to make students continuously examine when they are using various social skills and when they will be using newly learned skills. The Personal Page may need to be adapted for use with low-functioning students. The students should keep an ample supply of Personal Pages in their journals for daily use (See *SSS:* JOURNAL DESCRIPTION below).

SSS: JOURNAL DESCRIPTION

The authors suggest that each student in the class have a three-ring binder to be used as a journal. The journal should contain the following: 1) the Pair Practice Record sheet (See description, page 13); 2) the Student Social Skill Summary Form (See description, page 9); 3) the Personal Page (See description, page 14). In addition, during each social skill unit, students may add completed activity pages to their journals. Students will use their journals at the beginning and end of each class period to complete the Pair Practice, Review Question, and Personal Page activities. They can easily refer to their journals when they wish to review for an upcoming test.

SSS: GRADING

The authors advocate using the "1/3 method" for grading student progress in a social skills class: one-third of the student's grade is determined by in-class and homework assignments, another one-third of the grade is determined by test/quiz scores, and the final one-third is determined by the student's participation in class. One method of recording participation involves use of the Daily Participation Point Sheet which is shown below and is included in Appendix J.

ATTENDANCE AND DAILY PARTICIPATION POINTS

Date:_____

Students' Names	Attendance (50%)	60%	70%	80%	90%	100%	Total Participation

If a student attends class but does not participate, he receives a daily participation grade of 50%. The student receives an additional 10% every time he appropriately participates in class. It is important that a positive classroom atmosphere be maintained and that students be positively reinforced often. Use of the Daily Participation Point Sheet will positively promote verbal participation. During classes when there is little opportunity for verbal discussion (e.g., students watching a videotaped program), students can be awarded participation points for positive behaviors other than verbal participation.

SSS: TEACHING A SOCIAL SKILL UNIT

After the educator and students have completed the reinforcement activities during the first five minutes of class (see *Reinforcement Time* on page 12), the instruction time may begin, which will be the major portion of the class period. The authors suggest using the following seven-step procedure for teaching each new social skill:

Step One: Social Skill Introduction
Step Two: Cognitive Planning Strategies
Step Three: Scripting
Step Four: Modeling
Step Five: Role Playing
Step Six: Homework And Concluding Activities
Step Seven: Transfer And Generalization Ideas

These seven steps have been separated and placed into a hierarchy for explanation purposes. In practice, however, the seven steps are integrated and do not have to be used in the exact sequence as shown above. The time required to address the seven steps will vary, depending on the complexity of the social skill being taught. Even the shortest units (e.g., eye contact) however, will take several class periods to complete. Each of the seven steps is described in detail below.

Step One: Social Skill Introduction

The educator must introduce each new social skill in a creative manner, using a method which will spark the students' interest. There are numerous ways to introduce a skill to enhance motivation for learning. A small sampling of ideas is provided below:

- The educator can role play the appropriate or inappropriate use of a social skill.
- The students can imagine a situation about the social skill.
- The students can listen to a short story about the social skill.
- The students can be shown a cartoon about the social skill.
- The educator can exaggerate the skill in a humorous and obvious manner.

Once educators have caught the students' interest, instruction of the social skill may begin. Each of the social skill units includes several activity pages which can be used during this skill introduction step, with the exception of the first and last pages of the unit, which are used at other times and will be described later. While a great deal of variability between the social skill units exists, some components remain constant. Each social skill unit includes:

1. The definition of the social skill. (Definitions can also be found in the Question Review pages in Appendix H.)
2. The skill steps or important "tips" about the social skill. Skill steps and important "tips" are also provided in the Question Review pages in Appendix H and on the Skill Homework Activity Page A at the beginning of every unit. The authors have identified the crucial skill steps for many of the social skills; however, some social skill units do not lend themselves to the development of ordered skill steps, so the essential points or "tips" to remember about the social skill are taught. The number of social skill steps have been limited because research indicates students are able to retain and transfer use of social skills better when there are fewer skill steps (Palincsar, 1986). In addition, mnemonic devices have been provided in some units to help the students memorize skill steps or tips.
3. Information which allows the students to understand why they need to learn the social skill and how it can be used at home, in school, and in the community.

Step Two: Cognitive Planning Strategies

Not only is it important to increase students' comprehension of social skills, but it is also essential to improve the cognitive planning strategies of learning how to identify which social skill to use and when to use it, and evaluating whether or not a social skill works appropriately. The need to incorporate cognitive planning strategies into social skill instruction was previously discussed (See SOCIAL COMMUNICATION SKILLS: GETTING THESE SKILLS TO TRANSFER AND GENERALIZE in Chapter One on page 6). Harris (1984) describes his **Making Better Choices Program**, which teaches a structured cognitive planning strategy during the first six lessons of his curriculum. Students learn the following sequence when planning the use of a social skill strategy:

STOP: Students monitor their tension level and take steps to calm down.
PLAN: Students decide which social skill to use and recall the skill steps.
DO: Students carry out their plan.
CHECK: Students evaluate how their plan worked and make necessary changes for the future.

This cognitive planning strategy is also incorporated into the remaining twenty social skill units of the **Making Better Choices Program**. Harris uses the following chart to depict his cognitive planning sequence:

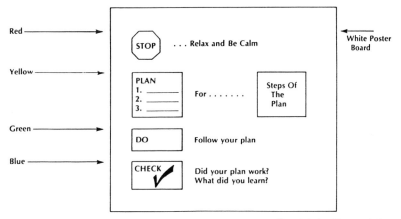

Reprinted with permission

FIGURE 1. The MBC Poster

To incorporate cognitive plannning strategies into a social skills curriculum, it is essential that the educator do the following:

1. Discuss cognitive planning strategies within every social skill unit.
2. Provide opportunities for students to consider different situations and identify which social skill would be appropriate to use and when to use it.
3. Discuss how to evaluate the success of each social skill used.

Step Three: Scripting

After providing the students with the essential information about the social skills, the educator is encouraged to have students read short scripts about the correct and incorrect use of social skills. The scripts should portray students using social skills in real-life situations, thereby providing relevancy for the students. The scripts will be helpful for those students who initially have difficulties role playing, and may clarify any confusion the students may have about the social skill after the initial instruction. The scripts are also useful with students who deny they have any social skill problems by allowing them to learn the proper use of social skills while not having to acknowledge their personal inadequacies.

Educators can write their own scripts for each social skill or use a commercially prepared program entitled **Scripting: Social Communication for Adolescents** (Waldo and Mayo, 1986). This resource provides scripts which demonstrate appropriate and inappropriate use of each social skill.

The scripting activity often increases students' participation. Students enjoy reading scripts because they are able to identify with many of the characters used in the scripts. In the authors' experiences with using social skill scripts, they have noticed that students with poor reading skills volunteer to read a part in a script just as often as average and above-average readers. The scripts may be used as the third step in teaching a unit or as an introduction to a new social skill unit. When doing the latter, the educator should ask the students to guess what social skill the script is depicting after it is read aloud.

Step Four: Modeling

It is essential that the educator model the social skill steps for the students. The authors suggest two methods of modeling:

1. Model the appropriate use of the social skill while simultaneously modeling the self-talk someone might say when using the social skill (e.g., "I wonder if these two people know one another? Maybe I should ask them if they know each other."). Self-talk is defined as the thoughts we have about ourselves and other people. In addition, the educator should model the cognitive planning self-talk that the students are taught to use for every social skill. (See description of **Making Better Choices Program** on page 17).
2. Model just the appropriate use of the social skill, phasing out the self-talk.

Research indicates that modeling is more effective when it is more realistic (Bandura, 1977). For example, the person modeling should act as though he is having a difficult time accepting NO from an authority figure, rather than just accepting the NO easily. In addition to modeling during Step Four, the educator should take every opportunity to model appropriate social skill usage throughout the school day.

Step Five: Role Playing

After modeling of the social skill has taken place, the students should practice and then role play situations where use of the social skill would be appropriate. Students should then be critiqued on how well they performed each social skill. Initially, a few students may be fearful of role playing; thus, the educator should take measures to help alleviate those fears (e.g., asking the class not to "make fun of" anyone who is role playing, letting the students initially role play without an audience). Some students will refuse to participate in the role play. Initially, these students can be given alternative assignments (e.g., writing role play situations, suggesting ideas for scripts), but every effort should be made to encourage them to participate as soon as possible.

Educators may develop their own role play situations for use with the class or may use already prepared role play situations found in social skill programs such as **Scripting: Social Communication for Adolescents** (Waldo and Mayo, 1986) or **Skillstreaming the Adolescent: A Structured Learning Approach to Teaching Prosocial Skills** (Goldstein et al., 1980). The role play situations must be relevant for the students. The educator might ask the class to brainstorm role play situations or ask for suggestions from individual students.

To begin this activity, educators are encouraged to give the students three role play situations. One should be a situation which could take place at school, one at home, and one in the community. Following are sample situations from the *Agreeing/Disagreeing* unit taken from **Scripting: Social Communication for Adolescents** (Waldo and Mayo, 1986).

(Home)   1. Your parents think you should not be involved in any after school activities so you can devote all your time to studies. Demonstrate how you would disagree with them in an appropriate way.

(School)   2. Your teacher gives you two days to complete a big homework assignment. Everyone in class, including you, thinks that will not be enough time. Show how you could express your disagreement in an appropriate way.

(Community) 3. You are shopping for your dad's birthday present. The salesclerk suggests that you buy him a shirt. Demonstrate how you could agree.

Reprinted with permission

The educator should read through and model all three situations with the students before asking them to work with a partner to practice role playing each one. While the partners are practicing, the educator should spend time with each group, making certain that everyone is staying on task and is correctly role playing each situation. When everyone is ready, the entire group should meet together. Partners should take turns coming to the front of the class to perform one or more of the situations they were given to practice.

Goldstein et al. (1980) advocate having the social skill steps (or tips) displayed at the front of the room during role plays for students who may forget the skill steps. This can be done by writing the skill steps on the chalkboard, putting the steps on a poster, or listing the steps on pages of a large sketch book. The sketch book allows educators to keep all social skill steps together in one place, and they can easily flip to each social skill when necessary. Students often refer to the skill steps (tips) before they do their role plays and during the role play if they get confused.

The educator should determine which students might have difficulty following the skill steps during the role play. Those students should role play using self-talk (aloud) to help display appropriate use of the social skill. Verbalized self-talk should be faded as soon as possible to ensure appropriate skill acquisition.

The partner for the role play should be carefully chosen. When practicing social skills that involve interactions with adults (e.g., accepting NO, accepting consequences), the role play situation should occur with an adult to promote transfer (See SOCIAL COMMUNICATION SKILLS: GETTING THESE SKILLS TO TRANSFER AND GENERALIZE in Chapter One on page 6). It is also suggested that other school staff members (e.g., school principal, regular educators) be involved in role plays to further promote transfer and generalization of skills. For social skills that involve the student interacting with peers (e.g., resisting peer pressure, starting a friendship), peers may be selected as partners. Educators are cautioned to choose only those students who take role playing seriously to be partners, because the person being critiqued must be serious.

Stokes and Baer (1977) recommend the *multiple exemplar strategy* which involves students role playing with several different people instead of with just one person. This will help to ensure transfer across settings. For additional strategies and research on role playing, refer to

Skillstreaming the Adolescent: A Structured Learning Approach to Teaching Pro-social Skills (Goldstein et al., 1980).

It is important that the educator and student review the student's performance during the role play. The educator should provide positive verbal feedback immediately after the student finishes the role play. The student may also receive feedback from the Role Play Critique Sheet (See Appendix K). This sheet may be completed by a variety of people. The educator may use it to grade the student, or other students in the class who acted as observers may use the sheet to critique the role play. Students who role play may conduct a self-evaluation if the role play is videotaped. The authors suggest using videotaping as often as possible because it gives the students a chance to see themselves actually performing the social skill. They can observe body language, volume, tone of voice, and the skill steps for the given social skill.

Step Six: Homework and Concluding Activities

Homework assignments are a means of reinforcing the skills the students have been taught. One type of homework assignment is the Skill Homework Activity Page A, which is the first page of every unit. After instruction of each social skill unit, students should complete the homework assignment with a parent. Page A contains the name of the social skill, the skill steps (or tips) for each social skill, and a role play situation. Parents are asked either to act out the role play situation with their child or to observe their son/daughter using the social skill in a real-life situation and describe that situation. Parents are then asked to evaluate their child's performance by circling *needs more help, good,* or *excellent* on the homework sheet and sign the sheet. The students should submit their papers to the teacher for a homework grade.

The educator must contact parents and explain the Skill Homework Activity pages before students take any sheets home. (See *Step Seven: Transfer and Generalization Ideas* on page 21.) There will still be a number of students who have difficulty getting their parents to complete the Skill Homework Activity. These students may complete the activity with some other adult (e.g., a teacher, a youth leader, a neighbor). Occasionally, the educator may want to allow all the students to choose the adult with whom they would like to complete the activity.

During the instruction of the social skill unit, various **SSS** activity pages may also be used as homework assignments. Educators should assess, through guided practice, whether the students have mastered the concepts before assigning an activity page or part of an activity page as homework.

The authors have developed an end-of-the-unit Student Evaluation Form (See Appendix L) for students to complete. Students should use this form to rate how much they learned from the social skill unit and give suggestions on ways to improve the unit. While this sheet helps promote student involvement, students do not need to complete this form after every unit.

Another concluding activity involves having the students play a board game called **Communicate** (Mayo and Waldo, 1986). This educational activity reinforces important concepts discussed during each social skill unit.

Concluding activities could also include giving students tests and quizzes. Evaluating student performance on a regular basis will 1) assess student progress; 2) promote transfer of skills, and 3) impress upon the students that social skills class is as important as academic classes. The authors have found that testing students after every four social skill units is effective. A short quiz is beneficial after every social skill unit.

A review guide has been included at the end of every unit. Each review guide contains one question written at each of the six levels of Bloom's taxonomy of educational objectives (Bloom, Engelhart, Furst, Hill, and Krathwohl, 1954). The taxonomy includes the following six levels: knowledge, comprehension, application, analysis, synthesis, and evaluation. Unfortunately, most of the questions asked by teachers are at the knowledge and comprehension levels only. The authors believe that every student, including those with special educational needs, should be taken through all six levels of the taxonomy in order to improve their upper level thinking skills and to promote transfer and generalization of the social skill.

Students should be encouraged to refer to their journals when completing the first few questions of the review guides. Educators may need to help the students with the questions written at the levels of application, analysis, synthesis, and evaluation. Educators can use the same review guide for the test or quiz, or develop their own by referring to the review guide, activity pages, and review questions (See Appendix H) for the unit.

The following section includes ideas for concluding activities that will help to promote transfer of social skills.

Step Seven: Transfer and Generalization Ideas

Getting students to transfer their skills is the most important step in the process of teaching a social skill unit. Sadly, it is a step that is often forgotten. Numerous authors have recently addressed the lack of specific planning to promote transfer (Adelman and Taylor, 1982; Mayo and Gajewski, 1987; McConnell, 1987; Schumaker and Hazel, 1984b; Simpson, 1987). Educators need to ensure that a plan for transfer of skills is included in every social skill unit. The authors have compiled a list of strategies that can be used to promote transfer of social skills to areas outside of the classroom. Educators should incorporate several of the following ideas into each social skill unit to ensure generalization of skills:

1. *Initial and Ending Class Activities* - The following activities, Pair Practice, Visualization, Review Questions, Positive Comments, and the Personal Page, are set up to help students transfer the social skills outside the classroom. They are designed to help students overlearn skills, transfer the use of skills to the home, school, and community; and to change their self-talk/mental imagery to be more positive. (See *SSS*: STRUCTURING A SOCIAL SKILLS CLASS on page 12).

2. *Cognitive Planning* - This strategy teaches the student to monitor personal performance by assessing 1) when he should use a specific social skill; 2) how others respond to his use of the social skill; 3) if he performed the skill correctly, and 4) if he should do something differently the next time. Cognitive planning also helps the student calm himself down enough so that he can actually perform the social skill. The *Making Better Choices Program* (Harris, 1987) is an example of a program which incorporates cognitive planning with the instruction of social skills. (See *SSS*: TEACHING A SOCIAL SKILL UNIT on page 15).

3. *Practice Day* - The students need to receive numerous opportunities to practice newly learned skills. One method involves using the first 15 minutes of class on Monday for a review session and setting aside one entire class session each month for a cumulative review (Good and Grouws, 1985). The students can review social skill steps and tips and practice all of the past social skills they have learned.

4. *Red Flag* - Educator must integrate social skill instruction throughout the entire school

day. McGinnis, Sauerbry, and Nichols (1985) describe a *Red Flag* strategy in which the educator tells a student that he will be "set up" later in the day (or the next day). Being "set up" means that the educator will purposely do something which will cause the child to demonstrate his use of a particular social skill. For example, the educator might tell the student that sometime later in the day, she will make a false accusation to the student. The student is expected to demonstrate the proper way to handle a false accusation. After the *Red Flag* situation has taken place, the educator and the student should discuss how the social skill situation was handled.

5. **Similarity of Environment and People** - Try to make the practice environment as similar as possible to where the students will actually be using the skill. For example, if a student is often disciplined for misbehaving in the hallways, have the student practice "accepting consequences" out in the hallway in addition to in the classroom. Try to involve people the student will actually be dealing with (e.g., mainstream teacher, principal) in the role play activities. This will help the student transfer the social skills when dealing with these people.

6. **Make Others Aware** - It is important to make other school professionals (e.g., regular education teachers, counselors, principals, secretaries) aware of the social skills you are teaching to your students. Hand out a list of each social skill taught to help them better understand how social skills are defined and broken into skill steps. Educators would benefit from an inservice which explains social skill instruction and gives helpful hints for them to use with all of their students. A weekly memo can be sent to school personnel, which discusses the social skill currently being taught in your class. Encourage the staff to praise students when they see them using social skills appropriately. For example, the school secretary might praise a student for interrupting appropriately (e.g., "Wendy, when you interrupted me just now, you did it very appropriately."). If you are using a certain strategy with a student (e.g., not becoming impulsive), make sure that other people know the exact words and steps you are using (e.g., "Wendel, tell yourself to calm down. Take a deep breath. Take another deep breath and count to five."). Then others will be able to use the same strategy with the student and, hopefully, help him to transfer his skills to areas outside the classroom.

7. **Parental Involvement** - Parents must understand and become involved in social skill instruction. The educator may want to meet with parents at the beginning of the school year and go through the Social Communication Skills Rating Scale - Adult Form (See Appendix A). It is important to get parental input as to which skills their child needs to work on. The educator can also explain the Skill Homework Activity pages to the parent (See description on page 20). The educator should give pointers to parents about role playing, and emphasize that parents should reinforce their children any time they see them using appropriate social skills.

8. **Self-Reinforcement and Monitoring** - Several authors have recently advocated the use of student-centered strategies (Anderson-Inman, 1986; Fowler, 1986). A self-monitoring checklist is a reminder to the students of skills learned and where they are expected to use those skills. The students could write a personal contract which tells when, where, and how often they plan to use the skill. The students can self-monitor by keeping a record of how often they use various social skills. Educators should initially model how to self-monitor. The students should also be taught to self-reinforce (reward) themselves for completing a task or having responsible behavior. **Transfer Activities: Thinking Skill Vocabulary Development** (Mayo and Gajewski, 1987) contains a unit on motivation which helps students move from extrinsic to intrinsic motivation.

9. **Reward/Behavioral Programs** - Many students have not reached the level in which they can self-monitor, and they need more external controls to help them use ap-

propriate behavior. Behavioral programs which provide rewards and consequences may be necessary. Educators should have a plan for helping students move from the external behavioral program to taking responsibility for their own behavior.

10. **Group Contingencies** - McConnell (1987) emphasizes that social interaction involves the interrelated behavior of two or more people. While a student may be able to perform a specified social skill (e.g., he can begin a conversation), others may not interact with the student, thus making it almost impossible for him to demonstrate skill competence. A socially isolated student such as this would not receive the natural reinforcement that comes from positive interaction with one's peers. It is often necessary to set up group contingencies (e.g., the class will receive a reward if John initiates conversation with three people) so that the other students will encourage the student to perform the skill, and interact with him so that he is able to perform the skill. Educators are cautioned to choose a reward criteria that is set at a level the given student is able to meet.

11. **Peer Reminders** - Students should be encouraged to remind fellow students about using social skills (e.g., "Come on, John. Remember how we learned to control our anger. You can do it."). In addition, students should praise each other for using appropriate social skills (e.g., "You really handled it well when the teacher was criticizing you.").

12. **A-U Sheets** - An A-U (Acceptable-Unacceptable) sheet is a system that helps the student use appropriate social skills in every class (See Appendix M). The sheet can be designed to meet the needs of any student. The student takes his A-U sheet to each of his classes and his teachers rate whether he was successful at the goals listed on the sheet. An "A" from the teacher means acceptable, while a "U" means unacceptable. There is also a section for teachers to comment and write down the next day's assignment. The student turns his A-U sheet in to his teacher at the end of the day. The teacher keeps a record of how successful the student has been with the goals listed on the A-U sheet. The student may earn points based on how many "A's" he received during the day. The student also takes the A-U sheet home each night to show his parents. Additional uses of the A-U can be found in **Transfer Activities: Thinking Skill Vocabulary Development** (Mayo and Gajewski, 1987).

13. **Student Mediators** - *Mediated Dispute Resolution* involves student conflicts being resolved by the students themselves with the help of a trained peer mediator (Koch and Miller, 1987). When a conflict arises, the students are asked if they would like to "get mediated." Students then put the disagreement "on hold" until a peer mediator is found. In a mediation session, the peer mediator first explains the ground rules. Then each student takes turns telling "his side of the story." The students then come up with a list of solutions, decide upon a solution and sign a written agreement. This strategy, which can be used any time throughout the school day, teaches students to compromise and negotiate. Transfer of social skills occurs when students learn to solve problems on their own rather than needing to have adults intervene.

14. **Transfer Contest** - The educator can hold "transfer contests" to motivate the students to transfer their newly learned social skills. One type of contest would involve the students writing about different times when they used their newly learned social skills outside of class. Another type of contest would be to have "social skill coupons" printed and distributed to parents and regular educators. Whenever these people observe the students using a social skill appropriately, they give them a coupon. The child turns in his coupons to his social skills teacher. The student who has collected the most coupons in an agreed upon amount of time wins the contest.

15. **Real-Life Outings** - While it is necessary to isolate social skills for direct instruction in the skills, the educator must remember that in *real life,* students must identify when

and which social skills to use and must use a combination of social skills at all times. It is important to take students on community outings in which they have the chance to demonstrate success in being socially appropriate. Such outings might include tours of area attractions, trips to restaurants, and sports activities.

SSS: USE OF COOPERATIVE LEARNING TECHNIQUES

As stated in Chapter One, social skill acquisition and use should be promoted through group interaction rather than through teacher-directed activities. The use of cooperative learning techniques is an effective way to encourage group interaction. For further information about the definition and history of cooperative learning, refer to SOCIAL COMMUNICATION SKILLS: HOW TO TEACH THESE SKILLS in Chapter One on page 4. Johnson and Johnson (1984) state 18 aspects an educator should consider when structuring a cooperative learning lesson:

1. Specifying academic and collaborative objectives
2. Deciding on the size of the group
3. Assigning students to groups
4. Arranging the room
5. Planning materials
6. Assigning roles
7. Explaining the academic task
8. Structuring positive goal interdependence
9. Structuring individual accountability
10. Structuring intergroup cooperation
11. Explaining criteria for success
12. Specifying desired behaviors
13. Monitoring students' behavior
14. Providing task assistance
15. Intervening to teach collaborative skills
16. Providing closure to the lesson
17. Evaluating the quality and quantity of students' learning
18. Assessing how well the group functioned

For a brief description of each of these 18 aspects, refer to Appendix N.

SSS includes four units which are structured in a cooperative learning manner. (See units A-28, A-31, B-9, and B-24.) When using any of the four units, the educator must keep in mind that several of the 18 aspects listed above will still need to be considered and planned for. The educator is encouraged to learn more about cooperative learning by reading **Circles of Learning** (Johnson et al., 1984), **Cooperation in the Classroom** (Johnson and Johnson, 1984), or **Learning Together and Alone: Cooperative, Competitive, and Individualistic Learning** (Johnson and Johnson, 1987), or by contacting the Cooperative Learning Center, University of Minnesota , 202 Pattee Hall, Minneapolis, MN 55455, (612) 624-7031. The educator is also encouraged to teach other units from *SSS* using a cooperative learning approach.

REFERENCES

Adelman, H. and Taylor, L. Enhancing the motivation and skills needed to overcome interpersonal problems. *Learning Disability Quarterly,* 5: 438-446, 1982.

Anderson-Inman, L. Bridging the gap: Student-centered strategies for promoting the transfer of learning. *Exceptional Children,* 52(6): 562-572, 1986.

Arkowitz, H. Assessment of social skills. In M. Herson and A. Bellack (Eds.), *Behavioral assessment,* 296-327. New York: Pergamon Press, 1981.

Aronson, E., Blaney, N., Stephan, C., Sikes, J., and Snapp, M. *The jigsaw classroom.* Beverly Hills, CA: Sage, 1978.

Baer, D., Wolf, M., and Risley, T. Some current dimensions of applied behavior analysis. *Journal of Applied Behavior Analysis,* 1: 91-97, 1968.

Bandura, A. *Social learning theory.* Englewood Cliffs, NJ: Prentice-Hall, 1977.

Bloom, B., Engelhart, M., Furst, E., Hill, W., and Krathwohl, D. *Taxonomy of educational objectives: The classification of educational goals.* New York: David McKay Company, Inc., 1954.

Bohlmeyer, E. and Burke, J. Selecting cooperative learning techniques: A consultative strategy guide. *School Psychology Review,* 16(1): 36-49, 1987.

Clark, B. *Optimizing learning.* Columbus, OH: Merrill Publishing Co., 1986.

Dale, E. and Chall, J. A formula for predicting readability: Instructions. *Educational Research Bulletin,* 27: 11-20 and 37-54, 1948 (Jan. 21 and Feb. 17).

Dembrowsky, C. *Affective skill development for adolescents.* Jackson, WY: Self-published, 1983.

Deshler, D. and Schumaker, J. Social skills of learning disabled adolescents: Characteristics and intervention. *Topics in Learning and Learning Disabilities,* 3(2): 15-23, 1983.

Foster, S. and Ritchey, W. Issues in the assessment of social competence in children. *Journal of Applied Behavior Analysis,* 12: 625-638, 1979.

Fowler, S. Peer-monitoring and self-monitoring: Alternatives to traditional teacher management. *Exceptional Children,* 52(6): 573-582, 1986.

Fry, E. Fry's readability graph: Clarifications, validity, and extension to level 17. *Journal of Reading,* 21(3): 242-252, 1977.

Galyean, B. *Mind sight: Learning through imaging.* Santa Barbara, CA: Center for Integrative Learning, 1983.

Gelzheiser, L., Shepherd, M., and Wozniak, R. The development of instruction to induce skill transfer. *Exceptional Children,* 53(2): 125-129, 1986.

Goldsmith, J. and McFall, R. Development and evaluation of an interpersonal skill-training program for psychiatric inpatients. *Journal of Abnormal Psychology,* 19(2): 120-133, 1975.

Goldstein, A. and Glick, B. *Agression replacement training: A comprehensive intervention for agressive youth*. Champaign, IL: Research Press, 1987.

Goldstein, A., Sprafkin, R., Gershaw, N., and Klein, P. *Skillstreaming the adolescent: A structured learning approach to teaching prosocial skills*. Champaign, IL: Research Press, 1980.

Good, T. and Grouws, D. Effective mathematics teaching in elementary grades. In D. Chambers (Ed.), *Effective teaching of mathematics, Bulletin No. 7447*. Madison, WI: Department of Public Instruction, 1985.

Gorovitz, E. The creative brain II; A revisit with Ned Herrmann. *Training and Development Journal*, 36(12): 74-77, 1982.

Greenspan, S. and Shoultz, B. Why mentally retarded adults lose their jobs: Social competence as a factor in work adjustments. *Applied Research in Mental Retardation*, 2: 23-31, 1981.

Gresham, F. Assessment of children's social skills. *Journal of School Psychology*, 19(2): 120-132, 1981a.

Gresham, F. Social skills training with handicapped children: A review. *Review of Educational Research*, 51(1): 139-175, 1981b.

Gresham, F. Misguided mainstreaming: The case for social skill training with handicapped children. *Exceptional Children*, 48(5): 422-431, 1982.

Hatcher, M. Whole brain learning. *The School Administrator*, 40(5): 8-11, 1983.

Harris, W. The making better choices program. *The Pointer*, 29(1): 16-19, 1984.

Harris, W. *Making better choices: A cognitive-behavioral approach for teaching social skills and cognitive planning*. Orono, ME: MBC Publications, 1987.

Hazel, J., Sherman, J., Schumaker, J., and Sheldon, J. Group social skills training with adolescents: A critical review. In D. Upper and S. Ross (Eds.), *Handbook of behavioral group therapy*. New York: Plenum Publishing, 1985.

Jackson, N., Jackson, D., and Monroe, C. *Getting along with others: Teaching social effectiveness to children*. Champaign, IL: Research Press, 1983.

Johnson, D. and Johnson, R. *Cooperation in the classroom*. Edina, MN: Interaction Book Company, 1984.

Johnson, D., Johnson, R., Holubec, E., and Roy, P. *Circles of learning*. Alexandria, VA: Association for Supervision and Curriculum Development, 1984.

Johnson D. and Johnson R. *Learning together and alone: Cooperative, competitive, and individualistic learning - Revised*. Englewood Cliffs, NJ: Prentice-Hall, 1987.

Johnson, R. and Johnson, D., Action research: Cooperative learning in the science classroom. *Science and Children*, 24(2): 31-32, 1986.

Kauffman, J. *Characteristics of children's behavior disorders.* Columbus, OH: Charles E. Merrill Publishing Co., 1977.

Kazdin, A. and Matson, J. Social validation in mental retardation. *Applied Research in Mental Retardation,* 2(1): 39-53, 1981.

Kendall, P. and Braswell, L. *Cognitive - behavioral therapy for impulsive children.* New York: The Guildford Press, 1985.

Keystone Area Education Agency. *Dubuque management system.* Dubuque, IA: Dubuque Community Schools, 1990.

Koch, M. and Miller, S. Resolving student conflicts with student mediators. *Principal,* 66: 59-62, 1987.

Mayo, P. and Gajewski, N. *Transfer activities: Thinking skill vocabulary development.* Eau Claire, WI: Thinking Publications, 1987.

Mayo, P. and Waldo, P. *Communicate.* Eau Claire, WI: Thinking Publications, 1986.

McCarthy, B. *4Mat in action: Creative lesson plans for teaching to learning styles with right/left mode technique.* Oak Brook, IL: Excel., 1983.

McConnell, D. Entrapment effects and the generalization and maintenance of social skills training for elementary school students with behavioral disorders. *Behavioral Disorders,* 12(4): 252-263, 1987.

McGinnis, E., Sauerbry, L., and Nichols, P. Skill-streaming: Teaching social skills to children with behavioral disorders. *Teaching Exceptional Children,* 17: 160-167, 1985.

O' Leary, S. and Dubey, D. Applications of self-control procedures by children: A review. *Journal of Applied Behavior Analysis,* 12: 449-465, 1979.

Palincsar, A. Metacognitive strategy instruction. *Exceptional Children,* 53(2): 118-124, 1986.

Paris, S. and Oka, E. Self-regulated learning among exceptional children. *Exceptional Children,* 53(2): 103-108, 1986.

Pearl, R., Donahue, M., and Bryan, T. *The development of tact: Children's strategies for delivering bad news.* Unpublished manuscript, Chicago, IL: University of Illinois, 1983.

Perlmutter, B., Crocker, J., Cordray, D., and Garstecki, D. Sociometric status and related personality characteristics of mainstreamed learning disabled adolescents. *Learning Disability Quarterly,* 6: 20-30, 1983.

Roff, M. Childhood social interactions and young adult bad conduct. *Journal of Abnormal Psychology,* 63(2): 333-337, 1961.

Roff, M., Sells, S., and Golden, M. *Social adjustment and personality development in children.* Minneapolis, MN: University of Minnesota, 1972.

Schloss, P., Schloss, C., Wood, C., and Kiehl, W. A Critical review of social skills research with behaviorally disordered students. *Behavioral Disorders,* 12(1): 1-14, 1986.

Schumaker, J. and Hazel, J. Social skills assessment and training for the learning disabled: Who's on first and what's on second? Part I. *Journal of Learning Disabilities,* 17(7): 422-431, 1984a.

Schumaker, J. and Hazel, J. Social skills assessment and training for the learning disabled: Who's on first and what's on second? Part II. *Journal of Learning Disabilities,* 17(8): 492-499, 1984b.

Schumaker, J., Hazel, J., Sherman, J., and Sheldon, J. Social skill performances of learning disabled, non-learning disabled, and delinquent adolescents. *Learning Disability Quarterly,* 5: 388-397, 1982.

Shames, G. and Wiig, E. *Human communication disorders: An introduction.* Columbus, OH: Charles E. Merrill Publishing Co., 1982.

Simpson, R. Social interactions of behaviorally disordered children and youth: Where are we and where do we need to go? *Behavioral Disorders,* 12(4): 292-298, 1987.

Slavin, R. *The effects of teams in teams-games-tournament on the normative climates of classrooms.* John Hopkins University: Center for Social Organization of Schools, 1974.

Stephens, T. *Social skills in the classroom.* Columbus, OH: Cedars Press, 1978.

Stokes, T. and Baer, D. An implicit technology of generalization. *Journal of Applied Behavior Analysis,* 10: 349-369, 1977.

Vetter, A. *A comparison of the characteristics of learning disabled and non-learning disabled young adults.* Unpublished doctoral dissertation. Lawrence, KS: University of Kansas, 1983.

Wahler, R., Berland, R., and Coe, T. Generalization processes in child behavior change. In B. Lahey and A. Kazdin (Eds.), *Advances in clinical child psychology,* New York: Plenum Press, 1979.

Waldo, P. and Mayo, P. *Scripting: Social communication for adolescents.* Eau Claire, WI: Thinking Publications, 1986.

Walker, H. *The acting out child: Coping with classroom disruption.* Boston, MA: Allyn and Bacon, 1979.

Webb, G. Left/right brains, teammates in learning. *Exceptional Children,* 49(6): 508-515, 1983.

Wehman, P., Abramson, M., and Norman, C. Transfer of training in behavior modification programs: An evaluative review. *Journal of Special Education,* 11: 215-231, 1977.

White, W., Schumaker, J., Warner, M., Alley, G., and Deshler, D. *The current status of young adults identified as learning disabled during their school career. (Research report No. 21).* Lawrence, KS: University of Kansas Institute for Research in Learning Disabilities, 1980.

Wiig, E. *Let's talk: Developing prosocial communication skills.* Columbus, OH: Charles E. Merrill Publishing Co., 1982a.

Wiig, E. *Let's talk inventory for adolescents.* Columbus, OH: Charles E. Merrill Publishing Co., 1982b.

PEER INTERACTION SKILLS

SKILL HOMEWORK ACTIVITY

_____
(Due Date)

Dear Parent or Guardian of: _____

This week we are learning about the social communication skill:

REPUTATION

This social skill is very important in interpersonal relationships.

The students have learned that having a *good* reputation is important. Once someone gets a *bad* reputation, it is difficult to change that reputation. The students have also learned that some people get *bad* reputations because of rumors people tell.

Before the due date, please complete one of the following activities with your son or daughter: (put a check mark by your choice)

_____ A. We acted out the role play situation listed below.

_____ B. I observed my son/daughter using this social skill in a real-life situation. (I have described the situation below.)

Description of real-life observation:

Role play situation:

PRETEND YOU HAVE GOTTEN A *BAD* REPUTATION WITH SOME OF YOUR TEACHERS AT SCHOOL. DISCUSS WAYS YOU CAN CHANGE YOUR REPUTATION WITH ONE OF YOUR PARENTS.

- -

Please circle the word below which best describes how your son or daughter did while using this social skill in either the role play or real-life situation.

NEEDS MORE HELP   GOOD   EXCELLENT

It is important for you to reinforce your child's use of this social skill at home in a positive way. Encourage and praise your child when you see the skill appropriately used. Remind him/her to use the social skill when necessary.

Thank you for your assistance.

Sincerely,

* *

PARENT/GUARDIAN SIGNATURE: _____

Reputations

A **reputation** is *how other people view you.* It is what they think you are like. Reputations can be positive (e.g., Jean has the reputation of being a good singer), or reputations can be negative (e.g., Junior has the reputation of being a bully). Some reputations are the truth about people, while other reputations are not really what the person is like.

DIRECTIONS: Make a list of different reputations that people might have. An example has been done for you. Then, write the first names of people you know who have each of the reputations you have listed.

POSITIVE REPUTATIONS   **NEGATIVE REPUTATIONS**

EXAMPLE → *brain, Joe*   *slob, Gail*

_____ / _____   _____ / _____

_____ / _____   _____ / _____

_____ / _____   _____ / _____

_____ / _____   _____ / _____

_____ / _____   _____ / _____

Name:_____

Barb's Reputation

DIRECTIONS: Read the following story and answer the questions that follow.

Barb knocked on the door of her counselor's office. Her counselor, Mrs. Conway, told her to come in. Barb said, "Mrs. Conway, I need to talk with you about something. I am getting so tired of people starting rumors about me." "What do you mean?" Mrs. Conway asked. Barb looked as though she was going to cry. "Well, people think that I take drugs and get in trouble with the police all the time. I can just tell by the way some of my teachers look at me that they think I'm a troublemaker. I've never been in any trouble." Mrs. Conway thought for a minute and then asked, "Barb, why do you think people think those things about you?" "Oh, it's just because of who my friends are and the way I dress. Just because my friends have been in trouble, people think I'm that way, too. It's not fair." "No, it's not fair, but we get an impression of someone by who that person's friends are. Barb, why don't you stop in again tomorrow and we can discuss this further."

1. Why do you think people thought Barb was a troublemaker?

2. What would you do if you were in Barb's situation?

3. Do you know anyone like Barb? How does that person handle his or her situation?

Name:_____

Reputations Discussion

DIRECTIONS: Answer the following questions. We will be having a discussion about reputations. You may share your answers to questions during the discussion if you would like, but you do not have to.

1. Describe (in 3 or 4 sentences) the reputation you have in this school.

2. Do you have a different reputation with your teachers than you do with the students in school? _____ Explain your answer.

3. What is your reputation in your neighborhood?

4. What are the reputations of your older brothers and sisters (if you have any)?

5. Have the reputations of any of your family members made it difficult or easy for you? _____ Explain your answer.

6. Do you like your reputation? _____ Explain your answer.

7. If you could start all over again at this school, would you try to change your reputation? _____ Explain your answer.

8. What kind of reputations do your friends have?

9. Do you like your friends' reputations? _____ Explain your answer.

10. Do your friends' reputations have an influence on your reputation? _____ Explain your answer.

11. Have you ever considered not being friends with someone because you're afraid your reputation might be affected? _____ Explain your answer.

12. Do you know anyone who has gotten an undeserved reputation? _____ Explain your answer.

13. Write or tell a short story about a person who got an undeserved reputation.

Name:_____

YOUR REPUTATION

It *IS* possible to change a bad reputation. It may be difficult to do, but it is not impossible.

DIRECTIONS: Brainstorm with another student. List some things that could be done by someone who wants to change a bad reputation.

- •
- •
- •
- •
- •
- •
- •
- •
- •
- •

Changing a reputation may be difficult, but it can be done. The important thing to remember is that you are the person who counts the most. You have to be happy with yourself. There may be some people who will expect you to act in the old way. But, you will know the truth about yourself. You will know that you have changed.

Name:_____

REPUTATION - REPUTATION - REPUTATION - REPUTATION

1. Define the term *reputation*. _____

   _____

2. Explain why some people get *bad* reputations.

   _____

   _____

   _____

3. Write or think of the name of someone you know who has a *bad* reputation. Tell what reputation the person has and describe some of the problems he/she has because of that reputation.

   _____

   _____

   _____

   _____

4. Compare *good* reputations to *bad* reputations. Tell one similarity and one difference.

   (similarity) _____

   _____

   (difference) _____

   _____

5. Write either a poem or the lyrics to a song about reputations. Use the back of this page.

6. Read the following paragraph. Tell whether you agree or disagree with the statements about reputations. Explain why you answered as you did.

   People should not worry about getting a *bad* reputation. Most of the time reputations are not what the person is really like.

   AGREE   DISAGREE   (Circle one)

   (explanation) _____

   _____

   _____

SKILL HOMEWORK ACTIVITY

_____
(Due Date)

Dear Parent or Guardian of: _____

This week we are learning about the social communication skill:

STARTING A FRIENDSHIP

This social skill is very important in interpersonal relationships.

The students have learned many tips for starting a friendship (see attached _FRIENDSHIP TIPS_). The students have many positive qualities which can help to start a friendship. They learned to differentiate between people who want to be _true_ friends and people who just want to _use_ them.

Before the due date, please complete one of the following activities with your son or daughter: (put a check mark by your choice)

_____ A. We acted out the role play situation listed below.

_____ B. I observed my son/daughter using this social skill in a real-life situation. (I have described the situation below.)

Description of real-life observation:

Role play situation:

YOU ARE GETTING FRUSTRATED BECAUSE YOU'RE HAVING A HARD TIME MAKING FRIENDS. TALK WITH ONE OF YOUR PARENTS ABOUT YOUR PROBLEM. DISCUSS SOME WAYS YOU COULD GO ABOUT MAKING A NEW FRIEND.

- -

Please circle the word below which best describes how your son or daughter did while using this social skill in either the role play or real-life situation.

NEEDS MORE HELP   GOOD   EXCELLENT

It is important for you to reinforce your child's use of this social skill at home in a positive way. Encourage and praise your child when you see the skill appropriately used. Remind him/her to use the social skill when necessary.

Thank you for your assistance.

Sincerely,

* *

PARENT/GUARDIAN SIGNATURE: _____

38

Friendship Tips

1. Like Yourself First

It will be hard for you to make friends if you don't like yourself. If you're the type of person who's always putting yourself down, people won't want to be your friend.

2. Be Where the People Are

Put yourself in places where other people are (e.g., sports events, clubs, neighborhood activities). You can't meet new friends hiding in your bedroom.

3. Have Things in Common

One way to start a friendship is to find someone who has something in common with you (e.g., if you collect baseball cards, you'll have a lot to talk about with someone else who collects baseball cards).

crafts
swimming
soccer
fixing cars
drama club
musical instruments
reading
computers
fishing
collections

4. Talk to People

It's hard to talk to someone you don't know. But if you don't talk to people, there' no chance for a friendship to develop.

HI, I'M IN YOUR FIRST HOUR MATH CLASS!

DIRECTIONS: Write your own friendship tips for #7 and #8.

---

5. *Don't Be Pushy*

Don't be pushy or overbearing. Friendships take time to grow. Once you meet someone, don't stick to them like glue. Don't expect to be best buddies right away. People will not want you for a friend if you act like that.

6. *Try the "Out" Crowd*

Don't always try to get in with the most popular people, the so-called "in" crowd. There are many other fun, interesting people who would really like a friend. Try people in the "out" crowd.

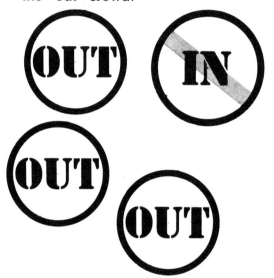

7.

8.

EDUCATOR PAGE: DO NOT DUPLICATE FOR STUDENTS

PURPOSE: To teach students the qualities people look for in a friend.

EDUCATOR INSTRUCTIONS: 1. Hold the discussion described below with students.

2. Have students complete the activity below.

DISCUSSION: 1. Read the following story to the students:

Lonnie Left Alone has no friends. Lonnie just can't figure it out. He's always telling other people about how tough he is and how many neat things his parents buy for him. The other kids always laugh at Lonnie when he makes fun of the teacher during class, but nobody seems to want to be Lonnie's friend. Lonnie thinks something must be wrong with everyone else. After all, you couldn't get a better friend than Lonnie.

2. Discuss some reasons why Lonnie may not have any friends.

3. Have students brainstorm the qualities they would like in a friend (e.g., kind, loyal, honest, fun).

ACTIVITY: 1. Hand out several small strips of paper to each student.

2. Tell the students to write the name of each student in class on the strips of paper (one name per strip).

3. Tell the students to think about each student in class and write down one personal quality each person has that would make him/her a good friend. They should write each person's quality on the strip of paper that contains that person's name.

4. Have the students give their "friendship quality strips" to the people the strips were written about.

Name:_____

What I Can Offer

What do you have to offer someone who may be considering you as a friend? Friendship is a two-way relationship. You want a friend who has good qualities, and other people will like you if you have good qualities. Think about it. What are your good qualities? Are you honest and loyal? Do you have a good sense of humor? What are your interests? Do you like sports or have any special hobbies? Each of us has something different to offer.

DIRECTIONS: Write your good qualities and interests inside of the giving hands below. Write at least three qualities in the left hand and at least three interests/hobbies in the right hand. (Remember, think about why someone would want to be your friend. What do you have to offer?) Fill both hands with things you have to offer.

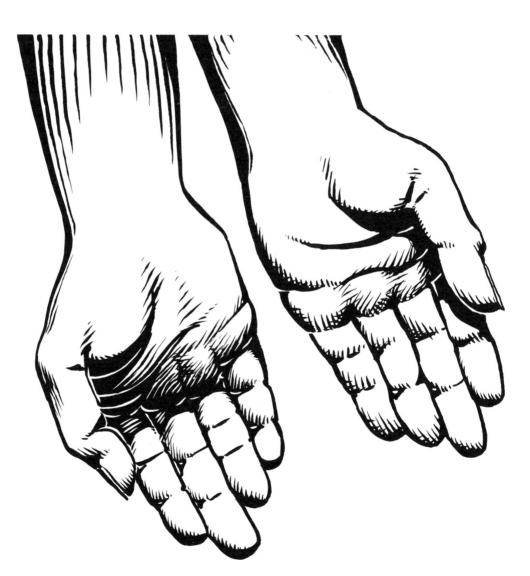

I Can Give . . .

Name:_____

DNEIRF

DIRECTIONS: Beware! When you are starting a friendship with someone, watch out for the *DNEIRF*. (That's *friend* spelled backwards). A *DNEIRF* doesn't like you for who you are. A *DNEIRF* may like you for the clothes you wear or how much money you have or what clique you belong to. A *DNEIRF* is not a true friend. Read about each friendship below. If the person is a true friend, write **FRIEND** on the line. If the person is not a true friend, write **DNEIRF** on the line.

_____ 1. Jim likes you because you have a car.

_____ 2. Linda sticks up for you when other people cut you down.

_____ 3. You and Bob do lots of things together (e.g., go to the movies, play baseball).

_____ 4. Carrie only likes to go with you when your mom gives you money.

_____ 5. Josh puts you down all the time.

_____ 6. Mary asks you over to her house a lot.

_____ 7. You and Robbie have a fun time when you're together.

_____ 8. Whenever you tell Jenny a secret, she tells everyone else.

_____ 9. Tina and Laurie like you because you drink alcohol.

_____10. Monica doesn't want to do things with you when your mentally retarded brother is around.

_____11. It seems that whenever Marty comes to your house, all he wants to do is talk to your older sister.

_____12. Shanna said she'll be friends with you now that you're a cheerleader.

_____13. Randy is always trying to talk you into doing funny things that get you in trouble.

_____14. You feel good when you're around Delia.

_____15. Paul is a good listener. He really listens when you need to talk with someone.

Name:_____

Friendship QUESTIONS

DIRECTIONS: Answer the questions below.

1. Are you good at starting new friendships? Tell why or why not.

2. Why is it sometimes scary to try to make new friends?

3. What would you do if you already had several friends, and you notice a new person in your class who doesn't have any friends and seems kind of shy?

4. Give at least four good tips for starting a friendship.

5. What are some things that you have to offer someone who is thinking about being your friend?

6. Explain what a *DNEIRF* is.

7. Choose one of your current friends. Tell how that friendship started.

44

STARTING A FRIENDSHIP - STARTING A FRIENDSHIP

1. Write the six tips for starting a friendship.

   (#1) _____

   (#2) _____

   (#3) _____

   (#4) _____

   (#5) _____

   (#6) _____

2. Explain why it's important to be able to make new friends.

   _____

   _____

   _____

   _____

3. Think of a person you would like to be friends with. Tell some strategies you could use to start a friendship with that person.

   _____

   _____

   _____

   _____

4. Read the situation and answer the question below:

   Maria had recently moved to a new school. She wanted to make some new friends, but she knew it would be difficult. Maria joined the track team and girls' choir. Maria tried to talk to at least one person in each of her classes every day. When Maria started to get discouraged, she told herself, "I'm a fun person to be with, and sooner or later I know I'll make some friends." After about a week, Maria had already made three new friends.

   What strategies did Maria use to make new friends?

   _____

   _____

   _____

5. Pretend you are a counselor. Make up a short lesson you could teach to students about starting a friendship. Write all the major ideas you would include in your lesson.

_____

_____

_____

_____

_____

6. Evaluate your friendship skills. Write down three personal qualities you have that make you a good friend. After each quality, give some reasons (or examples) of why you feel you possess that quality.

(quality #1)_____

(reasons) _____

_____

_____

(quality #2)_____

(reasons) _____

_____

_____

(quality #3)_____

(reasons) _____

_____

_____

SKILL HOMEWORK ACTIVITY

_____
(Due Date)

Dear Parent or Guardian of: _____

This week we are learning about the social communication skill:

MAINTAINING A FRIENDSHIP

This social skill is very important in interpersonal relationships.

In a previous unit, the students learned how to start a new friendship. In this unit, they have learned the following "tips" to help keep a friendship going once it has begun:

1. Communicate with your friend (in person, letters/notes, phone).
2. Be honest.
3. Be loyal.
4. Keep secrets unless someone is in danger.
5. Be supportive.
6. Try to be fun and optimistic as much as possible.
7. Remember that neither of you is perfect.
8. Expect that your friend will sometimes disagree with you.
9. Do nice things for your friend — offer a helping hand.
10. Remind your friend every once in a while how important the friendship is to you.
11. Share your friend — don't be jealous when he/she does things with others.

Before the due date, please complete one of the following activities with your son or daughter: (put a check mark by your choice)

_____ A. We acted out the role play situation listed below.

_____ B. I observed my son/daughter using this social skill in a real-life situation. (I have described the situation below.)

Description of real-life observation:

Role play situation:

PRETEND YOUR YOUNGER BROTHER/SISTER ASKS FOR ADVICE ABOUT MAINTAINING A FRIENDSHIP. DEMONSTRATE HOW YOU WOULD EXPLAIN EACH OF THE "TIPS" LISTED ABOVE TO HIM/HER.

Please circle the word below which best describes how your son or daughter did while using this social skill in either the role play or real-life situation.

NEEDS MORE HELP   GOOD   EXCELLENT

It is important for you to reinforce your child's use of this social skill at home in a positive way. Encourage and praise your child when you see the skill appropriately used. Remind him/her to use the social skill when necessary.

Thank you for your assistance.

Sincerely,

* *

PARENT/GUARDIAN SIGNATURE: _____

47

Name:_____

Ways To Keep It Going...

Friends are important in our lives. We should do everything we can to keep an important friendship going, once it has started.

Below is a list of eleven tips or strategies that will help you to keep your friendships going. A brief description for each tip is also provided.

---

1 | **Communicate with your friend**
(in person, letters/notes, phone).

Communicating with your friend can be easy, especially if you live close to each other, have classes together, eat lunch at school together, or are in a club or sport together. Suppose that one of you moves away, or that you don't have any classes together. Suppose that one of you starts dating a boyfriend/girlfriend, or starts spending a lot of time in a new club or sport. Then, setting aside time to communicate with your friend becomes very important if you want your friendship to continue.

---

2 | **Be honest.**

If you can't be honest with your friend, then who can you be honest with? If your friend learns that you are not being honest, then he/she will lose faith in you.

3 | **Be loyal.**

Be the person's friend when you are together and when you are apart. If your friend learns that you say bad things behind his/her back, it may end the friendship.

---

4 | **Keep secrets unless someone is in danger.**

If your friend tells something and asks you to keep it a secret, then it is your responsibility not to tell anyone else. If your friend finds out that you broke a secret, then you will lose his/her trust, and will not be told secrets anymore. If your friend tells you something that makes you believe he/she is in danger (e.g., is being abused, is taking drugs, is considering suicide) then it is your responsibility to seek help for your friend. Your friend may be mad at first, but in the long run it would be the best thing to do.

---

5 | **Be supportive.**

Try to encourage your friend whenever possible. We all need support, and friends are a great source.

6 | **Try to be fun and optimistic.**

Although a friend is a good person to talk to when you are depressed or worried, you should try to be fun and optimistic whenever possible. Nobody likes to be around someone who is always depressed and negative.

---

7 | **Remember that neither one of you is perfect.**

Apologize to your friend when you make a mistake and forgive your friend's mistakes. Nobody is perfect, and we all do things wrong. If you are looking for a friend who will never make you mad, you won't find one.

8 | **Expect that your friend will sometimes disagree with you.**

No two people are exactly alike. Your friend will think differently about certain things than you will. It is OK to disagree about some things and still be friends.

9 | **Do nice things for your friend — offer a helping hand.**

When your friend is feeling depressed, it might be a good time to do something nice to lift his/her spirits. Even if your friend isn't depressed, it can be fun to do something nice. When your friend is in need, it may be a good time to offer a helping hand.

10 | **Remind your friend every once in a while how important the friendship is to you.**

Now and again, it is nice to say something like, "I'm really glad you're my friend." You don't even have to tell your friend in person; you can tell him/her in a note or letter if that makes you feel more comfortable. We all need to be reminded that our friendship is special and that we are not being taken for granted.

11 | **Share your friend — don't be jealous when he/she does things with others.**

Try not to be "possessive" of your friend and expect that you are the only one he/she should do things with. Your friend can do things with other people and still be friends with you.

Write down any other tips you can think of for maintaining a friendship.

1.

2.

3.

4.

Name:_____

Dear Diary

REMEMBER: There are at least eleven ways to help keep a friendship going.

1. Communicate with your friend (in person, letter/notes, phone).
2. Be honest.
3. Be loyal.
4. Keep secrets unless someone is in danger.
5. Be supportive.
6. Try to be fun and optimistic as much as possible.
7. Remember that neither one of you is perfect.
8. Expect that your friend will sometimes disagree with you.
9. Do nice things for your friend — offer a helping hand.
10. Remind your friend every once in a while how important the friendship is to you.
11. Share your friend — don't be jealous when he/she does things with others.

DIRECTIONS: Read the following entry that Shannon wrote in her diary about her friend Jackie. At the bottom of the page, write the numbers for each of the strategies listed above that Jackie did not follow.

> Dear Diary: Monday
> Sometimes I wonder if Jackie is really my friend or not. Today I found out that she blabbed to Mark that I liked him. I told her not to tell anyone. Sometimes she really makes me mad! Last week she told me she likes my haircut, but then I overheard her telling Sandy she likes me better in long hair. She's probably still mad at me for the time I got ink on her shirt. I apologized up and down to her. I really felt bad. She gave me the silent treatment for a week! More tomorrow — Shannon

Write down the numbers for the strategies listed above that Jackie is not following:

_____

Name:_____

My Friend and I

DIRECTIONS: Think about whom you would consider to be one of your closest
friends. Complete the following table, by thinking about how you
treat this friend, and how this friend treats you.

	Communicate with your friend.	Be honest.	Be loyal.	Keep secrets.	Be supportive.	Share your friend.	Be fun and optimistic.	Remember neither one of you is perfect.	Allow your friend to disagree.	Do nice things — be helpful.	Remind your friend how important the friendship is.
Think about the way you usually treat your friend. Put an **x** under each rule that you generally follow with him/her.											
Think about the way your friend usually treats you. Put an **x** under each rule that he/she generally follows.											

DIRECTIONS: List the tips for maintaining a friendship that you feel you sometimes
ignore and need improvement on.

DIRECTIONS: Write a note below that you could give to one of your closest friends.
It should tell the reasons why you are glad he/she is your friend.
(You do not have to actually give the note to your friend. You can
if you want to. Remember, it is good to remind your friend every
once in a while how important the friendship is to you.)

©1989 THINKING PUBLICATIONS   51

Name:_____

Some Friends Aren't Worth Keeping!

Unfortunately, there are people who pretend to be our friends, but really they are just "using" us. You do not have to maintain a friendship with someone who pressures you or uses you.

For example, a friend might say to you, "If you're really my friend, you'll steal those tapes for me." If that happens, you might want to ask yourself if that person is a true friend.

DIRECTIONS: Add to this list of times when you may want to end a friendship.

1. When a friend is nice to you only when he wants something from you

2. When a friend tries to pressure you into smoking, even after you say *NO*

3. When a friend continues to tell others your secrets, even after you ask him not to

4.

5.

6.

7.

8.

9.

10.

MAINTAINING A FRIENDSHIP - MAINTAINING A FRIENDSHIP

1. Write eleven tips or strategies a person can use to help maintain friendships.

   (1)_____ (2)_____

   (3)_____ (4)_____

   (5)_____ (6)_____

   (7)_____ (8)_____

   (9)_____ (10)_____

   (11)_____

2. Choose three of the strategies listed above. Write the number for each strategy you choose, and then explain why it is important.

   (number)_____ (reason) _____

   (number)_____ (reason) _____

   (number)_____ (reason) _____

3. Describe a situation when you would not want to keep a secret that one of your friends told you.

   _____

   _____

   _____

4. Compare yourself to one of your friends. Tell one strategy you think you are better at, and one strategy your friend is better at.

   I am better at _____

   _____

   My friend is better at _____

   _____

5. Create a new strategy for maintaining a friendship which you could add to the list of eleven strategies discussed in this unit.

   _____

   _____

6. List the three strategies you believe you need to make the most improvement on.

   (1) _____

   (2) _____

   (3) _____

SKILL HOMEWORK ACTIVITY

_____
(Due Date)

Dear Parent or Guardian of: _____

This week we are learning about the social communication skill:

GIVING EMOTIONAL SUPPORT

This social skill is very important in interpersonal relationships.

The students have learned that _giving emotional support_ means letting people know you are thinking about them. It means recognizing when people need support.

Before the due date, please complete one of the following activities with your son or daughter: (put a check mark by your choice)

_____ A. We acted out the role play situation listed below.

_____ B. I observed my son/daughter using this social skill in a real-life situation. (I have described the situation below.)

Description of real-life observation:

Role play situation:

YOUR SISTER'S BEST FRIEND IS MOVING TO ANOTHER STATE. DEMONSTRATE HOW YOU CAN GIVE EMOTIONAL SUPPORT TO YOUR SISTER.

- -

Please circle the word below which best describes how your son or daughter did while using this social skill in either the role play or real-life situation.

NEEDS MORE HELP   GOOD   EXCELLENT

It is important for you to reinforce your child's use of this social skill at home in a positive way. Encourage and praise your child when you see the skill appropriately used. Remind him/her to use the social skill when necessary.

Thank you for your assistance.

Sincerely,

* *

PARENT/GUARDIAN SIGNATURE: _____

G.E.S.

Giving emotional support means *recognizing how people are feeling and letting them know you are thinking about them. It means supporting people when they need you.*

People need emotional support all the time, not just when something bad happens to them. If your friend wins an award, you can show your emotional support by telling him you're happy he won the award. If your sister is sick in bed with the flu, you can show your emotional support by telling her you hope she gets well soon. If your friend seems depressed about something, you can show your emotional support by talking with her.

Remember, you want to let people know you're thinking about them.

There are many ways to give support to someone. A few ideas are listed below.

- By listening to the person
- By telling the person you care
- By congratulating the person
- By sending flowers to the person

- By writing a note or sending a card
- By talking with the person
- By remaining loyal to the person
- By doing something nice

DIRECTIONS: List some other ways to provide emotional support for someone.

-
-
-
-
-

DIRECTIONS: In your own words, tell what *giving emotional support* means.

_____

_____

_____

IMPORTANT: IF YOU FEEL THAT THE PERSON IS SEVERELY DEPRESSED, YOU SHOULD ALERT AN ADULT RIGHT AWAY (e.g., COUNSELOR, TEACHER, PARENT).

Support

DIRECTIONS: Brainstorm times when you need to give emotional support to someone (e.g., when your brother doesn't make the baseball team). Write one idea inside each of the letters in the word **SUPPORT** below.

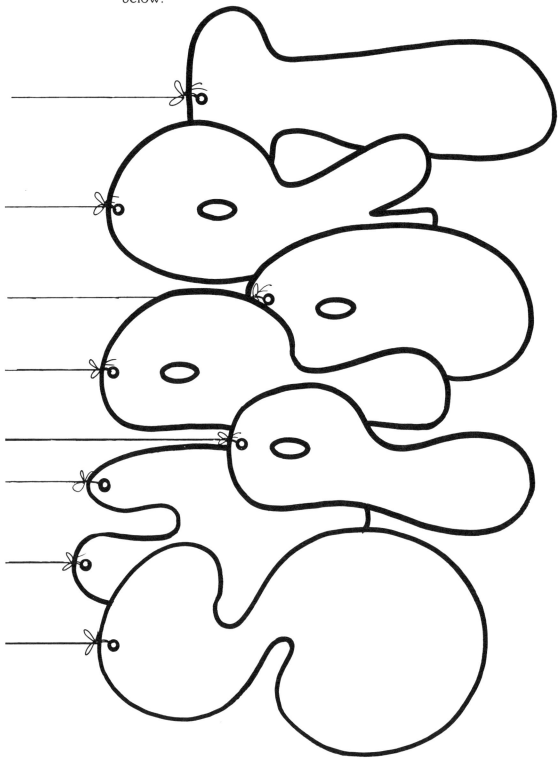

Name:_____

Supporting Someone

DIRECTIONS: Read the situations below. For each one, brainstorm some ways you could give emotional support to the person and list the ways below each situation.

1. Your friend's father died recently.	2. Your friend's girl/boy friend just broke up with him/her.
3. Your brother made it to the state wrestling competition.	4. Someone you know is in the hospital with a broken leg.
5. Your friend's parents are getting a divorce.	6. Your friend gets teased in a mean way by other people about her thick glasses.

Name:_____

Greeting Card

Some people earn their living by designing greeting cards. Do you think you would like such a job?

DIRECTIONS: Design a greeting card that you could give to someone for support. You may want to look at some cards to get ideas.

Draw/write on the front of your card.

Sorry you're not feeling well...

...wanted to let you know that I'm thinking of you.

Include a short verse on the inside.

Name:_____

What Would You Do?

DIRECTIONS: Fill in the last picture box (D) below. Draw a picture that shows what the person could do or say to give emotional support. You may write a paragraph explaining the support, if you prefer.

Emotional Support Record

DIRECTIONS: Keep a record during the next week of the various times when you provide emotional support to people. Remember, you can provide emotional support to someone when something good or bad happens.

Person I provided support to	The reason I provided support	What I did/said to provide support

Name:_____

GIVING EMOTIONAL SUPPORT - GIVING EMOTIONAL SUPPORT

1. Define *giving emotional support.*

   _____

   _____

2. Write three situations when you may want to give emotional support to someone.

   (1) _____

   (2) _____

   (3) _____

3. There is a girl in your class named Jesse. Her younger brother was recently in a bad car accident. Describe what you might do or say.

   _____

   _____

4. Read the following situation. Answer the questions at the end.

   > Julio was getting teased by two older students. Julio's friend Juan said, "Don't let it bother you, Julio. I think those guys are just jealous that you made the basketball team and they didn't. Come on. Let's go get something to eat."

   Who is the person giving emotional support?_____

   Who was the support given to? _____

   Why was the support given? _____

   How was the emotional support given? _____

5. Develop a plan for yourself in which you will provide emotional support to one person during the next week. Be specific about who you will provide support to and how you will do it. Write your plan on a separate sheet of paper.

6. Read the following situation. Decide if you think Kay provided emotional support or not. Explain your answer.

   > Anna felt it was wrong to drink. Lately, her friends had been putting pressure on her, though. One night, her friends were teasing her. One friend, Kay, didn't say anything. When Anna got up to leave, Kay told her she would walk her home.

   Did Kay provide emotional support? (circle one)   YES   NO

   (explanation) _____

   _____

SKILL HOMEWORK ACTIVITY

_____
(Due Date)

Dear Parent or Guardian of: _____

This week we are learning about the social communication skill:

GIVING ADVICE

This social skill is very important in interpersonal relationships and can be broken down into the following skill steps. Please watch for all of the steps in your role play practice or real-life observation.

1) Decide whether the person asked for your advice. (You may give advice without someone asking you for it, but it will be accepted better if it is asked for.)

2) Find out as many facts as you can before giving advice.

3) Try not to sound bossy when you give advice.

The students have also learned there are times when they should not try to give advice. They should tell their friend to talk to an adult (e.g., counselor, teacher, parent). If their friend is in danger, they should tell someone about their friend right away.

Before the due date, please complete one of the following activities with your son or daughter: (put a check mark by your choice)

_____ A. We acted out the role play situation listed below.

_____ B. I observed my son/daughter using this social skill in a real-life situation. (I have described the situation below.)

Description of real-life observation:

Role play situation:

YOUR SISTER TELLS YOU THAT SHE HID HER REPORT CARD BECAUSE SHE GOT AN "F" ON IT. SHE IS SCARED TO SHOW YOUR PARENTS AND SHE WANTS TO KNOW WHAT YOU THINK SHE SHOULD DO. DEMONSTRATE HOW YOU WOULD GIVE HER ADVICE.

- -

Please circle the word below which best describes how your son or daughter did while using this social skill in either the role play or real-life situation.

NEEDS MORE HELP   GOOD   EXCELLENT

It is important for you to reinforce your child's use of this social skill at home in a positive way. Encourage and praise your child when you see the skill appropriately used. Remind him/her to use the social skill when necessary.

Thank you for your assistance.

Sincerely,

* *

PARENT/GUARDIAN SIGNATURE: _____

Giving Advice

Here are some questions to ask when giving advice to someone. The skill steps are in parentheses in the right column.

1) Did the person ask for my advice?

(Decide whether the person asked for your advice. You may give advice without someone asking you for it, but it will be accepted better if it is asked for.)

2) Do I know all the facts?

(Find out as many facts as you can before giving advice.)

3) Do I sound bossy when I give advice?

(Try not to sound bossy when you give advice. Say something like, "Here's an idea you could try," or "If I were in your shoes . . . .")

These tips do not apply if someone is being hurt or thinking about hurting himself. You should immediately tell an adult about these two things.

DIRECTIONS: Read each situation below. Tell what the person giving advice did wrong.

1. Cindy and Joey were walking to class. Joey told Cindy that he thought Tricia Lane was cute and pretty nice. Cindy said, "If you want my advice, stay away from her. She's bad news! She hangs around with all the kids who get in trouble."

2. Junior told Karen that his social studies teacher, Mrs. Fair, was out to get him because she gave him a detention for not doing anything. Junior asked Karen what she thought he should do about the detention. She told him he should talk to the principal because he didn't do anything wrong. Karen didn't know Junior had sworn at Mrs. Fair.

3. Jenna asked her mom for advice about how to get her hair cut. Her mom said (in a snotty tone), "Your hair looked so ugly last time. It's stupid to wear your hair like that. This time you are going to get your hair cut very short."

4. Wendel told his best friend Jim that his dad was punching him in the face and leaving bruises. Jim told Wendel to wear sunglasses and borrow some make-up from his sister to cover up the bruises.

Giving Advice to Friends

Your friends are going to ask your advice about a lot of different things. Sometimes, they will ask your advice about simple things. Other times, they may ask your advice on difficult subjects.

Friends may ask your advice about . . .

SIMPLE TOPICS

- which shirt to wear
- what to do on Friday night
- what type of pizza to order
- which sport to try out for

DIFFICULT TOPICS

- their parents' drinking
- their boyfriend/girlfriend
- failing a class
- being abused

Be careful about giving advice on difficult topics. There are some topics that you should not give advice on. For example, if your friend asks your advice about being physically abused, don't try to be a counselor. Tell your friend to talk to a counselor or some other adult. (In a situation like this, where your friend is getting hurt, it would be a good idea for you to let an adult know about it even if your friend doesn't talk to someone.)

DIRECTIONS: Read each situation below. Decide if you should give advice to your friend or if you should tell them to see a counselor. Write **give advice** or **counselor** on the line. There are some situations where you should tell a counselor or other adult about how your friend is feeling. Put a circle around the situation if you should also tell an adult about your friend.

_____1. Your friend asks your advice about where to apply for a job.

_____2. Your friend asks your advice about whether or not he should run away from home.

_____3. Your friend asks your advice about what to do about his father's physically abusing him.

_____4. Your friend asks your advice about what record to buy.

_____5. Your friend asks your advice about where to take his girlfriend to eat.

_____6. Your friend asks your advice on what to do because she's failing her math and English classes.

_____7. Your friend asks your advice on what to do because he feels like killing himself.

_____8. Your friend asks your advice about how to get more friends.

Name:_____

ADVICE--Good or Bad?

DIRECTIONS: For each situation below, write some advice that would be good advice and some that would be bad advice.

1. Tony tells you that his friend John has a copy of the science test he has to take. He wants to know if you think he should use the stolen test.

    BAD ADVICE:

    GOOD ADVICE:

2. Eva is angry because April has been saying things behind her back. Eva wants to know if you think she should beat April up.

    BAD ADVICE:

    GOOD ADVICE:

3. Adam hates living at home. He is thinking about running away from home. He wants to know what you think he should do.

    BAD ADVICE:

    GOOD ADVICE:

4. Jesse is thinking about going out for the basketball team. None of his friends play basketball, though, and might start calling him a jock. He wants to know what you think he should do.

    BAD ADVICE:

    GOOD ADVICE:

Name:_____

BOSSY, BOSSY, BOSSY

Dear Jackie,

I sure miss you! I can't believe it's been a whole month since you left. Things are still the same around here. Linda and Jean are fine. Joyce is her usual BOSSY self. Do you know what she said to me the other day? She said, "Renee, can I give you some advice? You really shouldn't wear such big necklaces. They don't look good on you!" Can you believe her? I was really upset. Linda is angry with Joyce, too, because Joyce has been sticking her nose in Linda's business. Joyce is always trying to give advice. She thinks she is Ann Landers! I've got to go!

See ya,
Renee

Do you know any people like Joyce — someone who is always trying to give advice, even when people don't ask for it? People like Joyce usually end up losing friends because they act like *know-it-alls.*

DIRECTIONS: Write a letter to Ann Landers or Dear Abby about what you should do about your friend who is like Joyce (always giving advice, even when people don't want it). Use a separate piece of paper to write your letter.

GIVING ADVICE - GIVING ADVICE - GIVING ADVICE

1. Tell the skill steps for the social skill of giving advice.

   (step 1) _____

   (step 2) _____

   (step 3) _____

2. Explain what can happen if you give advice to people too often.

   _____

   _____

   _____

3. Describe a situation in which a friend might ask for your advice. Then write the advice you would give that person.

   (situation) _____

   _____

   (advice) _____

   _____

4. Explain the difference between giving advice about simple things (e.g., which shirt looks best) and giving advice about difficult topics (e.g., what to do about a parent who drinks).

   _____

   _____

   _____

5. Write a story about a person who gives good advice to another person. (Use the back of this page if you need more space.)

   _____

   _____

   _____

   _____

6. Rate how good you are at giving advice to other people. Then explain why you rated yourself as you did.

   POOR   **FAIR**   **GOOD**   **VERY GOOD**

   (reason)_____

   _____

SKILL HOMEWORK ACTIVITY

_____
(Due Date)

Dear Parent or Guardian of: _____

This week we are learning about the social communication skill:

IGNORING

This social skill is very important in interpersonal relationships.

The students have learned that _ignoring_ takes a great deal of self-control. They should ignore other students who are bothering them:

1) So they don't get in trouble, and

2) So they can show their good self-control.

Before the due date, please complete one of the following activities with your son or daughter: (put a check mark by your choice)

_____ A. We acted out the role play situation listed below.

_____ B. I observed my son/daughter using this social skill in a real-life situation. (I have described the situation below.)

Description of real-life observation:

Role play situation:

PRETEND THAT YOU ARE EATING DINNER WITH YOUR FAMILY. YOUR BROTHER/SISTER STARTS PICKING ON YOU. DEMONSTRATE HOW YOU WILL IGNORE HIM/HER.

- -

Please circle the word below which best describes how your son or daughter did while using this social skill in either the role play or real-life situation.

NEEDS MORE HELP   GOOD   EXCELLENT

It is important for you to reinforce your child's use of this social skill at home in a positive way. Encourage and praise your child when you see the skill appropriately used. Remind him/her to use the social skill when necessary.

Thank you for your assistance.

Sincerely,

* *

PARENT/GUARDIAN SIGNATURE: _____

IGNORE!

IGNORING = NOT PAYING ATTENTION TO OTHER PEOPLE

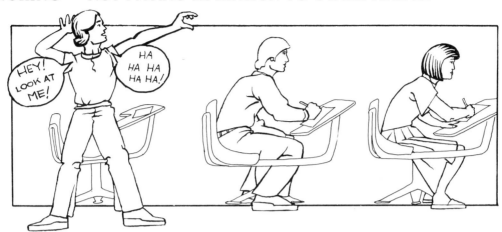

Ignoring takes a great deal of self-control. You must have good control over your own body. Some young people have not yet developed this control, because ignoring is a difficult, adult-like task.

Look at the cartoon below. Which student do you think will get in trouble when the teacher turns around and looks at the class? Mark started the trouble. He was whispering under his breath to Juan. Mark made Juan laugh. When the teacher turned around, she saw Juan laughing. She blamed Juan for causing the trouble. Mark just smiled nicely at the teacher. Mark didn't get in trouble.

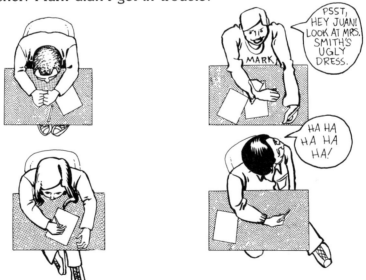

Beware of people like Mark. They know how to get other people in trouble while they look like innocent little angels. People like Mark will *set you up*. They know how to manipulate you so that **you** get in trouble and they don't. Don't be manipulated! There are two main reasons why you should ignore other students:

1) So you don't get in trouble, and

2) So you can show that you have self-control.

Name:_____

Can You Ignore?
- OR -
Are You In Control?

DIRECTIONS: Complete the Ignoring Rating Scale below. Pretend that you are in a class and the following 10 things happen to you. Mark each with a **1**, **2**, or **3** if it would be easy, hard, or very hard for you to ignore:

   1 = Easy for me to ignore
   2 = Hard for me to ignore
   3 = Very hard for me to ignore

_____ 1. My friend whispers a joke to me.

_____ 2. Someone drops his books.

_____ 3. I hear a fire engine outside.

_____ 4. Someone says a mean comment to me.

_____ 5. My friend makes a face at me.

_____ 6. The principal comes to the door to talk to the teacher.

_____ 7. My friend is calling my name.

_____ 8. The person behind me burps.

_____ 9. The class clown shouts out a silly answer.

_____ 10. Someone throws a spitball at me.

SCORING: 12 and below: You are a great ignorer! You are really in control!

   13-20:   You need work ignoring others. You can do it if you try.

   21 and above: You need help! You are not in control of your own body!

Ignoropoly

PREPARATION:
1) Put a chair in the front of the room facing the rest of the class.
2) Assign a timekeeper. The timekeeper should be the adult directing the activity. Make certain the timekeeper has a watch.
3) Each student should have this page and a magic marker.

ROUND ONE:
(2 seconds)
4) One student at a time should come up and sit in the chair.
5) The student needs to ignore the other students in the class for two seconds.
6) The timekeeper will tell the student when the two-second time period starts and ends.
7) The other students in the class should do things to try to get the person in the chair to laugh or watch them. The students may not throw anything or touch the person in any way. The students in the class must stay in their seats.
8) If the person ignores for two seconds, he has passed Round One and moves onto Round Two. He should color in the Round One mark below.
9) If the person does not ignore for two seconds, he is out of the game.
10) The timekeeper will be the judge of whether the student ignored or not.

ROUND TWO-
ROUND SIX:
11) Continue playing the same as above, increasing the ignoring time as indicated.
12) The person who can ignore for the longest period of time is the winner.

| ROUND SIX (60 Sec.) |
| ROUND FIVE (30 Sec.) |
| ROUND FOUR (15 Sec.) |
| ROUND THREE (10 Sec.) |
| ROUND TWO (5 Sec.) |
| ROUND ONE (2 Sec.) |

©1989 THINKING PUBLICATIONS   SSS: Social Skill Strategies (Book B)

Name:_____

𝕴𝕘𝕟𝕠𝕣𝕚𝕟𝕘 𝕼𝕦𝕖𝕤𝕥𝕚𝕠𝕟𝕤

1. What are two reasons why you should ignore someone?

    •

    •

2. Why is it hard for some students to ignore?

3. Tell one strategy you might use to help you ignore someone.

Self-Monitoring

Your teacher will help you practice ignoring and staying in control. There is also something that YOU can do on your own to help you ignore others. Keep your own record of all the times when you ignore someone. For example, you are in your math class and four times throughout the class period, you ignore distractions. Each time you ignore, you put a check (like on the sheet below) and write who or what it is you ignore.

MEAN IGNORING

When people ignore you, it usually hurts your feelings. They may be trying to tell you that they do not like the way you are behaving. If that is the reason, you can change your behavior. But sometimes people may ignore you just to be mean.

DIRECTIONS: Read Jane's story below. It is an example of how ignoring can hurt someone's feelings.

Jane

Jane was a very nice girl. She was friendly and well-behaved. Jane's friend, Laurie, got mad at Jane because she would not let Laurie copy her math assignment. Laurie made up some rumors about Jane and told Jane's other friends to ignore her. When Jane walked up to talk to her friends, they all ignored her. Jane did not know what was going on and felt very sad.

This type of ignoring is mean. It is also very childish. If you are upset with someone, you should talk about your problems instead of not saying anything.

_____

DIRECTIONS: Answer the questions below. Write in complete sentences.

1. How would you have felt if you were Jane?

2. When have you ever been mean and ignored someone? Explain why you did it.

3. Think of someone who is ignored by other students. Is that person ignored because he/she behaves poorly or because others are being mean? Explain your answer.

Name:_____

IGNORING - IGNORING - IGNORING - IGNORING - IGNORING

1. Define the term *ignoring* and give two reasons why you might want to ignore other
   people.

   (definition) _____

   (reason)_____

   (reason)_____

2. Explain why it is sometimes difficult to ignore other people.

   _____

   _____

   _____

3. Describe a situation when you should ignore someone at school.

   _____

   _____

   _____

4. Compare having to ignore a friend in class with having to ignore a student who
   is not your friend. Tell one similarity and one difference.

   (similarity) _____

   _____

   (difference) _____

   _____

5. Think of a new strategy you can use to help yourself ignore people during class
   time. Describe the strategy below.

   _____

   _____

   _____

6. Rate yourself from 1-10 (1 = poor, 10 = excellent) on how good you are at ignoring
   people during class:_____ Explain your answer below.

   (explanation) _____

   _____

SKILL HOMEWORK ACTIVITY

_____
(Due Date)

Dear Parent or Guardian of: _____

This week we are learning about the social communication skill:

RESPONDING TO TEASING

This social skill is very important in interpersonal relationships.

This skill can be broken down into the following skill steps. Please watch for all of the steps in your role play practice or real-life observation.

1. Decide if the person is teasing you in a _friendly_ way or a _mean_ way.
2. If the teasing is _friendly_, you have a choice:
   A. Laugh along to show that you don't take yourself too seriously.
   B. Tease the person back in a _friendly_ way.
3. If the teasing is _mean_, you have a choice:
   A. Ignore the person completely.
   B. Say, "You are putting me down. I don't like that. I want you to stop!"

Before the due date, please complete one of the following activities with your son or daughter: (put a check mark by your choice)

_____ A. We acted out the role play situation listed below.

_____ B. I observed my son/daughter using this social skill in a real-life situation. (I have described the situation below.)

Description of real-life observation:

Role play situation:

1. (FRIENDLY) YOU ALMOST ALWAYS GET AN "A" ON YOUR HISTORY TESTS. TODAY YOU GOT AN "A –" AND YOUR FRIEND TEASES YOU. SHOW HOW YOU WOULD RESPOND.

2. (MEAN) YOUR VISION IS POOR AND YOU WEAR GLASSES WITH THICK LENSES. YOUR BROTHER IS TEASING YOU ABOUT IT AND IT HURTS YOUR FEELINGS. DEMONSTRATE WHAT YOU WOULD DO OR SAY.

- -

Please circle the word below which best describes how your son or daughter did while using this social skill in either the role play or real-life situation.

NEEDS MORE HELP   GOOD   EXCELLENT

It is important for you to reinforce your child's use of this social skill at home in a positive way. Encourage and praise your child when you see the skill appropriately used. Remind him/her to use the social skill when necessary.

Thank you for your assistance.

Sincerely,

* *

PARENT/GUARDIAN SIGNATURE: _____

Teasing: Friendly or Mean?

There is a big difference between *friendly* teasing and *mean* teasing!

Friendly teasing *is when someone gives you a "hard time" about something, but they do it in a nice way. It is done to make you laugh, not to hurt your feelings.* Unfortunately, some people take themselves too seriously. They can't take any kind of teasing, even when it is done in a friendly way.

Mean teasing *is when someone gives you a "hard time" about something, and they want to hurt your feelings.*

DIRECTIONS: Read the stories below. At the end of each story, tell whether you think it includes friendly or mean teasing.

Story #1:   Jermane called to his friend Glenn, and said, "Hey Glenn, get over here! I want to show you something." Glenn walked over to Jermane and asked, "What's up?" "Look at that kid over there with the weird clothes on. Who is he?" asked Jermane. Glenn started to laugh and said, "I don't know, but let's go give him some grief. Anyone who dresses like that deserves it."

Story #2:   Roxanne is on the cheerleading squad and really is a good organizer. She writes down everything that needs to be done, and reminds everyone else on the squad about practice times, etc. The other girls on the squad appreciate having someone as organized as Roxanne, and often tell her so. One day the girls started teasing Roxanne about being the "mother hen" of the squad, taking care of all her little chicks. Roxanne started to laugh and said, "Believe me, taking care of all my little chicks is a full-time job!"

Story #3:   Malinda is a shy girl, and she loves to read. Every day after she finishes eating her lunch at school, she takes out a book instead of going outside with all the other students. She doesn't mind going to school, except for one thing: Two guys are always teasing her about reading so much. They come up to her, knock the book out of her hands, and say things like, "What's the matter, Malinda? Too afraid to take your nose out of your books?"

Name:_____

Rules for Teasing

DIRECTIONS: There are four rules to remember when someone teases you. Read each of the rules carefully. The cartoons will help explain each rule. At the bottom of the page, tell why each rule is important.

RULE #1
If someone teases you in a *friendly* way, laugh along to show that you are able to laugh at yourself.

RULE #2
If someone teases you in a *friendly* way, you may tease the person back in a *friendly* way.

RULE #3
If someone teases you in a *mean* way, completely ignore, and do not look like you are upset.

RULE #4
If someone teases you in a *mean* way, you may say, "You are putting me down. I don't like that. I want you to stop!"

DIRECTIONS: Explain why each rule is important.

Rule #1:

Rule #2:

Rule #3:

Rule #4:

Name:_____

Teasing--More Practice

Remember these four rules for responding to teasing:

1. If someone teases you in a *friendly* way, laugh along to show that you are able to laugh at yourself.

2. If someone teases you in a *friendly* way, you may tease the person back in a *friendly* way.

3. If someone teases you in a *mean* way, completely ignore and do not look like you are upset.

4. If someone teases you in a *mean* way, you may say, "You are putting me down. I don't like that. I want you to stop!"

DIRECTIONS: Read each of the situations below. If the person who gets teased follows one of the rules correctly, write **CORRECT** and the number of the rule that was followed. If the person who gets teased does not follow one of the rules correctly, write **INCORRECT** and the number for the rule(s) that should have been followed.

_____1. Ben was thinking about how much he loved to tease Joe. Joe would always get upset and start to cry. Not too many kids in junior high cried as easily as Joe, and that was why Ben never passed up a chance to bug him. Just as Ben was thinking about him, Joe walked by. "Hey, tinsel teeth! Have you brushed your teeth yet today?" asked Ben. Joe tightly made two fists, and got that goofy look on his face that meant he was about to cry again. Ben loved it when Joe got that goofy look. Just then a teacher walked by, so Ben left. Ben knew he could tease Joe later during lunch.

_____2. Jeanne and all of her friends were sitting together at lunch. They had just finished gym class where they had square danced with the guys. They were all teasing each other about different things that had happened during class, and they were all laughing. Jeanne was laughing right along with everybody else, until Beth teased her. Jeanne said, "Knock it off! There's nothing wrong with the way I dance." Beth said, "OK, OK! You don't have to be so touchy, Jeanne, I was just kidding around."

_____3. Mark was out driving with his friend Kevin. Mark had just gotten his driver's license, and wanted to take his buddy for a ride. They decided to stop at a store, but Mark had a hard time trying to parallel park. He had to repark the car four times. Kevin laughed and started to tease Mark. Mark started laughing too. Finally the car was close enough to the curb, so the guys got out and went into the store.

_____4. Craig was riding his bike down to the mall. He knew he would have to lock his bike in the rack by the main entrance. He was worried because he knew all the creeps hung out there during the summer. That gang of kids was always giving someone a hard time, and Craig wasn't looking forward to what he knew was coming. Sure enough, when he parked his bike, they all came out and started to tease him. Craig pretended that they did not even exist, and calmly walked into the mall.

Name:_____

How Do You Handle Teasing?

DIRECTIONS: Think carefully about the following questions and answer them honestly.

1. List three things that your family and friends can tease you about in a *friendly* way, without your getting upset.

   •

   •

   •

2. List three things that you have been teased about that you considered to be *mean* teasing.

   •

   •

   •

3. Are you usually able to laugh at yourself when someone teases you in a *friendly* way?

4. Tell about a time when you teased someone in a *friendly* way.

5. Tell about a time when you teased someone in a *mean* way.

6. List three things you can tease one of your family members about in a *friendly* way.

   •

   •

   •

7. List three things you should never tease one of your family members about because it would be *mean* teasing.

   •

   •

   •

Name:_____

BEWARE!

DIRECTIONS: In your own words, tell what you think the warning sign below means.

BEWARE OF TEASING
SOMEONE IN A *FRIENDLY* WAY!

WHAT MAY SEEM LIKE *FRIENDLY* TEASING TO YOU, MAY NOT FEEL FRIENDLY TO SOMEONE ELSE.

MEANING:

RESPONDING TO TEASING - RESPONDING TO TEASING

1. Write the four rules you should follow when someone teases you.

   (rule 1) _____

   (rule 2) _____

   (rule 3) _____

   (rule 4) _____

2. Explain what causes someone to be the kind of person who would tease another person in a *mean* way.

   _____

   _____

3. Describe something one of your family members gets teased about in a *friendly* way at home.

   _____

   _____

4. Tell one way that *friendly* teasing is similar to *mean* teasing, and one way that it is different.

   (similarity) _____

   (difference) _____

5. Write a short story about "Maggie The Mean Teaser." Make certain your story includes information about what causes her to be a mean teaser and about how other people feel about her. (Use the back of this page if you need more space.)

   _____

   _____

   _____

   _____

6. Read the short story below and then answer the questions.

   Jeanne got braces at the beginning of the school year. Her friends all call her "tinsel teeth" and tease her about having to brush her teeth after lunch at school. Jeanne laughs when they tease her, so they think it is all right to keep doing it.

   Question: Can Jeanne's friends be totally certain that she doesn't mind their teasing?
   YES   NO

   (reason)_____

   _____

SKILL HOMEWORK ACTIVITY

_____
(Due Date)

Dear Parent or Guardian of: _____

This week we are learning about the social communication skill:

PEER PRESSURE

This social skill is very important in interpersonal relationships.

Teen-agers must deal with a great deal of negative pressure from others. The students have learned that it is okay to say *NO*. There are six different ways to say *NO* to peers (see the attached sheet for the "six great ways to say *NO*").

> **Before the due date, please complete one of the following activities with your son or daughter: (put a check mark by your choice)**
>
> _____ A. We acted out the role play situation listed below.
>
> _____ B. I observed my son/daughter using this social skill in a real-life situation. (I have described the situation below.)
>
> **Description of real-life observation:**
>
> **Role play situation:**
>
> YOUR FRIENDS WANT YOU TO STEAL SOME MONEY FROM YOUR PARENTS. STAND UP TO THEM AND TELL THEM *NO*. DO THIS ROLE PLAY THREE TIMES. USE A DIFFERENT WAY TO SAY *NO* EACH TIME.
>
> -
>
> **Please circle the word below which best describes how your son or daughter did while using this social skill in either the role play or real-life situation.**
>
> NEEDS MORE HELP   GOOD   EXCELLENT

It is important for you to reinforce your child's use of this social skill at home in a positive way. Encourage and praise your child when you see the skill appropriately used. Remind him/her to use the social skill when necessary.

Thank you for your assistance.

Sincerely,

* *

PARENT/GUARDIAN SIGNATURE: _____

Name:_____

PEER PRESSURE

Teen-agers suffer from a horrible disease called *peer pressure*. Peer pressure can cause a great deal of damage. Some teen-agers have gotten in trouble at home, in school, and in the community. This has all been due to peer pressure. There is a simple cure for peer pressure. Teen-agers simply need to say a single word. That word is *NO*.

Peer pressure can make people do things they don't want to do. Some examples of negative peer pressure include:

- Your friends pressuring you into stealing or cheating.

DIRECTIONS: Give four more examples of negative peer pressure.

- •   •

- •   •

Peer pressure can also be positive. Your friends can be a good influence on you. Some examples of positive peer pressure include:

- Your friends pressuring you into joining a sports team or getting good grades.

DIRECTIONS: Give four more examples of positive peer pressure.

- •   •

- •   •

_____

Saying *NO* to friends is hard. It takes a very confident person to stand up for what she or he believes. Those people who can say *NO* are very strong individuals. Don't be afraid to stand up for what you believe!

What type of person are you? Are you a weak follower or are you a strong leader? Explain your answer.

Name:_____

6
Great Ways
To Say *NO*
or
How To Resist Peer Pressure
Without Going Crazy!

The "REPEAT"

Keep repeating your *NO* statement.

Joe: Here, have a drink of wine.
Mike: No thanks, I don't want any.
Joe: Don't be a chicken, come on!
Mike: No thanks, I don't want any.
Joe: You baby! Just a little.
Mike: No thanks, I don't want any.

The "OFFENSIVE"

Say something that will put some pressure back on the other person.

Joe: Here, have a drink of wine.
Mike: No thanks, I don't want any.
Joe: Don't be a chicken, come on!
Mike: Get off my back. Why are you pressuring me?
Joe.   Okay already. Gees.

The "COMPROMISE"

Give another idea that you both can live with.

Joe: Here, have a drink of wine.
Mike: No, but I will have a soda.
Joe: Okay, here you go.

The "DISCUSSION STOP"

Don't discuss it any further.

Joe: Here, have a drink of wine.
Mike: No, thanks.
Joe: Don't be a chicken, come on!
Mike: I'm not talking about it any more.
Joe: Aw, come on.
Mike: (walks away)

The "HUMOR"

Say something funny

Joe: Here, have a drink of wine.
Mike: My gosh Joe, didn't you hear? Drinking wine causes a loss of manliness!
Joe: Yeah, right.

The "REASON"

Tell the reason why you won't.

Joe: Here, have a drink of wine.
Mike: No thanks. If I get caught drinking, my parents said they will sell my 4-wheeler.
Joe: You're kidding?
Mike: No, and I don't think they are kidding either.

©1989 THINKING PUBLICATIONS

Name:_____

Peer Pressure Role Plays

DIRECTIONS: You and a partner should role play each of the situations several times. Use at least 2-3 different ways to say *NO* to the peer pressure each time. Check off each of the ways you use.

	The Repeat	The Offensive	The Compromise	The Discussion Stop	The Humor	The Reason
1. One of your friends is trying to pressure you into stealing a record from a store.						
2. You are having an argument with a kid at school. Your friend is pressuring you to fight this person.						
3. You are at a party. Your friend is pressuring you to drink.						
4. Your older brother/sister is trying to get you to tease the handicapped boy next door.						
5. Your friend is trying to get you to break up with your boyfriend/girlfriend.						
6. Your best friend is trying to talk you into going to the basketball game instead of studying for your science test.						
7. One of the popular kids at school is trying to talk you into pulling a prank on the substitute teacher						
8. Your friend wants you to have a party while your parents are gone.						
9. Your friend wants you to lie for him and tell his parents that he's sleeping over when he really isn't.						
10. A girl you work with wants you to cover for her and tell the boss that she was on time for work. It's the third time she was late this week.						

©1989 Thinking Publications   85   SSS: Social Skill Strategies (Book B)

Name:_____

Peer Pressure Questions

1. Give three examples of good peer pressure.

   ●

   ●

   ●

2. Give three examples of bad peer pressure.

   ●

   ●

   ●

3. Tell at least three different ways you could respond to peer pressure.

   ●

   ●

   ●

4. Tell about a recent situation when your friends tried to pressure you into doing something you didn't want to.

5. Tell how you responded to the above situation.

6. How do you feel when someone tries to pressure you into doing something?

7. Why do you think teen-agers always try to get their friends to do things?

8. Why is it often hard to say *NO* to your friends?

PEER PRESSURE - PEER PRESSURE - PEER PRESSURE

1. Tell six good ways to respond to negative peer pressure.

    (#1) _____

    (#2) _____

    (#3) _____

    (#4) _____

    (#5) _____

    (#6) _____

2. Explain why it is sometimes difficult to resist peer pressure.

    _____

    _____

3. Describe a situation when you may need to resist pressure from your friends.

    _____

    _____

4. Compare positive peer pressure to negative peer pressure. How are they alike and how are they different?

    (alike) _____

    _____

    (different) _____

    _____

5. Create the lyrics for a song about ways to resist peer pressure. Write the lyrics on the lines below. (Use the back of this page if you need more space.)

    _____

    _____

    _____

6. Rate yourself below on how well you feel you can resist peer pressure. (Place an "X" where you feel you are now.) Then, explain why you rated yourself as you did.

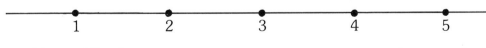

    1   2   3   4   5

    I have difficulties   I am good at
    resisting peer pressure   resisting peer pressure

    (explanation) _____

    _____

SKILL HOMEWORK ACTIVITY

_____
(Due Date)

Dear Parent or Guardian of: _____

This week we are learning about the social communication skill:

JOINING IN

This social skill is very important in interpersonal relationships and can be broken down into the following skill steps. Please watch for all the steps in your role play practice or real-life observation.

1. Decide if you would like to join in an activity.

2. Decide what you should do to join in (e.g., sign up, offer, ask, begin a conversation).

3. Try to join in before an activity starts or during a break, if possible.

Before the due date, please complete one of the following activities with your son or daughter: (put a check mark by your choice)

_____ A. We acted out the role play situation listed below.

_____ B. I observed my son/daughter using this social skill in a real-life situation. (I have described the situation below.)

Description of real-life observation:

Role play situation:

PRETEND YOU ARE JUST GETTING HOME AND YOU FIND YOUR FAMILY PLAYING CARDS. DEMONSTRATE WHAT YOU COULD SAY TO JOIN IN.

- -

Please circle the word below which best describes how your son or daughter did while using this social skill in either the role play or real-life situation.

NEEDS MORE HELP   GOOD   EXCELLENT

It is important for you to reinforce your child's use of this social skill at home in a positive way. Encourage and praise your child when you see the skill appropriately used. Remind him/her to use the social skill when necessary.

Thank you for your assistance.

Sincerely,

* *

PARENT/GUARDIAN SIGNATURE: _____

The Art of *Joining In*

Joining in means *finding a way of entering into an activity or conversation without disrupting those involved.*

Following is a list of situations when you may want to join in:

1. You hear an announcement at school that the track season will start in a week.

2. You see a bunch of neighborhood kids playing volleyball.

3. Your family is playing a game.

4. You would like to join in a new group of friends at school.

DIRECTIONS: Describe two more situations when a person may want to join in.

1.

2.

Below is a list of three skill steps you should follow if you want to join in appropriately.

1. Decide if you would like to join in an activity.

2. Decide what you should do to join in (e.g., sign up, offer, ask, begin a conversation).

3. Try to join in before an activity starts or during a break, if possible.

DIRECTIONS: Describe a situation when it would be best to join in by signing up, offering, asking, and beginning a conversation.

(signing up) _____

(offering)_____

(asking) _____

(beginning a conversation) _____

DIRECTIONS: Tell why it is important to try and join in an activity before it starts or during a break.

Group Members:_____
_____
_____
_____

COOPERATION ACTIVITY

DIRECTIONS: 1. You will be working in small groups. (Your teacher will assign the groups.)

2. Work cooperatively with your team members to complete the activities on the following three pages.

3. As a team, choose one of these two ways to complete the activities:

   a. Each team member completes one of the activities. Then the members exchange activities and double check another person's work.

   b. All team members complete the activities together. One team member does the writing.

4. Complete the activities by the end of the class period.

5. All team members should sign their names on each page.

6. Each team member will take a quiz on all of the activities.

7. Your quiz grade will be the average of the grades that everyone in your group earns.

8. Your teacher will also be giving you a group cooperation grade. It will be based on how well each member of your group cooperates and participates during the activity.

Group Members:_____
_____
_____

Activity A - Home/School/Community

There is a difference between joining in when you want to, and joining in when you should. There are situations when you want to join in. For example, when you see your friends playing a softball game, you want to play too. There are situations when you should join in. For example, if your teacher asks for more help cleaning up after a class party, you should offer to join in, even if you really don't want to. This type of joining in is more like "pitching in" to help.

DIRECTIONS: List five situations when you would want to join in and five situations when you should join in at home, at school, and in the community.

HOME

(Want to)

1.

2.

3.

4.

5.

(Should)

1.

2.

3.

4.

5.

SCHOOL

(Want to)

1.

2.

3.

4.

5.

(Should)

1.

2.

3.

4.

5.

COMMUNITY

(Want to)

1.

2.

3.

4.

5.

(Should)

1.

2.

3.

4.

5.

Activity B - Joining In or Butting In?

There is a big difference between *joining in* and *butting in*. When you butt into an activity, it means that you push your way in without asking or signing up. When you butt into an activity, you upset the people who are already involved.

DIRECTIONS: Read each of the following situations. If the person joined in a good way, write ***Joined in***. If the person butted into the activity, write ***Butted in***.

_____1. Randy saw a group of kids talking in the hall on the first day of school. He wanted to join in, so he walked over, slapped one of the guys on the back, and interrupted by saying, "Hey, everybody! Let me show you this great new watch I got last week."

_____2. Samantha heard on the announcements that anyone interested in joining the volleyball team should sign up in the physical education office. Samantha decided she wanted to join in, so she went to the office after school. She knocked on the door and said, "Excuse me, but I was wondering if I could join the volleyball team."

_____3. Jim saw a bunch of guys trying to organize a game of softball after school. Jim walked up to them and said, "I'd sure like to play, if you could use another person."

_____4. Nancy saw a group of kids she didn't know very well playing cards. She wanted to join in, so she walked up to them and said, "Hey, why don't you deal me in? I'll show you how this game is really played."

_____5. Kari found out that the group of students cooking for the class picnic needed some extra help. Kari found the group and said, "I knew you wouldn't be able to do this without me! Here I am to help save the day."

_____6. Adam's brother Chuck and his dad were going shopping for a new suit for Chuck's dance. Adam really wanted to go along, so he said to them, "Hey, would you mind if I came along with you?"

_____7. Cindy saw her sister helping her dad do the dishes. Cindy decided that she should join in and help too. She said to them, "Is there anything I can do to help?"

Group Members:_____

_____

_____

_____

Activity C - Putting It In Words

Sometimes, when people want to join in an activity, they just stand close by and hope that someone will ask them. Many times, just standing close isn't enough. When you want to join in an activity, you need to ask, or sign up, or begin a conversation, or offer (depending on what the situation is).

DIRECTIONS: Describe five situations when you may want to join in. Write each of them below, and then write down what you would actually say when joining in.

SITUATION	WHAT YOU WOULD SAY

93

Name:_____

Joining In QUIZ

1. Explain the difference between *joining in* and *butting in*.

2. List one situation when you might want to join in at home, at school, and in the community.

    a. (home)

    b. (school)

    c. (community)

3. Why is it important to try to join in an activity before it begins, or during a break in the activity?

4. Pretend that your friends are trying to construct a building with a deck of cards. It looks like fun and you would like to join in. Tell what you could say to join in.

©1989 THINKING PUBLICATIONS

SSS: Social Skill Strategies (Book B)

JOINING IN - JOINING IN - JOINING IN - JOINING IN

1. Write the definition for *joining in*, and the three skill steps for joining in correctly.

   (definition) _____

   _____

   (step 1) _____

   (step 2) _____

   (step 3) _____

2. Tell why you can sometimes feel uncomfortable when you want to join in.

   _____

   _____

3. Describe a situation when you should join in an activity at home, at school, and in the community.

   (home) _____

   _____

   (school) _____

   _____

   (community) _____

   _____

4. Compare joining in when you *want to* and joining in when you *should*. Tell one way they are the same and one way they are different.

   (same) _____

   (different) _____

   _____

5. Create a mnemonic device to help yourself remember the four ways you can join in (sign up, offer, ask, begin a conversation).

   _____

   _____

   _____

   _____

6. Describe the last time you can remember joining in an activity. Tell whether you think you joined in appropriately or not. Explain your answer.

   (situation) _____

   _____

   Did you join in correctly?   YES   NO

   (explanation) _____

   _____

SKILL HOMEWORK ACTIVITY

_____
(Due Date)

Dear Parent or Guardian of: _____

This week we are learning about the social communication skill:

BEING LEFT OUT

This social skill is very important in interpersonal relationships and can be broken down into the following skill steps:

1. Try to determine if you are being left out on purpose or by mistake.

2. If a mistake was made, talk to the person who forgot you, or just ignore it.

3. If you were left out on purpose, choose a strategy to make yourself feel better. (Refer to the attached sheet for a list of strategies.)

Before the due date, please complete one of the following activities with your son or daughter: (put a check mark by your choice)

_____ A. We acted out the role play situation listed below.

_____ B. I observed my son/daughter using this social skill in a real-life situation. (I have described the situation below.)

Description of real-life observation:

Role play situation:

YOU WERE SUPPOSED TO MEET YOUR FRIENDS AT THE VIDEO ARCADE. YOU WAITED THERE FOR AN HOUR. FINALLY, YOU STARTED BACK HOME. AS YOU WALKED PAST THE SWIMMING POOL, YOU SAW YOUR FRIENDS SWIMMING. YOU THINK THEY LEFT YOU OUT ON PURPOSE. TALK WITH YOUR MOTHER/FATHER ABOUT HOW YOU ARE FEELING AND WHAT YOU SHOULD DO ABOUT IT.

Please circle the word below which best describes how your son or daughter did while using this social skill in either the role play or real-life situation.

NEEDS MORE HELP   GOOD   EXCELLENT

It is important for you to reinforce your child's use of this social skill at home in a positive way. Encourage and praise your child when you see the skill appropriately used. Remind him/her to use the social skill when necessary.

Thank you for your assistance.

Sincerely,

* *

PARENT/GUARDIAN SIGNATURE: _____

96

Being Left Out

Being left out from an activity, or a group of people, can be painful for children and adults alike. People wonder why they were left out. Many people start to think something is wrong with them. They think people don't like them.

Sometimes people are mistakenly left out of something. Maybe someone forgot to call them or to send them an invitation. These kinds of things happen. But other times, people are intentionally left out. Teen-agers often leave others out of their group on purpose.

Many teen-agers belong to *cliques*. A clique is a group of people who associate only with the other members of the clique. The people in the clique can be very mean to other people outside of the clique. Teen-agers are often inconsiderate of other people's feelings. Even those people who are in a clique get left out at times.

Describe how the people in the illustration are feeling.

Name:_____

How People *Feel*

DIRECTIONS: Read each situation. Try to put yourself in the place of the person who is left out. (e.g., What is the person thinking? How does the person feel?) Then answer each question.

1. Robin really enjoys hanging around with the guys on the basketball team. He just found out that all the guys got together over the weekend and never asked him.

   What do you think Robin is thinking about?

   How do you think Robin is feeling?

2. Nicky's friend Joan asked her if she had gotten her invitation yet. Nicky said, "What invitation?" Joan said, "For Amanda's party." Nicky told Joan she had not received an invitation. Joan said, "Well, I got mine in the mail two days ago. I wonder why you didn't get one?"

   What do you think Nicky is thinking about?

   How do you think Nicky is feeling?

3. Travis' friends are all going on the ski trip. Travis can't go because he has to work. He really wants to go on the trip.

   What do you think Travis is thinking about?

   How do you think Travis is feeling?

4. Melissa's friends all made it for the cheerleading squad. Melissa was happy for them, but she realized they would be doing a lot of things together without her.

   What do you think Melissa is thinking about?

   How do you think Melissa is feeling?

Name:_____

A Sad Story

DIRECTIONS: Write or tell a story about a teen-ager who is left out of an activity or a group of people. Tell how the teen-ager feels about being left out.

_____

_____

_____

_____

_____

_____

_____

_____

_____

_____

_____

_____

_____

_____

_____

_____

_____

_____

_____

_____

_____

Being Left Out STRATEGIES

When you are left out, try the following three skill steps:

1. Try to determine if you are being left out on purpose or by mistake.

2. If a mistake was made, talk to the person who forgot you, or just ignore it.

3. If you were left out on purpose, choose a strategy to make yourself feel better.

DIRECTIONS: Look at the drawing below to discover ways to make yourself feel better when you are left out on purpose.

TRY TO BE POSITIVE

1. You are an important person.

2. TRY TO BE POSITIVE!

3. There are people who would like to be with you. Seek them out!

4. Do something nice for yourself! You deserve it!

5. ASK YOURSELF: Was I left out on purpose? Maybe it was just a mistake. If you think it was a mistake, ask someone!

6. Find a new friend: Maybe someone else who's been left out.

7. Remember — Things will probably be different soon!

8. Talk to someone about how you feel.

9. Remember — Teen-agers can be cruel. They change their minds often. You won't be left out forever.

Name:_____

When You're Left Out...

DIRECTIONS: In each section below, write a time when you were left out. Then tell how you felt when you were left out. Tell whether you were left out intentionally (on purpose) or not intentionally. Remember, all people are left out at times.

_____

One time when I was left out was . . . _____

_____

_____

_____

I felt . . . _____

_____

_____

I was left out (circle one) . . .   intentionally   not intentionally

_____

One time when I was left out was . . . _____

_____

_____

_____

I felt . . . _____

_____

_____

I was left out (circle one) . . .   intentionally   not intentionally

_____

Name:_____

BEING LEFT OUT - BEING LEFT OUT - BEING LEFT OUT

1. List the three skill steps for being left out.

   (step 1) _____

   (step 2) _____

   (step 3) _____

2. Describe how a person might feel if he/she is left out of something.

   _____

   _____

   _____

   _____

   _____

3. Describe a recent situation when either you or someone else was left out of something. Tell whether the person was left out by mistake or intentionally.

   _____

   _____

   _____

   _____

   _____

4. Compare being left out on purpose to being left out by mistake. Tell how they are the same and how they are different.

   (same) _____

   _____

   _____

   (different) _____

   _____

5. Write some things you could say to yourself when others intentionally leave you out. Write them in the thought bubble below.

6. Read the following story. Evaluate how Chan handles being left out.

> Chan overheard some of his friends talking about going to Mia's birthday party on Friday night. He hadn't heard anything about a birthday party. Chan thought to himself, "Oh boy, I'm not invited. I knew Mia didn't like me. I wonder why she didn't invite me. I've never done anything to her. Everyone probably thinks it's a big joke that I didn't get invited. Why doesn't she like me?" Just then Mia walked up and handed Chan an invitation to her birthday party and said, "Sure hope you can make it, Chan."

How do you feel Chan handled being left out? Give reasons to support your answer.

_____

_____

_____

_____

_____

_____

SKILL HOMEWORK ACTIVITY

_____

(Due Date)

Dear Parent or Guardian of: _____

This week we are learning about the social communication skill:

TATTLING

This social skill is very important in interpersonal relationships and can be broken down into the following skill steps. Please watch for all of the steps in your role play practice or real-life observation.

1. Ask yourself, "Is what happened important enough for me to tell someone"?
2. If it is, decide whom you should tell and choose a good time and place.

Before the due date, please complete one of the following activities with your son or daughter: (put a check mark by your choice)

_____ A. We acted out the role play situation listed below.

_____ B. I observed my son/daughter using this social skill in a real-life situation. (I have described the situation below.)

Description of real-life observation:

Role play situation:

YOUR BROTHER HAS BEEN STEALING MONEY FROM YOUR SISTER. YOU WANT TO TELL SOMEONE ABOUT IT. DECIDE WHOM YOU SHOULD TELL AND THEN CHOOSE A GOOD TIME TO TELL THAT PERSON.

Please circle the word below which best describes how your son or daughter did while using this social skill in either the role play or real-life situation.

NEEDS MORE HELP   GOOD   EXCELLENT

It is important for you to reinforce your child's use of this social skill at home in a positive way. Encourage and praise your child when you see the skill appropriately used. Remind him/her to use the social skill when necessary.

Thank you for your assistance.

Sincerely,

* *

PARENT/GUARDIAN SIGNATURE: _____

Name:_____

TATTLING

Mrs. Wildman, Adam stepped on my toe and then he hit Jean. Sara took Josh's pencil from him. Tell Brian to leave us... Etc. Etc. Etc. Etc.

Tattling means *telling what someone else has done or is going to do.* When you hear the word *tattler*, you usually think of someone who tells silly, little things like the person on the left. This type of person can get on your nerves. Every time you turn around, that person is telling on someone for something.

Actually, there *are* times when you should tell on others, but many students have difficulty deciding which things are important enough to tell someone about. They are afraid the other students will make fun of them or be upset with them, so they don't say anthing.

Nick! Who took the markers off my desk? I know you saw who did it. Can you help me out?

I didn't see a thing. Nope, I didn't see anything. I'm not a <u>squealer!</u>

This unit will help you decide when you shouldn't tell someone and when you should tell someone. It will help you understand why people don't like tattlers. The unit will teach you which things you need to tell someone about and it will help you decide upon the right time and place to do it.

Here are the skill steps for this skill:

1. ASK YOURSELF, "IS WHAT HAPPENED IMPORTANT ENOUGH FOR ME TO TELL SOMEONE"?

2. IF IT IS, DECIDE WHOM YOU SHOULD TELL AND CHOOSE A GOOD TIME AND PLACE.

Name:_____

It's Necessary to Tell

There Are Times When You Must Tell Someone!

Sometimes it's necessary to tell someone about what another person has done. If someone is in danger, it's necessary to tell an adult. For example, if a person you know is going to hurt someone else, you should tell an adult. Or if a person you know is going to hurt himself, you should tell an adult. Someone may be doing something that is hurting you. If this is the case, you should tell someone even though you may not want to. These are emergency situations when you should tell someone right away. You should also tell an adult when you witness someone damaging property or stealing something. Can you think of any other times when you would always want to tell an adult?

DIRECTIONS: Read each heading and give three specific examples that could go under each. An example is done for you.

EXAMPLE ➡

1. A person you know is going to hurt someone else.

   • *My friend is going to beat up another person after school.*

   •

   •

2. A person you know is going to hurt himself/herself.

   •

   •

   •

3. Someone is hurting you or is making you feel uncomfortable.

   •

   •

   •

4. You observe someone damaging property or stealing something.

   •

   •

   •

EDUCATOR PAGE: DO NOT DUPLICATE FOR STUDENTS

DIRECTIONS: 1. The educator should have a discussion with the students about tattling. Before the discussion begins, the educator should give a Discussion Behavior Sheet (see next page) to each student.

2. The educator should decide ahead of time which discussion behavior(s) the students will rate themselves on. Some examples of discussion behaviors include: having eye contact with the person who is speaking, raising your hand to talk, making relevant comments, leaning slightly forward in your seat to show your interest, nodding at the speaker, giving support to others. The educator should then model the discussion behavior the students will be rating themselves on.

3. The educator should explain that each time the student does the specified discussion behavior appropriately, the student should put a " **+** " in the positive column. Each time the student fails to do the specified discussion behavior, the student should put a " **−** " in the negative column. The educator should model how to do this for the students. Many of the students will not realize when they are NOT doing the specified behavior and will fail to give themselves a " **−** ." This is acceptable, since the purpose of this activity is not for students to do a serious critique of their discussion, but rather to become more aware of it.

4. The educator should then discuss the following situations with the students. The class should discuss whether or not they would tell someone about what happened in each situation.

SITUATIONS

A. The student sitting behind you pokes you with his pencil. Would you tell the teacher? What if he poked you and your arm started bleeding? What if he poked you thirty times during the class? If you did decide to tell the teacher, when would be the right time and place to tell the teacher?

B. You see someone vandalize something in the school bathroom. Does it make a difference what was vandalized (e.g., a sink being broken vs. someone writing on the wall)? Would you tell someone about it? Who would you tell? When would you tell?

C. Someone taped a funny poster on the outside of your locker. Would you tell someone about this? Explain why or why not.

D. One of your friends steals money from another one of your friends. Would you tell? Why or why not? How will each friend feel if you tell? If you do not tell?

E. You work in an ice cream shop. A person you work with just showed up ten minutes late for work. Would you tell the boss? Explain why or why not.

F. Your parents go away for the weekend. Your sister has a party. Would you tell your parents? Why or why not?

Tattling - D (Con't)

Name:_____

Discussion Behavior Sheet

NAME: _____

DATE:_____

DISCUSSION BEHAVIOR:_____

POSITIVE (+)	NEGATIVE (−)

The *RIGHT* Time and Place

DIRECTIONS: When it's necessary to tell someone what happened, you should choose the right time and place. Read the script below. Then answer the questions.

Characters: Billy .a boy in class
Victor . . . . a boy in class
Mrs. LaVanway . . . . .the teacher

Scene: Billy has just observed Victor stealing money from Mrs. LaVanway's purse while she's out of the room.

Mrs. LaVanway: (walking back into the room) Thank you for waiting class. Now would you please take out your math assignments.

Billy: (shouting) Mrs. LaVanway, Victor just stole five dollars from your purse. I saw him take it while you were out of the room.

Victor: (yelling) I did not take it you liar.

Billy: (shouting) Yes, you did.

Mrs. LaVanway: Thank you for letting me know that Billy. Victor, I'd like you to go to the principal's office right now.

Victor: (making a fist at Billy) You are dead today after school. I'm going to kill you. Just wait!

QUESTIONS:

1. Do you think it was right for Billy to tell Mrs. LaVanway about Victor's stealing her money?

2. Do you think Billy chose the right time and place to tell her?

3. How could Billy have been more discreet when he told Mrs. LaVanway? (Look up the word *discreet* in a dictionary if you do not know what it means.)

TATTLING - TATTLING - TATTLING - TATTLING - TATTLING

1. Tell the two skill steps involved in "good" tattling.

   (step 1) _____

   (step 2) _____

2. Tell what can happen if you "tattle" all of the time.

   _____

   _____

3. Describe a situation at home when you would need to tell someone about what you know.

   _____

   _____

4. Compare *"bad" tattling* with *telling someone when you need to.* Tell how the two are alike and how they are different.

   (alike) _____

   _____

   (different) _____

   _____

5. Write a short article for your school newspaper explaining when it's necessary to "tattle" and how students should go about telling. (Use the back of this page if you need more space.)

   _____

   _____

   _____

6. Evaluate yourself. Are you a tattler? Do you tell someone when it's necessary to tell? Do you go about telling in the right way? (Use the back of this page to explain your answer, if you need more space.)

   _____

   _____

MANAGEMENT SKILLS

SKILL HOMEWORK ACTIVITY

_____
(Due Date)

Dear Parent or Guardian of: _____

This week we are learning about the social communication skill:

BEING ASSERTIVE

This social skill is very important in interpersonal relationships.

This skill can be broken down into the following skill steps. Please watch for all of the steps in your role play practice or real-life observation.

1. Decide if your rights have been violated.
   (If they have been, then continue to step 2)

2. State your feelings in a firm/confident way, without making threats.

3. Listen to what the other person says.

Before the due date, please complete one of the following activities with your son or daughter: (put a check mark by your choice)

_____ A. We acted out the role play situation listed below.

_____ B. I observed my son/daughter using this social skill in a real-life situation. (I have described the situation below.)

Description of real-life observation:

Role play situation:

YOU SHOULD BE THE NEXT PERSON THAT THE SALES CLERK HELPS, BUT SHE KEEPS WAITING ON ALL THE ADULTS FIRST. DEMONSTRATE HOW YOU COULD BE ASSERTIVE.

- -

Please circle the word below which best describes how your son or daughter did while using this social skill in either the role play or real-life situation.

NEEDS MORE HELP   GOOD   EXCELLENT

It is important for you to reinforce your child's use of this social skill at home in a positive way. Encourage and praise your child when you see the skill appropriately used. Remind him/her to use the social skill when necessary.

Thank you for your assistance.

Sincerely,

* *

PARENT/GUARDIAN SIGNATURE: _____

Name:_____

To Be **ASSERTIVE** or Not To Be?

When your rights have been violated, it is important to learn to be assertive. **Being assertive** means *that you make your feelings known in a firm and confident way without making threats.* This activity page will give you practice identifying times when your rights have been violated.

DIRECTIONS: For each situation below, decide whether or not your rights have been violated. (REMEMBER: When your rights are violated, you should be assertive.) If they have not been violated, then write **NO**. If they have been violated, then write **YES**, and tell why.

1. You and your brother are supposed to do dishes together every day after supper. He said that if you did them by yourself on Monday, he would do them by himself on Tuesday. You agreed. When Tuesday night came, he acted like he forgot all about the agreement. Have your rights been violated? _____ (If *yes*, explain why.)

2. It is a school policy that you should be given an after-school detention on your third tardy to class. You were tardy for the third time in math class today, and the teacher gave you a detention. Have your rights been violated? _____ (If *yes*, explain why.)

3. Your teacher has several pairs of both right and left-handed scissors in his drawer. You're left-handed, and he gave you a pair of right-handed scissors to work with for your art project. Your teacher knows you are left-handed. Have your rights been violated? _____ (If *yes*, explain why.)

4. Your friends at school are constantly pushing you to try drugs. Deep down inside, you know that you do not want to get involved with drugs. Have your rights been violated? _____ (If *yes*, explain why.)

5. Your parents have a house rule that you will be grounded for one week, if you come home after your curfew without prior permission. Last night, you were watching a movie at your friend's house and forgot all about the time. You got home 45 minutes late, and your parents grounded you. Have your rights been violated? _____ (If *yes*, explain why.)

6. Your parents signed you up for summer camp without asking you if you were interested. Have your rights been violated? _____ (If *yes*, explain why.)

Name:_____

Passive-Assertive-Aggressive: What's the Difference?

When your rights are violated, whether in a big way or a small way, it is important to be assertive. ***Being assertive*** means *that you state your feelings in a firm and confident way, without making threats.* Unfortunately, many people don't know how to be assertive. They make the mistake of being either passive or aggressive when their rights are violated. This activity page will help you learn the difference between being assertive, passive, and aggressive.

DIRECTIONS: Read the three stories below. Based on what you learn in those stories, match the words ***PASSIVE***, ***ASSERTIVE***, and ***AGGRESSIVE*** to their correct definitions on the following page and then answer the questions that follow.

STORY #1: PASSIVE PATTY

Passive Patty loaned four hot lunch tickets to Pushy Paul. He said he would pay her back as soon as he could. After waiting a couple of weeks, Passive Patty asked Paul for the tickets. Pushy Paul said, "You can forget about getting those hot lunch tickets back, because I don't have any money." All Passive Patty said was, "Oh, OK" and left.

STORY #2: ASSERTIVE SANDY

Assertive Sandy bought a stereo that came with a full one-year warranty. It worked fine for about two weeks, but then went on the blink. When she returned it to the store, the sales clerk said he would not honor the warranty, because nobody ever had any problems with that stereo before. Assertive Sandy said in a firm and confident manner, "This stereo came with a full one-year warranty. The fact that you have had no problems in the past is irrelevant. By law you are required to repair it." She made certain not to raise her voice, because she did not want to make the clerk angry. Her technique paid off, because the clerk ended up honoring the warranty, and had it repaired at no cost to Assertive Sandy.

STORY #3: AGGRESSIVE GAIL

Aggressive Gail was not happy when she found out that Blabbermouth Beth was spreading rumors about her. Aggressive Gail stomped up to Blabbermouth Beth and said, "Look, if you ever tell another lie about me, I am going to smash your face in. You understand me?" All that Gail's aggressive statement accomplished was to get Blabbermouth Beth upset. She said, "You want to smash my face in? I'd like to see you try! I'll meet you outside after school, and we'll see who smashes who."

MATCHING:

_____1. PASSIVE

_____2. AGGRESSIVE

_____3. ASSERTIVE

A. Standing up for your rights by making your feelings known in a confident and firm way, without making threats.

B. Not standing up for your rights at all.

C. Standing up for your rights by making threats.

QUESTIONS:

1. Which of the three techniques do you think is best, and why?

2. Tell what is wrong with the other two techniques.

3. Think about how you handle situations when your rights are violated. Put a circle around the word that best describes how you react most of the time.

   PASSIVE -------------------------ASSERTIVE -------------------------AGGRESSIVE

   Tell why you answered as you did.

4. Identify another person in your life and write down his/her first name on the following line: _____ Think about how that person usually handles situations when his/her rights are violated. Put a circle around the word that best describes how that person reacts most of the time.

   PASSIVE -------------------------ASSERTIVE -------------------------AGGRESSIVE

   Tell why you answered as you did.

Name:_____

Which Is Which?

DIRECTIONS: Read each situation below and answer the questions that follow.

Situation #1: Yolanda babysits for her neighbor every day after school. She wants to earn money for Christmas presents. Christmas is only two weeks away, and the neighbor hasn't paid her in over a month. The neighbor says, "I'm sorry I haven't paid you in so long, Yolanda! With Christmas coming up, I just don't have the money to pay you. I'll give you the money as soon as I can in January." Yolanda says, "No way! Why do you think I took this stupid babysitting job? Pay me now, or I quit!"

1) Yolanda's comment was:

A. Passive
B. Assertive
C. Aggressive

2) What do you think the neighbor said back to Yolanda?

Situation #2: Larry is babysitting for three rowdy boys. It is time for them to go to bed, and they don't want to. Larry says, "I'm sorry, but 9:30 is your bedtime. You need to get into bed now."

1) Larry's comment was:

A. Passive
B. Assertive
C. Aggressive

2) Do you think the boys knew that Larry was serious about their going to bed?   YES   NO   (circle one)   Why?

Situation #3: Juan's parents promised him a dog, if he kept his grades at C's or better all year at school. Juan really wanted a dog, so he worked hard in all of his classes. Juan reached his goal, but after school was out, his parents said they changed their minds and would not be getting him the dog. Juan walked away and said nothing.

1) The way Juan reacted was:

A. Passive
B. Assertive
C. Aggressive

2) By walking away without saying anything, do you think Juan's parents understood just how disappointed he was?
YES   NO   (circle one)   Why?

Name:_____

What Words Would You Say?

DIRECTIONS: Read each situation below, and answer the questions that follow.

Situation #1: Mitchell's boss promised him a 25 cent raise after he had been working for six months. Mitchell waited for quite a while after the sixth month, and still hadn't received his raise.

    1)   What could Mitchell say or do that would be passive?

    2)   What could Mitchell say or do that would be assertive?

    3)   What could Mitchell say or do that would be aggressive?

Situation #2: Kelly should have been the next customer to be waited on, but the sales clerk kept waiting on all of the adults first.

    1)   What could Kelly say or do that would be passive?

    2)   What could Kelly say or do that would be assertive?

    3)   What could Kelly say or do that would be aggressive?

Situation #3: Bruce's science teacher never seemed to call on him when he raised his hand to answer a question in class. It seemed that if anyone else had his hand raised, the other person would get called on instead of Bruce. He was really getting frustrated.

    1)   What could Bruce say or do that would be passive?

    2)   What could Bruce say or do that would be assertive?

    3)   What could Bruce say or do that would be aggressive?

BEING ASSERTIVE - BEING ASSERTIVE - BEING ASSERTIVE

1. Define *being assertive* and write the three skill steps for this social skill.

    (definition) _____

    _____

    (step 1) _____

    (step 2) _____

    (step 3) _____

2. Explain why it is important for a person to know how to be assertive.

    _____

    _____

    _____

3. Describe a situation when you would need to be assertive at home, at school, and in the community.

    (home) _____

    _____

    (school) _____

    _____

    (community) _____

    _____

4. Compare being assertive to being passive and aggressive. Tell one way they are the same and one way they are different.

    (same) _____

    _____

    (different) _____

    _____

5. Write a short story about "Aggressive Gordy." Include information about how others feel toward him. (Use the back of this page if you need more space.)

_____

_____

_____

_____

6. Think about how you handle situations when your rights are violated. Put a circle around the word that best describes how you react most of the time.

PASSIVE --------------------------ASSERTIVE --------------------------AGGRESSIVE

Put a circle around the word that best describes how you would like to react when your rights are violated.

PASSIVE --------------------------ASSERTIVE --------------------------AGGRESSIVE

Explain your answers. _____

_____

_____

_____

_____

SKILL HOMEWORK ACTIVITY

_____
(Due Date)

Dear Parent or Guardian of: _____

This week we are learning about the social communication skill:

MAKING A COMPLAINT

This social skill is very important in interpersonal relationships. This skill can be broken down into the following skill steps. Please watch for all of the steps in your role play practice or real-life observation.

1. Decide if you have a reason to make a complaint. If you do, then see Step Two.
2. Make the complaint in an assertive manner.
3. Tell what you want to happen.

The students use the word **RAT** to remember:
Reason
Assertive
Tell

Before the due date, please complete one of the following activities with your son or daughter: (put a check mark by your choice)

_____ A. We acted out the role play situation listed below.

_____ B. I observed my son/daughter using this social skill in a real-life situation. (I have described the situation below.)

Description of real-life observation:

Role play situation:

YOUR MOTHER/FATHER HASN'T SPENT MUCH TIME WITH YOU LATELY. MAKE A COMPLAINT IN AN ASSERTIVE MANNER AND THEN TELL HER/HIM WHAT YOU WANT TO HAPPEN.

- -

Please circle the word below which best describes how your son or daughter did while using this social skill in either the role play or real-life situation.

NEEDS MORE HELP   GOOD   EXCELLENT

It is important for you to reinforce your child's use of this social skill at home in a positive way. Encourage and praise your child when you see the skill appropriately used. Remind him/her to use the social skill when necessary.

Thank you for your assistance.

Sincerely,

* *

PARENT/GUARDIAN SIGNATURE: _____

Making a Complaint

Sometimes, complaints are necessary. Here are some things to remember about making a complaint:

1) Decide if you have a REASON to make a complaint. Do you have a fair complaint? If you do, then see Step Two.
2) Make the complaint in an ASSERTIVE manner. (See skill steps for being assertive in Unit #B-12.)
3) TELL what you want to happen. (After you make the complaint, tell what you would like to have happen.)

We have a good memory device to help you remember the steps in making a complaint. Think of the word **RAT**.

R = REASON (Decide if you have a good reason.)

A = ASSERTIVE (Do it in an assertive manner.)

T = TELL (Tell what you want to happen.)

You can also think of the sentence, "I'll be a *rat* and complain," to help you remember the steps. Don't get the wrong impression. We don't think you're a rat if you make a complaint. You should make a complaint about some things.

There is something else you should remember about making a complaint. Choose the right time and place to make the complaint. For example, you probably wouldn't make a complaint to your brother about messing up your bedroom if he is with his girlfriend or if he's with his friends.

DIRECTIONS: Tell a good time and place to make each of the complaints below.

1. You want to make a complaint to your parents about not going on a vacation this year.

2. You want to make a complaint to your friend about how he/she has been treating you lately.

3. You want to make a complaint to your teacher because this is the third paper of yours he has misplaced.

4. You want to make a complaint to the auto mechanic who fixed your car because it's not working again.

FAIR?

There are some things that you SHOULD complain about and some things that you SHOULD NOT complain about. You can ask yourself two questions:

Is it fair to complain about this?
Do I have a right to complain about this?

Examples: It would be fair to complain about sour milk if
you had just bought it.
It would not be fair to complain about sour milk
if it had been at your house for three weeks.

It would be fair to complain about your friend's using your locker without permission.
It would not be fair to complain about your friend's using your locker if you use his/her locker without permission.

It would be fair to complain about not getting a seat to see a movie if you had bought a ticket.
It would not be fair to complain about not getting a ticket to see a movie if the theatre is full.

DIRECTIONS: Read each situation and decide if it would be fair to make a complaint. If it is fair, then write **FAIR** on the line. If not, write **NOT FAIR**.

_____ 1. Your teacher just gave you a homework assignment.

_____ 2. The check-out clerk was very rude to you for no reason.

_____ 3. Your parents have a curfew for you.

_____ 4. Your parents won't let you go out any week nights or on the weekend.

_____ 5. There isn't any salt or pepper on the table you're sitting at in a restaurant.

_____ 6. Your boss scheduled you to work weekends. You knew you would have to work weekends when you got the job.

_____ 7. You took a test in science this morning. Your teacher didn't get the test corrected yet.

_____ 8. Your father asked you to mow the lawn.

Name:_____

What's Your Complaint IQ?

DIRECTIONS: Take the quiz below and see if you make complaints in the right way.

1. Your brother has been going into your room and using your things. You . . .

    a. Tell him that you do not want him going into your bedroom anymore without your permission.

    b. Don't say anything to him.

    c. Call him a big jerk and punch him.

2. You are eating at a restaurant. The waitress forgets to bring you your glass of milk. You . . .

    a. Forget about it. You didn't really need the milk.

    b. Tell her she forgot your milk.

    c. Tell her what a bad waitress she is.

3. The people you babysit for haven't paid you for the last three times you babysat. You . . .

    a. Tell them you are quitting and their kids are brats.

    b. Tell them that you really need to be paid.

    c. Wait and see if they will pay you.

4. One of your classmates has been spreading untrue rumors about you. You . . .

    a. Complain to your friends but say nothing to that person.

    b. Get a bunch of people to beat up that person.

    c. Tell that person you do not like the rumors being spread and you want them stopped.

5. You purchase a shirt from a store. When you get home you see that it is ripped. You . . .

    a. Take the shirt back to the store.

    b. Keep the shirt.

    c. Call the store and tell them you won't shop there again.

6. Your friend has been putting his books in your locker. You don't like it. You . . .

    a. Throw his books on the floor.

    b. Tell him to put his books in his own locker.

    c. Don't say anything because he'll get mad.

7. Your teacher told you that he would give you extra credit for the report you did. You didn't get the extra points. You . . .

    a. Ask him about it and tell him you deserve the extra credit.

    b. Complain to the person sitting next to you.

    c. Shout out that the teacher is unfair.

SCORING (Question #)

ANSWER	1	2	3	4	5	6	7
a	3	1	5	1	3	5	3
b	1	3	3	5	1	3	1
c	5	5	1	3	5	1	5

You are too wishy-washy. Stand up for your rights.
0-7

You're getting better. Be assertive.
8-14

You know how to complain.
15-25

You're a little too pushy.
26-29

You're too aggressive. You get out of hand!
30-35

124

Name:_____

COMPLAINT Questions

DIRECTIONS: Answer the questions.

1. Tell three situations at school when you may need to make a complaint.

    •

    •

    •

2. Tell three situations at home when you may need to make a complaint.

    •

    •

    •

3. Tell three situations in the community when you may need to make a complaint.

    •

    •

    •

4. Tell why it is important to choose the right time and place to make the complaint.

5. Tell a time when it would be fair to make a complaint and a time when it would not be fair to make a complaint.

    FAIR:

    NOT FAIR:

Name:_____

MAKING A COMPLAINT - MAKING A COMPLAINT

1. Write the three skill steps for the social skill of making a complaint.

(step 1) _____

(step 2) _____

(step 3) _____

2. Explain why it is important to make a complaint in the appropriate way.

_____

_____

_____

_____

3. Describe a recent situation when you made a complaint to someone.

_____

_____

_____

_____

4. Compare making a complaint in an assertive way to making a complaint in an aggressive way. Tell one similarity and one difference.

(similarity) _____

_____

(difference) _____

_____

5. Develop a short, five-question quiz you could give to students about making a complaint appropriately.

6. Evaluate whether the people below have a good reason to make a complaint. Explain your answers.

(#1) Jojo bought a new pair of tennis shoes. When he got them home, he noticed that the side of one tennis shoe was ripped. Does Jojo have a good reason to make a complaint to the store? _____

Explanation:

(#2) Gigi bought a new shirt. When she got home, she used a pair of scissors to cut the tags off the shirt. She accidently cut a hole in the shirt. Does Gigi have a good reason to make a complaint to the store? _____

Explanation:

SKILL HOMEWORK ACTIVITY

_____
(Due Date)

Dear Parent or Guardian of: _____

This week we are learning about the social communication skill:

RECEIVING A COMPLAINT

This social skill is very important in interpersonal relationships.

This skill can be broken down into the following skill steps. Please watch for all of the steps in your role play practice or real-life observation.

1. Listen carefully to the complaint.
2. Decide if you are responsible for what the person is complaining about.

IF *YES*

3. Apologize.

4. Tell what you will do about
the complaint.

OR

5. Ask the person to suggest
what to do about the complaint.

IF *NO*

Follow the skill steps for dealing
with a false accusation.

(See Unit B-18.)

Before the due date, please complete one of the following activities with your son or daughter: (put a check mark by your choice)

_____ A. We acted out the role play situation listed below.

_____ B. I observed my son/daughter using this social skill in a real-life situation. (I have described the situation below.)

Description of real-life observation:

Role play situation:

YOUR MOM/DAD MAKES A COMPLAINT TO YOU ABOUT NOT DOING YOUR CHORES AND YOU REALLY HAVEN'T BEEN DOING THEM. DEMONSTRATE HOW TO RESPOND CORRECTLY TO THE COMPLAINT.

- -

Please circle the word below which best describes how your son or daughter did while using this social skill in either the role play or real-life situation.

NEEDS MORE HELP   GOOD   EXCELLENT

It is important for you to reinforce your child's use of this social skill at home in a positive way. Encourage and praise your child when you see the skill appropriately used. Remind him/her to use the social skill when necessary.

Thank you for your assistance.

Sincerely,

* *

PARENT/GUARDIAN SIGNATURE: _____

Name:_____

Are You RESPONSIBLE?

It is important to know how to receive a complaint correctly. NOBODY IS PERFECT! We all make mistakes and, therefore, we all receive complaints.

Here are the first two steps to follow when someone makes a complaint to you:

1. LISTEN CAREFULLY TO THE COMPLAINT.

2. DECIDE IF YOU ARE RESPONSIBLE FOR WHAT THE PERSON IS COMPLAINING ABOUT.

For example, pretend you are assigned to do a project in English with another student. When the assignment is due, your partner has his part done, but you don't. You just couldn't get yourself to do the project. When your partner complains to you about not having it done, you know that you are responsible. You were the one who was supposed to do half of the project.

For another example, pretend your brother makes a complaint to you about not turning the stereo off. You did not touch the stereo. You remember seeing your sister turn it on earlier in the day. You know that you are not responsible.

DIRECTIONS: Read each of the situations below. If you are responsible, write **RESPONSIBLE**. If you are not responsible, write **NOT RESPONSIBLE**.

_____ 1. You were supposed to rake the leaves this afternoon. Instead, you watched TV. Your dad makes a complaint to you about not doing your job.

_____ 2. You didn't remember to turn on the air conditioner before you left the house. It was your job. Your family complained to you about how hot it was in the house.

_____ 3. You never vandalize public property. The owner of the roller skating rink made a complaint to you by saying, "Kids have been writing on the walls in the bathrooms again. If you're one of them, I want you to knock it off."

_____ 4. You share a bedroom with your brother/sister. You cleaned up the room after you got up. Your brother/sister messed it all up again in the afternoon. Your mom made a complaint to you about how messy it was.

_____ 5. You were in charge of hiring the disk jockey for the dance Friday night. You told the D.J. to be there at 8:00. The dance started at 7:30, so there was no music for the first 30 minutes. The students really complained.

_____ 6. You had a party at your house. You had the music really loud, because you wanted everyone to hear it. Your neighbors came over and complained about the noise.

Name:_____

What NOT To Do

You have learned these two steps for receiving a complaint:

1. Listen carefully to the complaint.

2. Decide if you are responsible for what the person is complaining about.

If you decide that you are responsible, here are two things you should **NOT** do:

1. *Don't make "a million excuses"!*

2. *Don't get defensive!*

Remember, nobody is perfect! We all make mistakes, so receiving complaints is a part of life. If someone makes a complaint to you, and you make a million excuses or get defensive, it shows you are not willing to admit that you make mistakes.

What TO DO!

You have learned these two steps for receiving a complaint:

1. Listen carefully to the complaint.

2. Decide if you are responsible for what the person is complaining about.

If you decide that you are responsible, here are steps you should follow:

3. Apologize,

4. Tell what you will do about the complaint,

      OR

5. Ask the person to suggest what to do about the complaint.

The cartoons below give examples of these steps.

Cartoon #1:

Apologize.   **Tell what you will do about the complaint.**

Cartoon #2:

Apologize.   **Ask the person to suggest what to do about the complaint.**

𝔚𝔯𝔦𝔱𝔢 𝔍𝔱

Remember, when you know you are responsible for a complaint, you should do the following:

- Apologize,

- Tell what you will do about the complaint,

        OR

- Ask the person to suggest what to do about the complaint.

DIRECTIONS: Pretend that you are responsible for all of the following complaints. Write down what you would say.

1. "That radio is on too loud! I'm trying to study for a test."

2. "You have a bad habit of cracking your gum, and it drives me crazy!"

3. "This is the third day you've been late to class. You miss a lot of information when you come late."

4. "You told Jeff that I like him. You promised you wouldn't say anything!"

5. "This paper is written so sloppily that I can't read it to grade it."

6. "Just because you had a bad day doesn't give you the right to yell at us."

7. "This is the third time you've interrupted me. I really need to get this done."

"They Got the Wrong Person!"

If you receive a complaint and you are not responsible, these are the steps to follow:

- Tell the person you are not responsible.

- Tell who is responsible, if you know.

The cartoon below gives an example of these steps:

DIRECTIONS: Pretend you are not responsible for the following complaints. Write down what you would say.

1. "That bathroom sink is filthy, and we have company coming any minute."

2. "Please stop tapping your pencil. The other students are trying to concentrate."

3. "I heard you are spreading rumors about me that I stayed out all night last weekend."

4. "Look at that door! You left it unlocked again."

5. "Why did you cut into this pie? You knew it was for supper tonight."

Name:_____

RECEIVING A COMPLAINT - RECEIVING A COMPLAINT

1. Tell what *receiving a complaint* means. Then list the five skill steps for this social skill.

    (definition) _____

    (step 1) _____

    (step 2) _____

    (step 3) _____

    (step 4) _____

    (step 5) _____

2. Explain why it is important to receive a complaint correctly, without getting defensive or making a million excuses.

    _____

    _____

3. Describe a situation when you may receive a complaint at home, at school, and in the community.

    (home) _____

    (school) _____

    (community) _____

4. Compare *making a million excuses* to *getting defensive*. Tell how they are the same and how they are different.

    (same) _____

    (different) _____

    _____

5. Create a mnemonic device to help you remember the five skill steps for receiving a complaint.

    _____

    _____

    _____

    _____

    _____

6. Evaluate one person in your family. Decide if you think that person usually receives complaints in a good or bad way. _____ Explain your answer.

    _____

    _____

SKILL HOMEWORK ACTIVITY

_____
(Due Date)

Dear Parent or Guardian of: _____

This week we are learning about the social communication skill:

GIVING CONSTRUCTIVE CRITICISM

This social skill is very important in interpersonal relationships.

The students have learned that when they give constructive criticism, they should:

1. Tell what behavior they want to see improved (e.g., This room needs to be picked up better), rather than make a personal insult (e.g., You are such a slob. How can you stand to be in this room?).

2. Say something positive when giving constructive criticism (e.g., This room needs to be picked up better. You really did a nice job cleaning up the bathroom, though).

Before the due date, please complete one of the following activities with your son or daughter: (put a check mark by your choice)

_____ A. We acted out the role play situation listed below.

_____ B. I observed my son/daughter using this social skill in a real-life situation. (I have described the situation below.)

Description of real-life observation:

Role play situation:

YOU WANT TO GIVE SOME CONSTRUCTIVE CRITICISM TO YOUR SISTER ABOUT HER POOR STUDY HABITS. REMEMBER TO TELL THE BEHAVIOR THAT YOU WOULD LIKE TO SEE IMPROVED AND SAY SOMETHING POSITIVE.

- -

Please circle the word below which best describes how your son or daughter did while using this social skill in either the role play or real-life situation.

NEEDS MORE HELP   GOOD   EXCELLENT

It is important for you to reinforce your child's use of this social skill at home in a positive way. Encourage and praise your child when you see the skill appropriately used. Remind him/her to use the social skill when necessary.

Thank you for your assistance.

Sincerely,

* *

PARENT/GUARDIAN SIGNATURE: _____

Constructive Criticism

Sometimes, it is necessary to give other people suggestions for improvement. We call this constructive criticism. The word constructive means *leading to improvement*. *Constructive criticism* means *telling someone something that will lead to improvement*.

There is a right way and a wrong way to give constructive criticism. Tell the person what BEHAVIOR you want improved (e.g., "I really don't like it when you're late. Please call the next time"). Don't give a personal insult (e.g., "You jerk. You're always late. Everyone hates that!"). It's important to let people know what you don't like, but you don't have to hurt their feelings by insulting them.

DIRECTIONS: Fill in the chart below by completing the RIGHT WAY column (tell the behavior you don't like) or the WRONG WAY column (give a personal insult).

EXAMPLE →

RIGHT WAY	WRONG WAY
1. These boxes should be stacked a little neater.	Are you blind? Stack those boxes again.
2.	You slob! Your shirt has a big spot on it. What a pig!
3. I wish you wouldn't put your books in my locker anymore.	
4. This casserole isn't my favorite.	
5.	You eat just like a pig. Oink, oink, oink.
6. It would be a good idea to rewrite this paper.	
7.	Boy, do you stink!
8.	Why do you wear so much make-up? To cover the pimples? You look like a clown.
9. Please try to keep our bedroom a little cleaner.	

Name:_____

Say It a Better Way!

DIRECTIONS: Read each criticism. Tell whether it is said in the right way (telling what behavior you want the person to improve) or the wrong way (a personal insult). Write **Right** or **Wrong** on each line. Correct the **Wrong** items.

_____ 1. I really wish you would come over to my house more.

_____ 2. Thanks a lot! You ruined our project with that sloppy report you did.

_____ 3. I am not going to the dance with you if you're going to dress like such a nerd.

_____ 4. Mom, that wig looks terrible on you. You look so ugly.

_____ 5. Mrs. Glee, I can't read your comment on my book report.

_____ 6. You are so gross! Do you have to burp in my ear?

_____ 7. You would look so nice if you washed your hair more often.

_____ 8. I'd appreciate it if you didn't set your glass of cola by my computer.

_____ 9. Mr. Ink, I can't read your crummy handwriting. Where'd you learn how to write?

_____10. You really smell horrible!

Name:_____

Add a Touch of Positive

Nobody enjoys getting criticism (even it it's said in the right way). It's a good idea to follow this rule when giving someone constructive criticism:

RULE: Add a positive comment when giving criticism.

Example: Brad, I really think you should rewrite this report because your handwriting is hard to read. But, it's a very good report. You'll probably get a good grade if you rewrite it.

When you add something positive, people accept criticism easier.

DIRECTIONS: Read each situation. Then write what you would say to give constructive criticism. Underline the positive comment.

1. You just cleaned the family room and now your brother is messing it up.

2. Your friend has been coming to school with really greasy hair.

3. Your friend flunked the science test because he/she didn't study and went to a movie instead.

4. Your brother made a lopsided cake which looks very funny. He asks what you think of it.

5. Your teacher asks you to evaluate her at the end of the year. You think she is unorganized.

Name:_____

YOU Are the Teacher!

DIRECTIONS: You will be assigned a partner. You and your partner should complete the following activity.

1. You and your partner are going to develop a short lesson (3-4 minutes) on a topic. You will teach your lesson to the rest of the class.

2. Choose one of the following topics. Let your teacher know which topic you will be teaching.

   - Why personal insults hurt people
   - How constructive criticism can be helpful
   - Saying something positive along with the negative

3. Write down as many things as you can think of about your topic (brainstorm ideas).

4. Decide which things you want the rest of the class to know about your topic. Your teacher will help you if you need it. Write those things on a piece of paper.

5. Get your lesson approved by your teacher.

6. Next, write your major points on an overhead transparency (or on a large piece of poster board, if you do not have an overhead projector).

7. Plan out exactly what both of you are going to say during your lesson. Remember, you only have 3-4 minutes. Are you going to have the students take notes? What questions will you ask the rest of the class?

8. Practice going through your lesson.

9. Give your lesson to the class.

GRADING

Your teacher will grade your lesson on the following criteria:

Cooperation between partners   _____/20 points

Behavior while preparing lesson   _____/20 points

Content of lesson   _____/20 points

Neatness of transparency/poster board   _____/10 points

Practice session   _____/10 points

Presentation of lesson   _____/20 points

TOTAL SCORE   _____/100 points

GIVING CONSTRUCTIVE CRITICISM

1. Write the two skill steps for the social skill of giving constructive criticism.

   (step 1) _____

   (step 2) _____

2. Explain why it is important to give constructive criticism in the appropriate way.

   _____

   _____

   _____

3. Give an example of a time when you may need to give constructive criticism to one of your friends.

   _____

   _____

4. Explain the difference between constructive criticism and a personal insult, and give an example of each.

   (difference) _____

   _____

   (constructive criticism) _____

   _____

   (personal insult) _____

   _____

5. Write a story about a person who learns to give constructive criticism rather than personal insults. (Use the back of this page if you need more space.)

   _____

   _____

   _____

   _____

6. Read the following story. Evaluate how well Anna gave constructive criticism. Explain your answer.

   One day, Anna's brother was complaining about not having any friends. Anna said to him, "I bet you'd have more friends if you didn't always try to show off to everyone. People don't like that. You're a nice guy. You don't need to prove anything to anyone."

   _____

   _____

   _____

SKILL HOMEWORK ACTIVITY

_____
(Due Date)

Dear Parent or Guardian of: _____

This week we are learning about the social communication skill:

ACCEPTING CONSTRUCTIVE CRITICISM

This social skill is very important in interpersonal relationships.

Accepting constructive criticism means that you respond appropriately when someone suggests a way for you to improve. This social skill can be broken down into the following skill steps:

1. Stay calm. (Remember, the person is trying to help you become better at something.)

2. Listen carefully. (If you do not understand the suggestion, ask questions.)

3. Thank the person for the suggestion.

4. Follow the suggestion for improvement.

Before the due date, please complete one of the following activities with your son or daughter: (put a check mark by your choice)

_____ A. We acted out the role play situation listed below.

_____ B. I observed my son/daughter using this social skill in a real-life situation. (I have described the situation below.)

Description of real-life observation:

Role play situation:

PRETEND YOU JUST PRACTICED GIVING YOUR BOOK REPORT TO YOUR PARENTS. WHEN YOU FINISH, THEY POINT OUT SEVERAL THINGS THEY LIKED ABOUT YOUR REPORT. NEXT, THEY SUGGEST THAT YOU STOP ROCKING BACK AND FORTH WHEN YOU TALK. DEMONSTRATE WHAT YOU WOULD SAY/DO TO ACCEPT THEIR CONSTRUCTIVE CRITICISM IN A GOOD WAY.

Please circle the word below which best describes how your son or daughter did while using this social skill in either the role play or real-life situation.

NEEDS MORE HELP   GOOD   EXCELLENT

It is important for you to reinforce your child's use of this social skill at home in a positive way. Encourage and praise your child when you see the skill appropriately used. Remind him/her to use the social skill when necessary.

Thank you for your assistance.

Sincerely,

* *

PARENT/GUARDIAN SIGNATURE: _____

141

Suggestions for Improvement

Accepting constructive criticism means *that you respond appropriately when someone suggests a way for you to improve.* For example, pretend that your teacher corrects your test and hands it back to you. On the top of the test, your teacher has written, "Your answers are good, but difficult to read. Please write more neatly next time." Your teacher has constructively criticized your penmanship.

When someone gives you constructive criticism, they are trying to be helpful. They are trying to help you become a better person.

DIRECTIONS: List four people in your life who would be most likely to give you constructive criticism.

1.

2.

3.

4.

Receiving constructive criticism is similar to receiving a complaint, but there are differences between them. When someone makes a complaint to you, he is not really interested in helping you become a better person; he just wants you to quit doing something so he won't be bothered by it any more. When someone constructively criticizes you, he cares about you and wants to help you be the best person you can be.

DIRECTIONS: Read each of the situations below. Decide if you are receiving constructive criticism or receiving a complaint. Write **CC** for constructive criticism, and **C** for complaint.

_____1. You are having a party. Someone calls the police because you are playing your music too loudly.

_____2. You are practicing your lines for the play that you are going to be in next week. Your brother suggests that you use more inflection in your voice, so it will sound more interesting to the audience.

_____3. Your teacher points out to you that if you came into class with a smile, it would help you to present yourself more positively.

_____4. You are tapping your pencil while you are thinking during a test. One of the other students says to the teacher, "I can't concentrate because of that tapping sound."

_____5. Your mom points out that you have several "split-ends" on your hair. She gives you some suggestions to help make your hair healthier.

How Good Are You
At This Social Communication Skill?

DIRECTIONS: Answer each of the following questions honestly.

1. Your parents tell you they think you would get better grades if you studied more. What would you do?

   a. Let them finish what they are saying, and then leave without saying anything.

   b. Stay calm, and listen to their suggestion. Tell them you agree, and really try to study more in the future.

   c. Get angry and tell them that if you want to fail it is none of their business.

2. Your teacher says she really enjoys having you in class, but thinks you could do better if you started keeping your schoolwork organized. What would you do?

   a. Interrupt and say that you hate her class.

   b. Thank her for the suggestion. Think about getting organized but forget to do it.

   c. Listen carefully and thank her for the suggestion. Take all your materials home that day, and get yourself organized.

3. Your uncle compliments you by saying he thinks you are a very good-looking person. He says he notices that you bite your finger nails and thinks they would look nicer if you let them grow longer. He asks if you have ever tried the product called *Stop Bite* to help you stop biting your nails. What would you do?

   a. Get embarrassed and decide to avoid seeing your uncle from now on.

   b. Stay calm and ask questions to learn more about the product and how it works. Go to a store and buy some to try.

   c. Say, "I've tried to stop and I just can't do it."

4. Your best friend talks to you in private and suggests in a nice way that you should start washing your clothes more often, because they smell bad. What would you do?

   a. Thank your friend for caring enough about you to be honest. Start to shower once a day, and wash your clothes more often.

   b. Try to change the subject right away, so you don't have to talk about it.

   c. Get really mad and give your friend the "silent treatment."

5. Your brother is a very good basketball player. You are on the basketball team at your school, but the coach hardly ever puts you in the games to play. Your brother tells you he thinks you could be a good player if you practiced more. What would you do?

   a. Get really angry and say, "Just because you are better than I am, you think you know everything. Why don't you just leave me alone?"

   b. Agree with him, but make no changes in how often you practice.

   c. Agree with him, and be happy that he is trying to help you. Ask if he could show you some new techniques to practice.

6. Your grandmother is concerned because you are arguing more often with your parents. She suggests that you try to work things out with your parents. What would you do?

   a. Let her talk, but not listen to a word she says.

   b. Yell at your grandmother and tell her she is as "nosey" as your parents are.

   c. Realize that she cares about you and is trying to help. Ask if she ever got into fights with her parents when she was growing up.

DIRECTIONS: Use the scoring chart below, to calculate your score.

(Question #)

(Answers)

	1	2	3	4	5	6
a	3	1	1	5	1	3
b	5	3	5	3	3	1
c	1	5	3	1	5	5

DIRECTIONS: Find your score below and read what it says about your score.

1 - 10 points	11 - 20 points	21 - 30 points
You really need to work on improving your ability to accept constructive criticism.	Not bad, but not good either. There are some techniques you should learn about this social skill.	Good! You are accepting constructive criticism in a mature way.

Name:_____

How To Do It The Right Way

When someone constructively criticizes you, there are four things you should do to accept it in a good way. The four skill steps for this social skill are listed below:

1. Stay calm. (Remember, the person is trying to help you become better at something.)

2. Listen carefully. (If you do not understand the suggestion, ask questions.)

3. Thank the person for the suggestion.

4. Follow the suggestion for improvement.

DIRECTIONS: Read each of the situations below. Write **good** if the person accepted the constructive criticism in a good way and **bad** if the person accepted it in a bad way. If you write **bad**, then write the number of the skill step that was not followed. (If more than one skill step was not followed, then write more than one number.)

1. Kelly's mom said to him, "Kelly, you are a very good-looking guy. I think you could look your best if you washed your hair more often. I notice that some days it looks greasy." Kelly listened carefully while his mom was talking, and realized that she was making a good suggestion to him. Kelly said, "I guess I should wash it more often. Thanks for the suggestion." Kelly started getting up earlier in the morning so he would have time to wash his hair.

   Did Kelly accept his mom's constructive criticism in a good or bad way?

2. Bart's wrestling coach was weighing everyone on the team at the beginning of the season. When Bart stepped on the scale, the coach noticed that he had gained ten pounds over the summer and was really out of shape. The coach talked to Bart privately and said, "Bart, I think you should work on losing ten pounds if you want to be able to wrestle varsity this year." Bart knew the coach was right, but didn't like having someone point out one of his weaknesses. Bart got angry and told the coach to mind his own business.

   Did Bart accept his coach's constructive criticism in a good or bad way?

3. Trudy asked her best friend why guys didn't seem to like her very much. Her friend said, "Trudy, I think you should just watch some of the things you say when you are around guys." Trudy did not understand the suggestion, but said, "OK, I'll work on that, thanks."

   Did Trudy accept her friend's constructive criticism in a good or bad way?

EDUCATOR PAGE: DO NOT DUPLICATE FOR STUDENTS

DIRECTIONS: Discuss the following ideas with your students to help them to consider the source of constructive criticism, and realize that they do not need to "soak in" everything said to them when it comes to input from other people.

Discuss These Ideas:

1. Sometimes other people don't have a right to criticize you (e.g., a stranger who doesn't know enough about you to make a judgement).

2. When you receive constructive criticism from someone you do not respect, you may choose to reject it.

3. Sometimes constructive criticism is actually a "put-down" and, therefore, may be rejected.

(You may want to divide your class into three or more groups. Give each group one of the topics listed above and ask them to make a list of examples or reasons for the statement they were given. Ask one member from each group to present the group's ideas to the entire class.)

Name:_____

SELF EVALUATION

DIRECTIONS: Try to pay attention to times you receive constructive criticism from someone at home, at school, or out in the community during the next week. When someone constructively criticizes you, record it on the chart below and answer all the questions.

Date	Who constructively criticized me?	What did the person criticize me about?	Did I accept it in a good way? (Yes or No)	Why or why not?
#1				
#2				
#3				

©1989 THINKING PUBLICATIONS

SSS: Social Skill Strategies (Book B)

ACCEPTING CONSTRUCTIVE CRITICISM

1. Explain what it means when someone gives you *constructive criticism* and write the four skill steps for the social skill of accepting constructive criticism.

    (definition) _____

    (step 1) _____

    (step 2) _____

    (step 3) _____

    (step 4) _____

2. Explain why a person constructively criticizes you.

    _____

    _____

3. List three things that people have constructively criticized you about in the past.

    (1) _____

    (2) _____

    (3) _____

4. Describe how receiving constructive criticism and receiving a complaint are the same and how they are different.

    (same) _____

    (different) _____

5. Write about a situation that could be role played to show how to accept constructive criticism in an appropriate way. (Use the back of this page if you need more space.)

    _____

    _____

6. Write down whether you think you need to work on improving your ability to accept constructive criticism or not. Explain why.

    _____

    _____

SKILL HOMEWORK ACTIVITY

_____
(Due Date)

Dear Parent or Guardian of: _____

This week we are learning about the social communication skill:

MAKING AN ACCUSATION

This social skill is very important in interpersonal relationships.

The students have learned that there are situations when they will need to blame someone for doing something wrong. They have learned, however, that they need to be careful when they make an accusation. It is possible to falsely accuse someone by "jumping to conclusions."

The students have learned the following skill steps for making an accusation:

1. Decide if you should gather more information before making the accusation.

2. Decide whom you will make the accusation to.

3. Decide on the best time and place to make the accusation.

4. Decide what you will say.

Before the due date, please complete one of the following activities with your son or daughter: (put a check mark by your choice)

_____ A. We acted out the role play situation listed below.

_____ B. I observed my son/daughter using this social skill in a real-life situation. (I have described the situation below.)

Description of real-life observation:

Role play situation:

ONE OF YOUR FRIENDS SAW YOUR YOUNGER BROTHER/SISTER WEARING YOUR FAVORITE SHIRT DOWNTOWN. YOU CHECK YOUR CLOSET AND THE SHIRT IS GONE. TELL WHOM YOU WOULD ACCUSE AND THEN DEMONSTRATE WHAT YOU WOULD SAY.

Please circle the word below which best describes how your son or daughter did while using this social skill in either the role play or real-life situation.

NEEDS MORE HELP   GOOD   EXCELLENT

It is important for you to reinforce your child's use of this social skill at home in a positive way. Encourage and praise your child when you see the skill appropriately used. Remind him/her to use the social skill when necessary.

Thank you for your assistance.

Sincerely,

* *

PARENT/GUARDIAN SIGNATURE: _____

Jumping to Conclusions

Making an accusation means blaming someone for doing something wrong. For example, pretend that you walk into an ice cream shop. You see two teen-agers who have just placed their order. You get into line behind them. While the sales clerk is making their cones, you see them steal some candy. They don't realize that you are watching. After they leave the store, you decide to make an accusation and you quickly tell the sales clerk what you saw.

In the example listed above, it would be fairly easy for you to make the accusation. You saw the theft occur and you would have little doubt about what happened. In many situations, however, it is difficult to be totally certain that someone has done something wrong. It is sometimes possible to jump to conclusions and falsely accuse someone.

Jumping to conclusions means *that you make your decision about a situation before you have all the facts*. Read the cartoon below, which gives you an example of someone who jumped to conclusions.

Things are not always the way they seem to be. Sometimes it is easy to jump to conclusions and end up falsely accusing someone. It can be very embarrassing when this happens! Remember, the first thing you should do before making an accusation is:

Step 1

> Decide if you should gather more information before making the accusation.

EDUCATOR PAGE: DO NOT DUPLICATE FOR STUDENTS

The activity described below will help your students realize that things are not always the way they seem to be.

DIRECTIONS: Read each of the following situations to your students. Each situation makes it appear as if one of the characters did something wrong. Next, ask your students to guess who is to blame. They may write down or tell whom they would accuse. After all students have made their choice, then read the answer. The answer will be an unlikely candidate, to help stress the point that things are not always what they seem to be.

After completing the three situations, lead a discussion about the importance of deciding if you have enough proof or if you should gather more information before making an accusation. Discuss the idea that a person can seldom be 100% certain before making an accusation. Help students understand that there will be situations when they should make an accusation even without having proof. For example: If a student "thinks" he knows who called and made a bomb threat to the school, but doesn't have much proof, he should report it anyway.

SITUATION #1: Shannon has a crush on a guy at school named Ben. She tells her best friend, Kerstin, about it before school. Kerstin promises not to tell anybody. Later that day, Shannon sees Kerstin whispering something to Beth. They both look Shannon's way and start laughing. Shannon runs into Beth on her way home from school and Beth says, "Hey Shannon, I heard you like Ben." Shannon gets very angry because Beth found out about her secret.

QUESTION: Who do you think told Beth that Shannon likes Ben?

ANSWER: Shannon's brother found her diary, and read it. He found out about her crush on Ben, and told Beth about it.

SITUATION #2: Malcolm is working on his math assignment at the end of math class. He asks for permission to go to the bathroom and leaves the room. When he gets back, he sees that his pencil is gone. He starts looking all over for it. The student sitting next to him starts laughing.

QUESTION: Who do you think took Malcolm's pencil away from him?

ANSWER: Nobody took it. Malcolm has his pencil resting on top of his ear.

SITUATION #3: Carol sees her sister, Ruth, sneaking out of her bedroom. When Carol asks why she was in her bedroom, Ruth says, "Well, let's see, I was . . . looking for some tape." When Carol goes to her closet to get her new sweater, she discovers it isn't there.

QUESTION: Who do you think took Carol's sweater out of her closet?

ANSWER: Carol's mom took it, because she was going shopping and wanted to buy Carol a new pair of pants to match it.

Gathering Information

DIRECTIONS: Match each situation described in the column on the left with the best way to gather information in the column on the right. Draw a line connecting the matching items.

Situation	**Ways To Gather Information**
Someone has started a bad rumor about you at school. You want to find out who started it.	Ask your friends if they saw anyone at your locker. Ask them to help you watch to see if anyone goes in it again.
While you were at work, someone took your jacket. You want to find out what happened to it.	Talk to people who heard the rumor and ask who told them.
While you were at your friend's house, someone broke the lamp that sits on your desk in your bedroom at home. You want to find out who broke it.	Try to remember if you took it to the drinking fountain with you. Quietly ask the teacher if she picked up your book. Ask the students who sit by you if they know what happened to it.
Lunch tickets have been disappearing from your locker at school. You want to find out who has been taking them.	Talk to the people you work with. See if anyone accidently took your jacket by mistake, or if anyone else is missing a jacket too.
While you were getting a drink, someone took a book off your desk in the classroom. You want to find out who took it.	Find out who was at home while your were gone. Talk to each member of your family and ask them questions about the lamp.

DIRECTIONS: For each of the following situations, write down at least two things the person could do to gather information before making an accusation.

1. The math teacher noticed that someone damaged the top of the second desk in the back row in his classroom. How can the teacher gather information?

   A.

   B.

2. Someone at school pulled a fire alarm as a prank. The school principal needs to find out who did it. How can the principal gather information?

   A.

   B.

Steps 2 + 3

Remember: It is very important to stop yourself from jumping to conclusions and falsely accusing someone! You need to gather enough information so you can be reasonably certain before you make an accusation.

The second thing you should do before making an accusation is to **decide whom you should make the accusation to**. You need to decide if you will make your accusation directly to the person you think has done something wrong, or if you will report the problem to someone else.

The third thing you should do before making an accusation is to **decide on the best time and place to make the accusation**. Usually, it is best to make your accusation in private, so that it will be less embarrassing to the person involved.

DIRECTIONS: Circle the best person to make the accusation to, and the best time and place to make the accusation for each of the situations.

1. You see a man stealing food from a grocery store.

   The best person to make the accusation to is:

   A. The store manager

   B. The thief

   C. Your parents

   The best time and place to make the accusation is:

   A. At the store right after the man steps outside the store

   B. At the store the next day

   C. At your house after you get home

2. You are almost certain that your best friend told someone else one of your secrets.

   The best person to make the accusation to is:

   A. Your best friend's mom

   B. Your favorite teacher

   C. Your best friend

   The best time and place to make the accusation is:

   A. When your best friend and you are with the "gang" after school

   B. When your friend and you are alone

   C. During class

3. Your class is taking a test. You see the student sitting in front of you cheating.

The best person to make the accusation to is:

A. Your parents

B. The teacher

C. Your principal

The best time and place to make the accusation is:

A. During class so all the other students can hear

B. After class when all the students have left

C. When you get home from school

4. You are almost certain that your boy/girl friend has been dating someone else behind your back. You had both agreed not to date anyone else.

The best person to make the accusation to is:

A. Your boy/girl friend

B. The person your boy/girl friend has been dating

C. Your school guidance counselor

The best time and place to make the accusation is:

A. When the two of you are alone

B. In front of his/her parents

C. In front of your other friends

DIRECTIONS: Answer the following questions.

1. Explain why it is usually best to make an accusation in private.

2. Describe a situation when you would not want to make an accusation in private.

BE CAREFUL NOT TO MAKE ACCUSATIONS ABOUT EVERY LITTLE THING THAT SOMEONE DOES WRONG. IF YOU MAKE TOO MANY ACCUSATIONS, PEOPLE WILL THINK YOU ARE A "TATTLETALE." REFER TO THE TATTLING UNIT (B-11.) FOR MORE INFORMATION.

Name:_____

Step 4

The fourth and final step for making an accusation is to **decide what you will say when making an accusation**. There are two things you should do:

1. Tell the person what you are accusing him/her of doing.

2. Tell what information you have that makes you think he/she has done something wrong.

The cartoon below gives an example of what you could say when making an accusation.

DIRECTIONS: Write down the exact words you would say when you make the following accusations.

1. You are accusing your sister of riding your bike without your permission.

2. You are accusing your teacher of losing a paper you turned in.

3. You are accusing your friend of gossiping about you behind your back.

It is very important to remain calm when you make an accusation. If you lose control and start yelling when you accuse someone, then the person you are accusing is more likely to get defensive. If you lose control, you make yourself look bad. Sometimes, it isn't easy to remain calm because what the person did wrong really makes you feel angry.

DIRECTIONS: List four things you can do to help yourself remain calm.

1.

2.

3.

4.

Evaluate Yourself

The four skill steps for making an accusation are:

1. Decide if you should gather more information before making the accusation.

2. Decide whom you will make the accusation to.

3. Decide the best time and place to make the accusation.

4. Decide what you will say.

DIRECTIONS: Evaluate your skills at making an accusation. Place an **X** in the box that best indicates where your skills are right now. Place an * in the box that best indicates where you would like your skills to be. (It is possible for you to put your **X** and * in the same box.)

Placing your **X** in this box means that you never, or hardly ever, accuse anybody, because:

a. You are afraid you might be wrong.

b. You feel that if someone wants to do something wrong, it's their business.

c. You feel uncomfortable about accusing someone, even when you are certain about what they have done.

Placing your **X** in this box means that you are pretty good at making an accusation because:

a. You try to have adequate proof before you make an accusation.

b. You make your accusation to the correct person.

c. You choose a good time and place to make an accusation.

d. You say the right words when you accuse someone.

Placing your **X** in this box means that you make accusations more often than you should because:

a. You tend to jump to conclusions and blame people before you have all the facts.

b. It is easier for you to blame things on other people than to blame yourself.

c. You don't trust people, and assume that they will do the wrong thing.

MAKING AN ACCUSATION - MAKING AN ACCUSATION

1. Tell what *making an accusation* means, and then write down the four skill steps.

   (definition) _____

   (step 1) _____

   (step 2) _____

   (step 3) _____

   (step 4) _____

2. Explain why jumping to conclusions can be a bad thing to do.

   _____

   _____

3. Describe a situation when you may need to accuse someone at home, at school, and in the community.

   (home) _____

   (school) _____

   (community) _____

4. Compare skill steps 2 and 3 for making an accusation. Tell one way they are the same and one way they are different.

   (same) _____

   (different) _____

5. Write a short story about Jacob, who jumps to conclusions and falsely accuses someone. (Use the back of this page if you need more space.)

   _____

   _____

   _____

6. Describe a time when you accused someone of doing something wrong. Indicate whether you think you did a good or a bad job making the accusation and tell why. (Use the back of this page if you need more space.)

   _____

   _____

   _____

SKILL HOMEWORK ACTIVITY

_____
(Due Date)

Dear Parent or Guardian of: _____

This week we are learning about the social communication skill:

DEALING WITH A FALSE ACCUSATION

This social skill is very important in interpersonal relationships. It can be broken down into the following skill steps:

1. Decide if you are guilty of doing what the person is accusing you of doing. (If _yes_, then apologize. If _no_, then follow steps 2-5.)

2. Judge whether the accuser is in or out of control. (If out of control, the person may need to cool off before listening.)

3. Think about why the person might be falsely accusing you.

4. Think about what you will say or ask to help clear things up.

5. Communicate with the person in a calm manner.

Before the due date, please complete one of the following activities with your son or daughter: (put a check mark by your choice)

_____ A. We acted out the role play situation listed below.

_____ B. I observed my son/daughter using this social skill in a real-life situation. (I have described the situation below.)

Description of real-life observation:

Role play situation:

PRETEND ONE OF YOUR PARENTS FALSELY ACCUSES YOU OF MESSING UP THE BATHROOM. DEMONSTRATE HOW YOU WILL RESPOND. (REMEMBER TO COMMUNICATE IN A CALM WAY.)

- -

Please circle the word below which best describes how your son or daughter did while using this social skill in either the role play or real-life situation.

NEEDS MORE HELP   GOOD   EXCELLENT

It is important for you to reinforce your child's use of this social skill at home in a positive way. Encourage and praise your child when you see the skill appropriately used. Remind him/her to use the social skill when necessary.

Thank you for your assistance.

Sincerely,

* *

PARENT/GUARDIAN SIGNATURE: _____

SKILL STEPS

When a person *falsely accuses you*, it means that *you are being blamed for doing something wrong that you have not done.* Everybody receives a false accusation from time to time. It is important that when you are falsely accused, you deal with it in a good way!

Below is a list of the skill steps for dealing with a false accusation and a description for each one.

Step 1: Decide if you are guilty of doing what the person is accusing you of doing.

• If you are guilty, then follow the skill steps for the social skill of making an apology.

• If you are not guilty, then follow skill steps 2-5.

Discuss situations when you have been falsely accused and how you felt when it happened.

Step 2: Judge whether the accuser is in or out of control.

• If the person is being assertive, and is in control, then he will probably be willing to listen to your side of the story.

• If the person is very angry, and is yelling, then he is being aggressive. The person will probably need time to cool off before listening to your side of the story. If the person is accusing you in a mean way, then it is best for you to tell him you will discuss it later.

Practice this skill step by completing Page C from this unit.

33

3 **Step 3: Think about why the person might be falsely accusing you.** 3

3
3 • Maybe the person is jumping to conclusions.   3

3 • Maybe you have a past reputation for doing things wrong, and the person is 3
3   assuming you did this thing wrong too.   3

3
3 • Maybe the person has received incorrect information.   3

3 • Maybe the person doesn't know the whole story.   3

3
3 Discuss other possible reasons why a false accusation might be made.   3

33333333333333333333333333333333333333333333333333333333333333333333

44444444444444444444444444444444444444444444444444444444444444444444

4 **Step 4: Think about what you will say or ask to help clear things up.** 4

4
4 • If the person is angry, then allow him time to regain control, before you tell your 4
4   side of the story.   4

4 • If you have proof that you did not do it, then tell the person what your proof is. 4

4 • If you know who did it, then you may want to tell who should be accused. 4

4 • If you can't understand why the person is accusing you, you may want to ask. 4

4 • You may want to help the person think of who else may have done it. 4

4 Practice this skill step by completing Page D from this unit.   4

44444444444444444444444444444444444444444444444444444444444444444444

5555555555555555555555555555555555555555555555555555555555555555555

5 **Step 5: Communicate with the person in a calm manner.**   5

5
5 If you are being falsely accused and you get so angry that you start yelling and 5
5 being aggressive, then you make yourself look guilty.   5

5 If you get very angry when someone falsely accuses you, then try one of the 5
5 following to calm yourself down: 5

5 • Take slow, deep breaths.   5

5 • Tell yourself to calm down.   5

5 • Count to ten or more.   5

5 • Tell the person you need to calm down and that you will talk later. 5

5 For more practice with this skill step, complete page E from this unit. 5

5555555555555555555555555555555555555555555555555555555555555555555

Accusing Activity

When a person falsely accuses you, it is important that you pay attention to how the person makes the accusation. Look at the person's body language and listen to the tone of voice and volume being used.

If the person is being assertive, and is "in control," then he will probably be willing to listen to your explanation of why you are not guilty of doing the thing you are being accused of doing.

However, if the person is very angry, and being aggressive, then the person probably has to "cool off" before listening to your side of the story. If the person is accusing you in a mean way, then it is best for you to say you will talk about it later.

DIRECTIONS: 1. You and a partner will work together to complete the following activity.

2. Take turns being the "giver" and "receiver" for the false accusations listed below.

3. When it is your turn to be the "giver" of a false accusation, choose any one of the accusations in the list. Decide if you will make the accusation in a way that shows you are *in control* and are willing to listen, or if you are *out of control* and need to "cool off" before listening to the "receiver." (Write down your choice on a piece of paper but do not show it to your partner.)

   If you choose to be *in control* when you make the false accusation, then be assertive. Do not yell or use a threatening tone of voice.

   If you choose to be *out of control*, then be aggressive by using a loud volume and a threatening tone of voice.

4. When it is your turn to be the "receiver," listen to the "giver" make the false accusation. If you think the "giver" is *in control*, say that you did not do it, and explain why. If you think the "giver" is *out of control*, say, "I did not do it. I'll talk to you about this later."

5. If the "receiver" correctly guesses how the accusation was made and responds in the right way, then the team of two people should award themselves a point. The pair of students who earn the most points will be declared the winners for this accusing activity.

LIST OF FALSE ACCUSATIONS:

1. Accuse your partner of taking your pen while you were out of the room.
2. Accuse your partner of spreading rumors about you.
3. Accuse your partner of trying to take away your girlfriend/boyfriend.
4. Accuse your partner of being jealous of your clothes.
5. Accuse your partner of copying answers from your test.
6. Accuse your partner of taking your last piece of gum while you were gone.
7. Accuse your partner of breaking into your locker.
8. Accuse your partner of copying your idea for a science report.
9. Accuse your partner of lying to you.
10. Accuse your partner of making prank phone calls to your house.

What To Say

If you are falsely accused, you need to talk to the person to clear things up. Below is a list of things you can say to help you.

- If you have proof that you did not do it, tell the person what your proof is.

- If you know who did it, tell the person who it is.

- If you can't understand why the person is accusing you, then ask.

- If you don't know who did it, you may want to help the person think of who else may have done it.

DIRECTIONS: Pretend you receive the following false accusations. Write down the exact words you would say to the person.

1. Your mom says to you, "That bathroom sink is filthy! You should clean it out when you make a mess." She does not say why she thinks it is you who made it messy. You didn't mess up the sink. Write down what you could say to her.

2. Your teacher says to you, "I understand you have been taking things from the 'lost and found' that don't belong to you. The secretary told me you asked to look at the 'lost and found' items yesterday." Someone was with you when you looked in the "lost and found." That person could be your proof that you didn't take anything. Write down what you could say to tell her you have proof.

3. Your friend says to you, "Why did you tell Mark who I like? You promised you wouldn't tell anyone!" You didn't tell anyone. Write down what you could say, to help your friend think of other possibilities for who may have told Mark.

4. Your dad says to you, "Why did you cut into this pie? You know it is for company tonight." You saw your sister eating a piece of the pie earlier. Write down what you could say to explain that it was your sister.

Name:_____

Loss of Credibility .

If you are a **credible person**, it means that *you are trustworthy and capable of being believed.*

If you have **lost your credibility**, it means that *because you have done wrong in the past, a person feels that he/she is no longer able to trust you.*

Pretend that last year you acquired the reputation at school of being a "trouble maker." This year you are trying to improve your reputation, so that your teachers and school principal will trust you again. Once you have lost your credibility, it takes time for people to believe you are trustworthy again. People may falsely accuse you of doing something wrong, because they assume you are still the way you were in the past.

DIRECTIONS: Read the letter below that someone wrote to a counselor. Pretend you are the counselor, and write a letter back on a piece of loose leaf paper, giving the person your advice. (You may tape record your advice instead of writing it, if you would prefer.)

Dear Counselor,

I am fifteen years old. Two years ago, I got caught shoplifting. Ever since that time, I feel like my parents believe everything I do is wrong. If something wrong happens in our house, I get blamed for it.

The other night, for example, my older brother borrowed the car after my parents went to bed. When my father heard the car leave, he checked my room. I wasn't in my room, so I got blamed for it. I tried to tell my parents the next day that I was in the basement studying. They didn't believe me until my brother got up for breakfast. He told my parents that he took the car.

I know I made a mistake two years ago. Do I still have to be punished for it now? Please write back and give me your advice.

Signed,

Miserable

Remember! When someone falsely accuses you, you need to communicate with the person in a calm way. If you get very angry and start yelling when you are falsely accused, you only make yourself look guilty.

FALSE ACCUSATION - FALSE ACCUSATION

1. Explain what *being falsely accused* means, and then write the skill steps.

   (definition) _____

   (step 1) _____

   (step 2) _____

   (step 3) _____

   (step 4) _____

   (step 5) _____

2. Explain what happens if you get aggressive and start yelling at the person who falsely accused you.

   _____

   _____

3. Write about a situation when you were falsely accused by someone at home and at school.

   (home) _____

   (school) _____

4. Rate the following people according to how good they are at dealing with a false accusation. Give a *1* to the best, a *2* to the second best, and a *3* to the worst.

   #_____ Willy does not get upset when someone falsely accuses him. He tries to offer proof that he didn't do it.

   #_____ Patty gets very upset when someone falsely accuses her. She usually starts yelling, which only makes her look guilty.

   #_____ Maggie gets upset when someone falsely accuses her. She takes a deep breath, says she didn't do it, and walks away.

5. Write down the name of a social skill you have learned in the past, which you should remember to use when you are being falsely accused.

   _____

6. Write down which of the techniques for calming yourself down (listed on Page B) you think would work best for you and why.

   _____

   _____

SKILL HOMEWORK ACTIVITY

_____
(Due Date)

Dear Parent or Guardian of: _____

This week we are learning about the social communication skill:

COMPROMISING/NEGOTIATING

This social skill is very important in interpersonal relationships. It can be broken down into the following skill steps:

1. Decide if you and someone else are having a conflict or disagreement.
2. Remind yourself to be flexible and calm, so you can come to an agreement.
3. Suggest a solution that might be acceptable to both of you.
4. Find out if your suggestion is acceptable to the other person.
5. If it is not acceptable, then continue to compromise and negotiate until an agreement is made.

(For more information about this social skill, refer to the attached sheet - _Compromising/ Negotiating - B_)

Before the due date, please complete one of the following activities with your son or daughter: (put a check mark by your choice)

_____ A. We acted out the role play situation listed below.

_____ B. I observed my son/daughter using this social skill in a real-life situation. (I have described the situation below.)

Description of real-life observation:

Role play situation:

PRETEND YOU WANT TO STAY AT A PARTY UNTIL 11:00 P.M., AND THEN WALK HOME. YOUR PARENTS WANT YOU TO CALL FOR A RIDE AND COME HOME AT 10:00. DEMONSTRATE HOW YOU COULD TRY TO NEGOTIATE WITH YOUR PARENTS.

- -

Please circle the word below which best describes how your son or daughter did while using this social skill in either the role play or real-life situation.

NEEDS MORE HELP   GOOD   EXCELLENT

It is important for you to reinforce your child's use of this social skill at home in a positive way. Encourage and praise your child when you see the skill appropriately used. Remind him/her to use the social skill when necessary.

Thank you for your assistance.

Sincerely,

* *

PARENT/GUARDIAN SIGNATURE: _____

CONFLICT

Compromising/negotiating is a social skill that is used when there is conflict. Before you learn the skill steps for this social skill, you need to learn more about the word *conflict*.

Conflict occurs *whenever there is a disagreement between two or more people.* Conflict is normal! There will always be conflict because no two people are exactly alike and, therefore, they will disagree about certain things. Conflict can be a good thing or a bad thing, depending on how it is handled.

The story below gives an example of a way to handle conflict in a bad way.

Toni and his friend Carl are trying to decide what to do Friday night. Toni thinks they should go to the basketball game because their school team made it to the regional finals. Carl thinks they should go to a movie he heard was supposed to be really good. Toni tells Carl he is crazy for wanting to go to a movie instead of the game. Carl tells Toni he is crazy for wanting to waste money on a stupid game. They end up getting mad at each other, and both boys stay home on Friday night.

In this story, Toni and Carl dealt with their conflict in a bad way. They made it a lose-lose situation, because in the end, neither ended up doing anything on Friday night.

The story below gives another example of a way to handle conflict in a bad way.

Tracy and Kathy want to do something fun today. Tracy says, "Let's go for a bike ride, I haven't used my bike in a long time." Kathy says, "No, I think we should stay home and play a card game instead. It's sort of cold out today." Tracy says, "Kathy, if you don't go bike riding with me, then I'll just find someone else to go with me. You're not my only friend in the world you know." Kathy ends up giving in and goes for a bike ride, but she doesn't have very much fun.

In this story, the conflict between Tracy and Kathy is handled in a bad way also, because they made it a win-lose situation. Tracy ended up being able to do exactly what she wanted to do, and Kathy didn't.

There is a way to deal with conflict in a good way. You can work with the person you are having the disagreement with, to make it a win-win situation. If Toni and Carl had decided to go to the basketball game this Friday, and then to the movie another day, they would have made their disagreement into a win-win situation. If Tracy and Kathy had decided to go for a short bike ride and then come back to play a card game, they would have made their disagreement into a win-win situation. You can turn a conflict situation into a win-win situation, by using the social skill called compromising/negotiating.

WIN -or- LOSE?

The social skill of compromising/negotiating is used when two people want to cooperate to solve a problem or resolve conflict. **Negotiate** means *to have a discussion with the person you are disagreeing with, to see if you can both come to an agreement.* **Compromise** means *coming to an agreement that is acceptable to both people, by each "giving in" a little.* Below is a list of four ways for two people to compromise:

1. Come to an agreement by deciding to do both things. (e.g., If you want to go fishing, and your friend wants to play cards, you could compromise by doing both things for a shorter length of time on the same day.)

2. Come to an agreement by deciding to do what one person wants this time, and what the other person wants the next time. (e.g., If you want to go to one movie, and your sister wants to go to another one, you could compromise by deciding to see one this week, and the other one next week.)

3. Come to an agreement by having both people give up part of what he or she wants. (e.g., If you want to go home at 9:00 and your friend wants to go home at 10:00, you could compromise by going home at 9:30.)

4. Come to an agreement by doing something completely different than either one initially suggested. (e.g., If you want to go to a mystery movie, and your friend wants to go to a horror movie, you could compromise by going to a comedy.)

DIRECTIONS: 1. Read the conflict situation below, and the six ways the situation could be handled.

2. For each, decide if it was handled in a *lose-lose*, *win-lose*, or *win-win* way and circle your choice.

3. If you circle *lose-lose*, or *win-lose*, explain your choice.

4. If you circle *win-win*, then indicate which of the four ways of compromising was used. (Write the number of the technique used.)

SITUATION: The Brown family had one radio. When Joe and Lou were doing their household chores, they disagreed about which radio station to listen to. Joe wanted to listen to a station that played rock-and-roll and Lou wanted to listen to a country music station.

1. The two boys started arguing, so their parents turned off the radio. The boys had to do their chores without music.

LOSE-LOSE   WIN-LOSE   WIN-WIN
                                                   (#_____)

2. The boys decided to listen to a radio station that played several different types of music.

    LOSE-LOSE   WIN-LOSE   WIN-WIN
                                                            (#_____)

3. Since Joe was bigger, he threatened to beat up Lou. Lou gave in and listened to the station that Joe wanted to hear.

    LOSE-LOSE   WIN-LOSE   WIN-WIN
                                                            (#_____)

4. The boys decided to listen to Joe's station this time and Lou's station next time they did chores.

    LOSE-LOSE   WIN-LOSE   WIN-WIN
                                                            (#_____)

5. The boys decided to listen to both stations, by switching back and forth every half hour.

    LOSE-LOSE   WIN-LOSE   WIN-WIN
                                                            (#_____)

6. The boys decided to listen to a radio station that played jazz music, because jazz music is each boy's second favorite.

    LOSE-LOSE   WIN-LOSE   WIN-WIN
                                                            (#_____)

Skill Steps

Compromising/negotiating can be broken down into five skill steps:

1. Decide if you and someone else are having a conflict or disagreement.

2. Remind yourself to be flexible and calm so you can come to an agreement.

3. Suggest a solution that might be acceptable to both of you.

4. Find out if your suggestion is acceptable to the other person. (Be a good listener.)

5. If the suggestion is not acceptable, then continue to compromise and negotiate until an agreement is made.

DIRECTIONS: 1) Work with a partner to devise a memory technique to help you remember the five skill steps. Practice until both of you have the steps memorized. When you are ready, say the skill steps to an adult, one person at a time.

2) Work with your partner to complete the activity below. For each situation, write down what you think would be a good compromise.

1. Samantha is staying at her friend's house. She wants to watch her favorite TV show at 8:00 p.m., but her friend wants to watch a different show at that time.

   A good compromise would be:_____

   _____

2. Mrs. Watson told her two sons that they needed to start doing some chores around the house. She said that one of them needed to do the dishes every night and one of them needed to straighten up the house every night. She left it up to her two sons to decide who would do what. They both wanted to straighten up and neither one of them wanted to do the dishes.

   A good compromise would be:_____

   _____

3. Mr. Klein asked his two daughters where they wanted to go to eat. One girl wanted to go to a pizza place, and the other wanted to go to a hamburger place.

   A good compromise would be:_____

   _____

4. The student council was trying to decide what kind of music to get for the next school dance. One group wanted to hire a disc jockey and another group wanted to hire a live band.

   A good compromise would be:_____

   _____

The *Mediator* Activity

Pretend you are having a conflict with someone, and you are not able to reach an agreement through compromise. Every time you both try to negotiate with each other, you just end up arguing. DON'T GIVE UP! Maybe you need a mediator.

A **mediator** is *someone who can act as a "go-between" and help you to reach an agreement with the person you are having a conflict with.* A mediator is a person who doesn't take sides, but instead asks questions that might help you to compromise. A mediator can be a friend, a teacher, a parent, a counselor, a brother or sister, or anyone else who would be interested in helping you solve a conflict you are having with someone. Take turns with the other people in your group and practice being a mediator by following the directions below.

DIRECTIONS: When it is your turn to be a mediator, follow these steps:

1. Choose one of the conflict situations listed on the following page.

2. Choose someone from your group to take "side one" of your situation. Choose someone else to take "side two." (Those two people need to pretend they are having a conflict and ask you to help them come to an agreement.)

3. When your role play begins, ask the questions listed below to help the two people in conflict to come to an acceptable agreement. The two people in conflict should actually answer the questions asked by the mediator.

MEDIATOR QUESTIONS

1) (Say this to the person taking "side one.") Tell me your side of the story. What is it that you want?

2) (Say this to the person taking "side two.") Tell me your side of the story. What is it that you want?

3) (Say this to the person taking "side one.") Tell me one way you can solve this conflict so you both can be happy.

4) (Ask this of the person taking "side two.") Is that idea acceptable to you or do you have another suggestion? (Continue asking question #4 to both people until they agree on a compromise.)

Note to the Mediator: If neither person in conflict is able to think of a compromise, you may want to make a suggestion, and ask how each person feels about it.

SITUATION 1 (Side One)	SITUATION 1 (Side Two)
You and your brother/sister have been given permission to repaint the study room you both share. You want to paint it blue.	You and your brother/sister have been given permission to repaint the study room you both share. You want to paint it yellow.
SITUATION 2 (Side One)	**SITUATION 2 (Side Two)**
You and your friend are going fishing. You want to go to Bass Lake.	You and your friend are going fishing. You want to go to Meyers Lake.
SITUATION 3 (Side One)	**SITUATION 3 (Side Two)**
You are going out to eat at a "fancy" restaurant with your mom/dad. You want to wear blue jeans.	You are going out to eat at a "fancy" restaurant with your son/daughter. You think dresses and suits should be worn.
SITUATION 4 (Side One)	**SITUATION 4 (Side Two)**
You want to go out on a date, but your mom/dad thinks you are too young to date.	Your son/daughter wants to go out on a date, but you want him/her to wait a few more years.

EDUCATOR PAGE: DO NOT DUPLICATE FOR STUDENTS

DIRECTIONS: 1. Before holding the three discussions listed below with the students, the educator should give a Discussion Behavior Sheet (see next page) to each student.

2. The educator should decide ahead of time which discussion behavior(s) the students will rate themselves on. Some examples of discussion behaviors include: having eye contact with the person who is speaking, raising your hand to talk, making relevant comments, leaning slightly forward in your seat to show your interest, nodding at the speaker, and giving support to others. The educator should then model the discussion behavior(s) the students will be rating themselves on.

3. The educator should explain that each time the student does the specified discussion behavior(s) appropriately, the student should put a " + " in the positive column. Each time the student fails to do the specified discussion behavior(s), the student should put a " – " in the negative column. The educator should model how to do this for the students. Many of the students will fail to realize when they are NOT doing the specified behavior and will neglect to give themselves a " – ." This is acceptable since the purpose of this activity is not for students to do a serious critique of their discussion, but rather to become more aware of it.

4. The educator should then hold the following three discussions with the students.

Discussion #1

Discuss the idea that when two people choose a mediator, it is important that they find someone who will be unbiased and impartial. Give your students example situations of times when two people cannot come to an agreement and need a mediator. Discuss who would and who would not make a good mediator for each situation given.

Discussion #2

Ask the students to discuss what they would do if negotiating is not working and there is no one around to be a mediator.

Discussion #3

Discuss the fact that we should not even try to negotiate with some people. Also, there are some situations when it would not be appropriate to negotiate. Ask for examples of each.

Name:_____

DISCUSSION BEHAVIOR SHEET

NAME: _____

DATE:_____

DISCUSSION BEHAVIOR:_____

POSITIVE (+)	NEGATIVE (−)

Name:_____

COMPROMISING/NEGOTIATING

1. Define *compromising/negotiating*, and then write the skill steps for this social skill.

   (compromising) _____

   (negotiating) _____

   (step 1) _____

   (step 2) _____

   (step 3) _____

   (step 4) _____

   (step 5) _____

2. Explain when it might be necessary to use a mediator, and how a mediator can help.

   _____

   _____

   _____

3. Describe a situation when you had a conflict with someone at home, and at school, and you were able to compromise.

   (home) _____

   _____

   _____

   (school) _____

   _____

   _____

4. Explain the differences among a win-win situation, a win-lose situation, and a lose-lose situation.

(win-win) _____

_____

(win-lose) _____

_____

(lose-lose) _____

_____

5. Think of a good compromise for the following conflict situation:

Mel and Gail decide to go to the dance together. Mel wants to double date, and Gail doesn't.

_____

_____

_____

6. Of all the members in your family, who do you think would make the best mediator? _____ Why?

_____

_____

_____

SKILL HOMEWORK ACTIVITY

_____
(Due Date)

Dear Parent or Guardian of: _____

This week we are learning about the social communication skill:

ACCEPTING CONSEQUENCES

This social skill is very important in interpersonal relationships. The skill steps include:

1. Accept the consequence without arguing or making excuses. Remain calm.

2. Be responsible and follow the consequence (e.g., if you are supposed to stay after school, be responsible and stay).

Before the due date, please complete one of the following activities with your son or daughter: (put a check mark by your choice)

_____ A. We acted out the role play situation listed below.

_____ B. I observed my son/daughter using this social skill in a real-life situation. (I have described the situation below.)

Description of real-life observation:

Role play situation:

YOU ARRIVED HOME AN HOUR LATER THAN YOU WERE SUPPOSED TO. YOUR PARENTS TELL YOU THAT YOU CANNOT GO OUT THIS WEEKEND. DEMONSTRATE HOW YOU WOULD ACCEPT THE CONSEQUENCE IN AN APPROPRIATE MANNER.

- -

Please circle the word below which best describes how your son or daughter did while using this social skill in either the role play or real-life situation.

NEEDS MORE HELP   GOOD   EXCELLENT

It is important for you to reinforce your child's use of this social skill at home in a positive way. Encourage and praise your child when you see the skill appropriately used. Remind him/her to use the social skill when necessary.

Thank you for your assistance.

Sincerely,

* *

PARENT/GUARDIAN SIGNATURE: _____

Name:_____

What are Consequences?

Consequences are *the results of our actions.* There are consequences for everything we do. Some consequences are positive (good), while other consequences are negative (not so good). Our behavior determines what type of consequence we will get. Below are some examples of behaviors and their associated consequences.

DIRECTIONS: Read over the first part of the chart. Then fill in the missing areas in the last part of the chart.

	BEHAVIOR	CONSEQUENCE	POSITIVE/NEGATIVE
EXAMPLES → → →	Carrie tried very hard in school. She studied hard.	Carrie received good grades in school.	Positive
	Jason lied to his mom.	Jason was grounded for a week.	Negative
	Mr. Gam stole money from where he works.	Mr. Gam lost his job and went to prison.	Negative
	Harriet lost 50 pounds.	Harriet felt better about her body.	
	Toby forgot to study for his English test.	Toby got an "F" on his test.	
		Mark earned his allowance this week.	
	Ashley was speeding down the highway.		Negative
		Brian's best friend is mad at him.	Negative
	Erik is always honest with his parents.		Positive
	Tami didn't get along with the customers where she worked.	Tami was fired from her job.	

Accepting Consequences

It is often difficult to accept negative consequences. In the picture below, it is obvious that Peter has a difficult time accepting the consequences for his actions.

★   There are two skill steps for accepting consequences:

1. Accept the consequence without arguing or making excuses. Remain calm.

2. Be responsible about the consequence (e.g., if you are supposed to stay after school, be responsible and stay).

DIRECTIONS: Complete the picture below to show how you could accept the consequence appropriately. Write what you would say.

Name:_____

ADDITIONAL TIPS FOR ACCEPTING CONSEQUENCES

● Show that you feel bad about what you did. (Sometimes people will give you a lesser consequence if they think you are sorry for what you did.)

● Don't apologize unless you are truly sorry for what you did. (After a while, people will get tired of hearing your "fake" apologies.)

● Think about what you did wrong so you don't do it again.

● Sometimes, it's best not to say too much (especially if you are afraid you will use a "snotty" tone of voice). You can make your consequence worse by being sarcastic.

● (Write your own tip) _____

DIRECTIONS: Read the cartoons and answer the questions below.

What consequence would you give to Jesse? Why?

_____

_____

_____

_____

_____

_____

_____

What consequence would you give to Tim? Why?

_____

_____

_____

_____

_____

_____

_____

EDUCATOR PAGE: DO NOT DUPLICATE FOR STUDENTS

DIRECTIONS: Discuss the following questions during class.

*

Why may different people receive different consequences for doing the same thing (e.g., two boys get into a fight and one boy gets suspended, while the other boy only gets a warning)?

*

Why is it difficult for children when their parents make threats and never carry out the threats (e.g., first time - "If you swear one more time, I'll take away your allowance"; second time - "If I hear you swearing again, I'll take away your allowance")?

*

Why is it difficult for children when adults set up outrageous consequences that they can't follow through (e.g., "You're grounded for the next six months")?

*

Why is it difficult for children when adults set up consequences for children, but the adults are not consistent about administering the consequences (e.g., one time Johnny comes home late and nothing happens; the next time he comes home late he gets grounded; the third time he comes home late and nothing happens)?

*

Why is it difficult for children when adults do not warn the children ahead of time about what the consequences will be (e.g., Kristin is not paying attention in class, so Mr. Jakes tells her to go to the principal's office; Kristin did not know she would have to go to the principal's office)?

ACTIVITY: Have the students tell about a time when they were confused by the consequence they received or how the consequence was carried out.

Giving Advice

DIRECTIONS: Read the stories below and give each person some advice on how to accept consequences better.

Melvin

Melvin started a fight with another student during lunch. When the principal asked Melvin to explain what had happened, Melvin yelled, "I didn't do anything. That jerk called me a name." The principal told Melvin that he was going to be suspended for a day. Melvin started yelling at the principal again. "I'm not going to be suspended! That's not fair!" Finally, the principal told Melvin that if he didn't stop yelling, Melvin would be suspended for two days instead of one day.

Write some advice you could give to Melvin about accepting consequences.

Harriet

Harriet was caught cheating on a test for the third time. When the teacher asked her about it, she said, "Oh, I'm so sorry. It'll never happen again." Harriet was thinking to herself, "Boy, how am I going to get out of this one?" Harriet started to cry. She told the teacher she had to babysit for her younger brother the night before and didn't get a chance to study. Harriet said again, "I promise, it'll never happen again. Please don't punish me."

Write some advice you could give to Harriet about accepting consequences.

The Consequence

DIRECTIONS: Read each situation. Decide what the best consequence would be for the person in each situation. BE PREPARED TO DISCUSS WHY YOU GAVE THE CONSEQUENCE YOU DID.

1. You are a teacher. One of your students, Josh, has been coming to class without a pen or pencil every day. You have reminded him several times. Tell him what will happen if he comes without a pen or pencil again.

   Consequence: _____

   _____

2. You are a parent. Your ten-year-old son missed his curfew by an hour. This is the second time this week that it happened. What consequence will you give to your son?

   Consequence: _____

   _____

3. You are a manager of a grocery store. One of the employees, Eva, has been very rude to the customers. You have warned her about this two times before. Now another customer just complained about Eva being rude to him. Tell what you will do to Eva.

   Consequence: _____

   _____

4. You are a principal. One of your students, Mark, just got into a fight with another student. Mark has never been in any trouble before. What do you think should happen to Mark?

   Consequence: _____

   _____

5. You are a teacher. One of your students, Anna, was caught cheating on a test. When you talk with her about it, she admits that she cheated and seems truly sorry. What do you think should happen to Anna?

   Consequence: _____

   _____

6. You are a parent. Your daughter, Maria, is talking to you in a very rude tone of voice. Tell what consequence you will give Maria.

   Consequence: _____

   _____

7. You are the owner of a restaurant. One of your employees, Mark, has been late for work several times. You had told Mark that the next time he was late for work, he would be fired. Mark was 10 minutes late for work today. What will you do?

   Consequence: _____

   _____

8. You are a principal. One of the students, Brad, was sent to your office by a teacher. Brad had been misbehaving in class. When you question Brad about it, he becomes very angry and yells at you. What consequence will you give Brad?

   Consequence: _____

   _____

9. You are a teacher. One of your students, Ashley, has not been turning in her homework assignments. What can you do to get her to do some work?

   Consequence: _____

   _____

10. You are a parent. Your son had a party over the weekend while you were gone. He was told not to have anyone over while you were away. What will you do?

   Consequence: _____

   _____

11. You are a parent. The neighbor girl has been babysitting for you for a year. You have asked her several times to stay off the phone in case there is an emergency and you need to phone home. You went out last night and when you tried to call home, the line was busy for forty-five minutes. When you arrived home, the babysitter was still on the phone. What will you do?

   Consequence: _____

   _____

EDUCATOR PAGE: DO NOT DUPLICATE FOR STUDENTS

The following scripted consequences should be recorded on an audio cassette tape player or on a video player. The scripts include various authority figures giving consequences to children. To promote transfer, it is suggested that the scripts be read by people who usually give the students consequences (e.g., teachers, principal). It is also more realistic if those people who normally give consequences can write their own scripts for giving consequences instead of using the ones below; that way the same wording and exact consequences can be used. Once the scripts are recorded, they can be used in a variety of ways. A few uses are listed below:

- A student can add to the script by verbalizing how he would accept the consequence. (This can be an educator-directed activity or the student can use the recording to practice independently.)

- A student can complete the script by writing the exact words he would say when accepting the consequence.

- A student can tell strategies for remaining calm when accepting the consequence.

Script # 1

Teacher: You've been disrupting the class. I'd like you to go and sit in the back of the room.

Script # 2

Teacher: This is the third time you forgot to bring your book to class. You'll have to spend your lunch hour with me.

Script # 3

Principal: This is the second time today that you've been sent out of class. I'm going to give you this writing assignment.

Script # 4

Principal: I believe that you were the one who started the fight, so I'm going to suspend you from school for one day.

Script # 5

Parent: You didn't clean your room this week so you don't get your allowance.

EDUCATOR PAGE: DO NOT DUPLICATE FOR STUDENTS

1. Give each student a blank game card page (see next page).

2. Tell the students to write a situation in each of the four spaces.

3. In each situation, the student will assume one of the following roles: teacher, parent, principal, and boss (employer).

4. The student should write four situations in which the above people must give a consequence to someone:

Example of blank and finished cards:

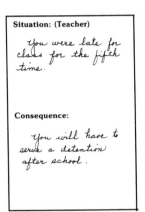

It is important that the educator model for the students the correct way to fill out the blank cards.

5. The students should write consequences that are reasonable for what happened in the situation.

6. After the students have finished completing the blank card sheet, cut the cards apart. Shuffle all the students' cards together.

7. The players should take turns reading the situation cards to one another.

8. When it is a player's turn, that person should listen to the situation and the consequence received. The player should then show how to respond to that consequence in a responsible manner. The player should also try to demonstrate a realistic response. If the player accepts the consequence too willingly (e.g., is smiling, says "sure, fine") the consequence has probably not been accepted in a realistic manner.

9. The educator and the other players should discuss whether they felt the player accepted the consequence in a responsible manner. They should also discuss whether the player accepted the consequences in a realistic manner.

10. The player scores one point if the group feels the consequence was accepted in a responsible manner and one point if the group feels the consequence was accepted in a realistic manner.

11. The person at the end of the game (when the cards run out or at the end of a given time limit) with the most points is the winner.

Situation: (Teacher)	**Situation: (Principal)**
Consequence:	Consequence:
Situation: (Parent)	**Situation: (Boss)**
Consequence:	Consequence:

ACCEPTING CONSEQUENCES - ACCEPTING CONSEQUENCES

1. Define the term *consequence*.

   _____

   _____

2. Explain why consequences are a part of everyone's life.

   _____

   _____

   _____

3. List two times in the past month when you received a consequence.

   (positive) _____

   (negative) _____

4. Compare two teachers. How are they the same about giving consequences? How are they different?

   (same) _____

   _____

   (different) _____

   _____

5. Tell three positive changes that can result when you improve your ability to accept consequences.

   (#1) _____

   _____

   (#2) _____

   _____

   (#3) _____

   _____

6. On a scale from one to ten (ten is the best), rate how well you accept consequences. #_____ Explain why you rated yourself as you did.

   (explanation) _____

   _____

EMOTIONAL EXPRESSION SKILLS

SKILL HOMEWORK ACTIVITY

_____
(Due Date)

Dear Parent or Guardian of: _____

This week we are learning about the social communication skill:

EXPRESSING FEELINGS

This social skill is very important in interpersonal relationships.

The students have learned that it is important to express their feelings in an acceptable manner. They have learned that they are in control of their feelings.

Before the due date, please complete one of the following activities with your son or daughter: (put a check mark by your choice)

_____ A. We acted out the role play situation listed below.

_____ B. I observed my son/daughter using this social skill in a real-life situation. (I have described the situation below.)

Description of real-life observation:

Role play situation:

YOU ARE FEELING BAD BECAUSE SEVERAL THINGS WENT WRONG AT SCHOOL TODAY. TELL ONE OF YOUR FAMILY MEMBERS ABOUT HOW YOU ARE FEELING AND WHY YOU FEEL THAT WAY.

- -

Please circle the word below which best describes how your son or daughter did while using this social skill in either the role play or real-life situation.

NEEDS MORE HELP   GOOD   EXCELLENT

It is important for you to reinforce your child's use of this social skill at home in a positive way. Encourage and praise your child when you see the skill appropriately used. Remind him/her to use the social skill when necessary.

Thank you for your assistance.

Sincerely,

* *

PARENT/GUARDIAN SIGNATURE: _____

Name:_____

FEELINGS BRAINSTORM

DIRECTIONS: 1. Work with a partner.
2. On a large piece of paper, trace the outline of one person's body.
3. Then, brainstorm as many "feeling" words as you can (e.g., relaxed, determined, exuberant).
4. Write all of the feeling words inside the sketch of the body. Try to fill the entire body with feeling words.

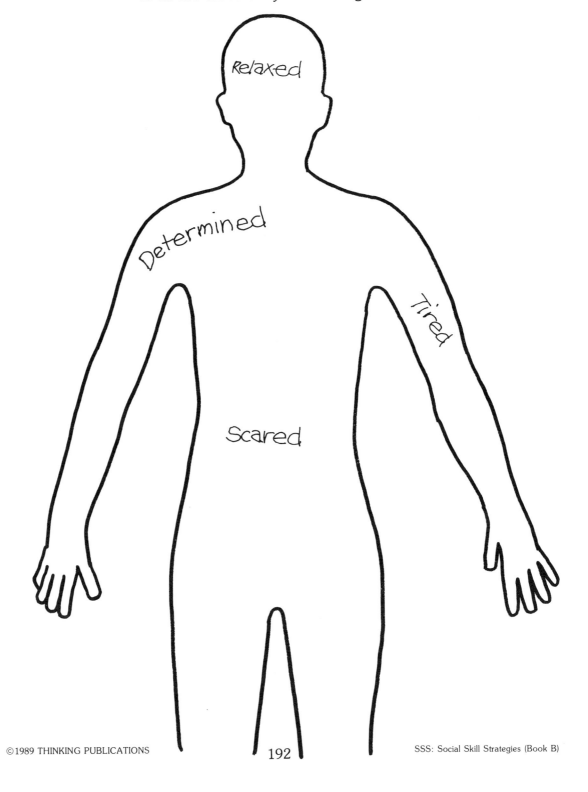

©1989 THINKING PUBLICATIONS

SSS: Social Skill Strategies (Book B)

Everyone Has Feelings

Every person has various feelings at different times. It's normal to feel happy, angry, embarrassed, and so forth, about different things.

We express our feelings by WHAT WE SAY and by OUR BODY LANGUAGE. Body language is an important part of how we express our feelings.

DIRECTIONS: Look at the pictures below. Answer the questions by each set of pictures.

A   **B**

1. How is the person in picture A different from in picture B?

2. In which picture does the person look like he is expressing his feelings through his body language? Explain why.

C   **D**

3. How is the person in picture C different from in picture D?

4. In which picture does the person look like she is expressing her feelings through her body language? Explain why.

Name:_____

Feelings

It's natural to have different feelings.

Everyone has feelings. No one ever feels one way all the time. For example, no one feels happy all the time. It's normal to feel angry, sad, and so forth. Some people feel they are "bad" if they feel angry about something. They say things like, "But when I'm angry, I always get myself in trouble." It's OK to FEEL angry. It's not OK to ignore your anger or let it get out of control. The problem arises when people do not know appropriate ways to express their feelings.

Here's an example:

Joe was feeling very angry. Therefore, he hit Matt. (Joe did not express his feelings in an appropriate way.)

Here's another example:

Joe was feeling very angry. Therefore, Joe told Matt why he was angry with him. (Joe expressed his feelings in a more appropriate way.)

REMEMBER . . . It's natural to have feelings. It's important to recognize our feelings and deal with them in an acceptable way.

DIRECTIONS: For each of the feelings below, tell some *appropriate* ways to express those emotions. (Include what you might say and do and what body language you might use.)

	FEELING SAD	FEELING HAPPY
What you might say:	_____	_____
What you might do:	_____	_____
What body language you might use:	_____	_____

	FEELING ANGRY	FEELING DEPRESSED
What you might say:	_____	_____
What you might do:	_____	_____
What body language you might use:	_____	_____

©1989 THINKING PUBLICATIONS

SSS: Social Skill Strategies (Book B)

　　　　　Name:_____

Time BOMB

It's important to EXPRESS your feelings. If you hide your feelings and keep them to yourself, you may become a "walking time bomb" like Bo in the picture below. (A **walking time bomb** means *you let your feelings build up until you can't take it any longer and then you explode.*)

QUESTIONS:

1. How did Bo's body language change from picture to picture?

2. Why did Bo explode when his mother asked him to take out the garbage?

3. What do you think Bo's mother thought about Bo's exploding like that?

4. What are some things Bo could have done to express his feelings more appropriately?

There are many different ways to express our feelings and not keep them "bottled up" inside of us. Below are a few examples of acceptable ways to express our feelings:
- Talk to the person you have the feelings about.
- Write about your feelings in a journal or diary.
- Exercise (e.g., jog, play tennis) to release negative feelings.

DIRECTIONS: List some more ways to express your feelings in an acceptable way. Use a separate piece of paper.

©1989 THINKING PUBLICATIONS　　　　　195

You Are in Control

> ## You are in control of your feelings.
> ## No one else can make you feel anything
> ## you don't want to feel!

This is very important to remember! You are in charge of how you feel. You cannot blame your feelings on someone else.

Example A: Jose was riding his bike when he saw Ben. Ben was always calling Jose names. As Ben passed Jose, he called Jose a name. Jose thought to himself, "There he goes again, that Ben is always ruining my day. Ben makes me feel so rotten all the time."

Example B: Jose was riding his bike when he saw Ben. Ben was always calling Jose names. As Ben passed Jose, he called Jose a name. Jose thought to himself, "I feel really bad when he calls me names. I wish he would stop it."

QUESTIONS:

1. How is Example A different from Example B?

2. In which example does Jose accept the responsibility for how he feels? _____ Why?

TAKING RESPONSIBILITY FOR YOUR FEELINGS

Remember, you are in charge of how you feel. It's a good idea to use the word "I" when expressing how you feel.

Example: I'm angry because the teacher yelled at me.

Instead of: That teacher makes me so angry.

Remember, no one can make you feel anything.

It's also a good idea to tell WHY you are feeling that way.

Example: I feel so good when you compliment me.

Instead of: I feel so good.

DIRECTIONS: Write five statements about how you feel. Use "I" statements and give reasons for why you are feeling that way.

©1989 THINKING PUBLICATIONS   196

EDUCATOR PAGE: DO NOT DUPLICATE FOR STUDENTS

DESCRIPTION: This activity is designed to help students become more aware of their feelings.

ACTIVITY: 1. Discuss the body cues a person exhibits that can help him identify how he is feeling (e.g., the person may have a clenched jaw and fists because he is angry; the person may shake his leg when he is nervous). The self-talk a person uses may also help him distinguish how he is feeling (e.g., a person who says to himself, "Oh, how could I have done something so stupid?" may be feeling embarrassed).

2. Have the students keep a "feelings diary" for a day. They may use either of the following formats for their diary.

Time of Day	Body Cues/Self-Talk	How I Was Feeling
9:15	Smiled, told myself I did well	proud
10:00	Sweaty hands, telling myself to calm down	nervous

Today during math class I felt worried when the teacher said she was handing back our tests. Then, I was happy because I got a B+.

3. When the students have completed their diaries, ask for volunteers to describe some of the feelings experienced throughout the day. Ask the students if they had a difficult time identifying their feelings. Explain to students that sometimes we may think we feel one way when we actually feel another way. (e.g., A student may be angry with the teacher for giving a difficult assignment when the student is actually feeling frustrated because of the assignment.)

Name:_____

You Have a Choice

It's important to know that you have a choice about your feelings. You can choose to feel happy or sad or angry or any other way you wish to feel. It's your choice. Look at the pictures below. Each of the people chose a different way to feel about the same situation.

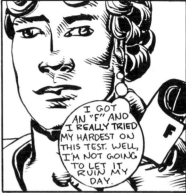

DIRECTIONS: For each situation, tell two different ways you could feel and tell what you would say to yourself.

Situation	Feeling	What you would say to yourself
1. You lose ten dollars.		
2. Your friend doesn't like you anymore.		
3. It's raining and you were going camping.		
4. You have to redo an assignment.		

©1989 THINKING PUBLICATIONS   SSS: Social Skill Strategies (Book B)

Name:_____

Feeling QUESTIONS

DIRECTIONS: Answer the questions below.

1. List six feelings/emotions.

   - •   •   •

   - •   •   •

2. Tell five types of body language that we use to express our feelings.

   - •

   - •

   - •

   - •

   - •

3. What are three acceptable ways of expressing your feelings when you feel bad?

   - •

   - •

   - •

4. Why is it important to express our feelings in an acceptable manner?

5. Tell what could happen when we hold our feelings inside of us.

6. What do we mean when we say, "We are in control of how we feel"?

7. Write a statement about how you feel right now using the "I" statement. Tell why you are feeling that way.

8. What do we mean when we say, "We have a choice about how we want to feel"?

9. How do you feel when you are with someone who is *usually* depressed?

10. How do you feel when you are with someone who is *usually* angry?

11. How do you feel when you are with someone who is *usually* happy?

12. Tell about a time when you would not want to express your true feelings (for example, when you have just gotten an "A" on your test and want to tell your friend about it, but you see that she is crying).

©1989 THINKING PUBLICATIONS
SSS: Social Skill Strategies (Book B)

EXPRESSING FEELINGS - EXPRESSING FEELINGS

1. List four feelings/emotions.

   (1) _____ (2) _____

   (3) _____ (4) _____

2. Explain how a person's body language may express feelings.

   _____

   _____

   _____

3. Explain why expressing our feelings in the appropriate way would be important to do:

   (at home) _____

   (in school)_____

   (in the community) _____

4. It was Juan's first track meet. He really wanted to do well in the hurdles. The announcer called the boys to the starting line. The gun went off. Juan was leading the race. All of a sudden, he fell over one of the hurdles. Juan got up and finished the race. He came in last.

   Identify the different ways you think Juan was feeling at various times. Explain your answer.

   _____

   _____

   _____

   _____

5. Write/tell a story about someone who keeps his feelings all "bottled up" inside of himself. Tell what eventually happens to the person. (Use the back of this page if you need more space.)

   _____

   _____

   _____

6. Evaluate how good you are at expressing your feelings in the appropriate manner. Explain your answer.

   _____

   _____

   _____

SKILL HOMEWORK ACTIVITY

_____
(Due Date)

Dear Parent or Guardian of: _____

This week we are learning about the social communication skill:

DEALING WITH ANGER

This social skill is very important in interpersonal relationships and can be broken down into the following skill steps. Please watch for the steps in your role play practice or real-life observation.

1. Be aware of what triggers your anger.
2. Recognize your body cues that let you know you're getting angry.
3. Use an anger control strategy to stay calm.
4. Evaluate how the control strategy worked.

Before the due date, please complete one of the following activities with your son or daughter: (put a check mark by your choice)

_____ A. We acted out the role play situation listed below.

_____ B. I observed my son/daughter using this social skill in a real-life situation. (I have described the situation below.)

Description of real-life observation:

Role play situation:

PRETEND YOUR BROTHER/SISTER IS TEASING YOU. WHEN YOU TELL YOUR MOM ABOUT IT, SHE BLAMES YOU AND TELLS YOU TO GO TO YOUR ROOM. YOU FEEL YOURSELF STARTING TO GET ANGRY. DEMONSTRATE HOW YOU COULD USE ONE OR MORE OF THE ANGER CONTROL STRATEGIES TO REMAIN CALM.

- -

Please circle the word below which best describes how your son or daughter did while using this social skill in either the role play or real-life situation.

NEEDS MORE HELP   GOOD   EXCELLENT

It is important for you to reinforce your child's use of this social skill at home in a positive way. Encourage and praise your child when you see the skill appropriately used. Remind him/her to use the social skill when necessary.

Thank you for your assistance.

Sincerely,

* *

PARENT/GUARDIAN SIGNATURE: _____

You must first know WHEN you are angry before you can use strategies to control your anger!
CUES help us know when we are angry.

We all have body signals or **CUES** which let us know when we are angry. These cues are different for each person. Below are some body cues many of us experience when we get angry.

- muscles tighten, tense up
- face feels hot, looks red
- breathing gets faster
- heart pounds hard
- stomach feels like it's in knots

- eyes narrow, squint
- jaw tightens
- body shakes
- fists clench

These are general body cues that occur when people get angry. Some people might experience most of the body cues above, while others may only experience one or two body cues. Each person is different. Some people may experience body cues that are not listed above. It is important for each person to figure out what his body cues are.

A **trigger** is something that happens that you choose to get angry about (e.g., when someone calls you a bad name). There are two types of triggers: external triggers and internal triggers.

EXTERNAL TRIGGERS are things that other people say or do that you feel angry about (e.g., another person's pushing you). An external trigger could also be something that happens (e.g., your pencil breaks).

INTERNAL TRIGGERS are things that you choose to say to yourself that cause you to get angry (e.g., "I know she's laughing at me. I'm going to get her. She'll be sorry." or "Why did I do that? I'm so stupid!").

There are different degrees of anger. Sometimes you are angry, but you are in control. Other times, you are so angry that you feel like you're going to lose control (or you do lose control). The anger control strategies listed below will help you calm down before you lose control. Some strategies work best when you are really upset. Other strategies work best before you get to the point of almost losing control. Each person is different and needs to find the strategy (or strategies) that work best.

1. **DEEP BREATHING:** Take a few deep, slow breaths. Try to slow down your breathing.

2. **CONSEQUENCES:** Think of what may happen if you lose control.

3. **SELF-TALK:** Tell yourself to *calm down and relax.* Tell yourself to *ignore it.* Say anything to yourself that will help you stay in control.

4. **COUNT:** Count to ten or more before you say or do anything. This will give you the extra time you may need to get back under control.

5. **REMOVE YOURSELF:** If you are afraid you're losing control and may hurt someone, it's a good idea to walk away from the person or situation. It is also helpful not to look at the person you are angry with. This strategy may get you in trouble in some situations (e.g., if you're in the principal's office and he's talking to you and you walk out before he's finished). Of course, it's better to walk away from the principal than it is to hurt the principal.

6. **VISUAL IMAGERY:** When you're upset about something and you can't stop thinking about it, try using visual imagery. Visual imagery means that you picture something in your mind. It is best to picture a calm, relaxing thought, such as a favorite place you may have. Visualization helps to take your mind off your anger.

7. **PLAN AHEAD:** If you know there is a certain situation or person that may trigger your anger, plan ahead to avoid the situation or practice control strategies you can use while you're in the situation.

EDUCATOR PAGE: DO NOT DUPLICATE FOR STUDENTS

Introduction

Teaching students to express their anger in an appropriate way is a complex issue. Some students we deal with express their anger in a variety of inappropriate ways. The following students have not yet learned to express their anger appropriately.

- Jess usually hits someone when he's angry.
- Allison yells and screams when she's upset.
- Toby thinks of different ways to get revenge on the person he's angry with.
- Paul keeps his anger "bottled up" inside himself until eventually he cannot take it any longer and explodes.
- Maria blames someone else whenever she's angry.

Two approaches for teaching students to handle anger will be discussed in this unit. The first approach should be used with students who handle their anger in an aggressive, rather than assertive, manner. This type of student is often verbally and/or physically aggressive when angry. The second approach should be used with students who handle their anger in a passive, rather than assertive, manner. This type of student does not let others know how he is feeling. He keeps his anger hidden for as long as he can until the anger is eventually expressed in some inappropriate way.

Aggressive ➡ Assertive Approach

The authors recommend the use of *anger control training*, which is described in **Aggression Replacement Training: A Comprehensive Intervention for Aggressive Youth** (Goldstein and Glick, 1987). Two chapters entitled "The Affective Component of ART: Anger Control Training" and "Trainer's Manual for Anger Control Training" describe a program which teaches students self-control in an attempt to reduce aggressive acts. The anger cycle of aggressive youth has been broken down and defined in concrete terms. Strategies for anger control are discussed and practiced.

Anger control training is one component of the broader program entitled *Aggression Replacement Training* (ART). The program includes two other components: Structured Learning (direct instruction of social skills) and Moral Education (discussion groups which attempt to help students progress to higher levels of moral reasoning).

The authors of **SSS** have provided a more simplified description of anger control training than what is provided in ART. Readers are urged to read the entire description of anger control training and the broader program entitled *Aggression Replacement Training*, if interested in gaining more information. The activity pages in this unit of **SSS** reinforce the vocabulary and strategies taught in Goldstein and Glick's anger control training program.

The **Making Better Choices Program** (Harris, 1984) (described on pages 7 and 17) reinforces the concepts of anger control training by teaching students to "stop and think." It helps students decrease their impulsive behavior by taking time to think about what is happening. The program encourages students to have a plan (a sequence of skills) to use to replace their impulsive behavior. More important, the **Making Better Choices Program** directs students to evaluate how their plan worked and make changes if necessary. Too often, when a plan does not work for a student, he gives up and discontinues use of the plan. Kendall and Braswell (1985) emphasize the need for training students to deal with relapses. They encourage students to use self-talk to reassure themselves that they can control their impulsiveness.

Passive ➡ Assertive Approach

The anger control strategies mentioned above for aggressive youth are also beneficial for children who express their anger passively (e.g., children who keep their anger hidden). Identification of "triggers" that cause anger and individual body signals (cues) which alert a person that he is becoming angered are valuable concepts for these students. With this type of student, a greater emphasis is placed on identifying and expressing one's feelings (see Unit B-21.). Instruction in being assertive (see Unit B-12.) is highly recommended.

Dealing With Anger - C   Name:_____

ANGER

Some people feel that it's bad to feel angry; everyone gets angry at different times. IT'S OK TO FEEL ANGRY! The important thing is HOW you deal with your anger. IT'S NOT OK TO HURT SOMEONE WHEN YOU ARE ANGRY.

People express their anger in different ways. Below are three ways people express their anger.

AGGRESSIVE

This type of person often hurts other people when he expresses his anger. He might say mean things to others and he may even get physically aggressive. This type of person gets out-of-control when he is angry.

Assertive

This type of person lets other people know when he is feeling angry. He does it in a way that respects the rights of other people. He expresses his anger without upsetting other people. ◁ RIGHT WAY

passive

This type of person keeps his anger to himself and does not let anyone know he is angry. It seems as if he's not upset, but he really is. The anger keeps building until the person cannot hold it in any longer. The person usually explodes or expresses his anger in some inappropriate way.

DIRECTIONS: Answer the following items.

1. Name someone you know who is aggressive when angry. Explain why you think that person is aggressive.

2. Name someone you know who is assertive when angry. Explain why you think that person is assertive.

3. Name someone you know who is passive when angry. Explain why you think that person is passive.

4. What type of person do you think you are? Explain your answer.

Name:_____

BODY CUES

RULE:

> # You must first know WHEN you are angry before you can use strategies to control your anger!

CUES help us know when we are angry.

We all have body signals or **CUES** which let us know when we are angry. These cues are different for each person. Below are some body cues many of us experience when we get angry.

- muscles tighten, tense up
- face feels hot, looks red
- breathing gets faster
- heart pounds hard
- stomach feels like it's in knots
- eyes narrow, squint
- jaw tightens
- body shakes
- fists clench

These are general body cues that occur when people get angry. Some people might experience most of the body cues above, while others may only experience one or two body cues. Each person is different. Some people may experience body cues that are not listed above. It is important for each person to figure out what his body cues are.

DIRECTIONS: List any other body cues you can think of that people experience when they get angry.

-

-

-

-

Name:_____

CUES, CUES, CUES

DIRECTIONS: Look at the picture of Angry Al. Label the body cues that tell Al he
is angry.

1. _____

2. _____

3. _____

4. _____

5. _____

DIRECTIONS: Choose a person you know (e.g., a parent, a friend). List the body
cues that person has when he/she becomes angry.

1._____

2._____

3._____

4._____

DIRECTIONS: List the cues your body gives you when you are angry. If you have
a difficult time figuring out what your own body cues are, ask another
person to describe what you look like when you are angry.

1._____

2._____

3._____

4._____

Name:_____

TRIGGERS

A **trigger** is *something that happens that you choose to get angry about* (e.g., when someone calls you a bad name). There are two types of triggers: external triggers and internal triggers.

EXTERNAL TRIGGERS are things that other people say or do that you feel angry about (e.g., another person's pushing you). An external trigger could also be something that happens (e.g., your pencil breaks).

INTERNAL TRIGGERS are things that you choose to say to yourself that cause you to get angry (e.g., "I know she's laughing at me. I'm going to get her. She'll be sorry." or "Why did I do that? I'm so stupid!").

DIRECTIONS: Brainstorm with a partner by adding to the list of **internal** and **external triggers**. (Use the back of this page if you need more space.)

External Triggers

1. Someone makes a face at you.

2. Someone gossips about you.

3. You fail a test.

4. Your teacher is keeping you after school.

5. Your father comes home drunk and starts yelling at you.

6. _____

7. _____

8. _____

9. _____

10. _____

Internal Triggers

1. You tell yourself people will think you're a sissy if you don't fight.

2. You tell yourself you're stupid and can't pass the test because you failed the last two tests you took.

3. You keep thinking about a fight you had with your brother. You think about how you can get revenge.

4. _____

5. _____

6. _____

7. _____

8. _____

Name:_____

YOUR Triggers

DIRECTIONS: 1) Think about times when you have been the most angry (times when you felt like you were going to lose control or did lose control).

2) Then, determine which things *triggered* your anger.

3) List those *triggers* below under the correct category. If specific phrases or words triggered your anger, write the exact words or phrases.

EXTERNAL TRIGGERS

_____

_____

_____

_____

_____

INTERNAL TRIGGERS

_____

_____

_____

_____

_____

©1989 THINKING PUBLICATIONS

SSS: Social Skill Strategies (Book B)

Name:_____

Triggers and Cues

DIRECTIONS: Read the situations. After each, write the triggers and the body cues.

1. Marvin was working as a bag boy at the grocery store. He was packing a woman's groceries when she started yelling at him. She was complaining about everything he did. He felt his face get hot and his jaw tighten.

   Triggers: **Body Cues:**

2. Malory was sitting at the kitchen table when her father walked in the door. Her dad started slamming things around in the kitchen and yelling at her. Malory tried to ignore him but he got upset because she was ignoring him. Malory tried not to get upset but her heart was beating faster and she felt very tense.

   Triggers: **Body Cues:**

3. Justin was walking down the hall when he saw another student make a face at him. Justin thought to himself, "That big jerk. He's going to get it now." Justin felt his muscles tighten. He clenched his teeth and his breathing got heavier.

   Triggers: **Body Cues:**

4. Mary was at home when the phone rang. When she answered the phone, there wasn't anyone on the line. Mary thought to herself, "I know it's Jill and Jessica playing a trick on me. Those two are really useless. They are always trying to get me upset." Mary was shaking and she felt sick to her stomach.

   Triggers: **Body Cues:**

Name:_____

You're In CONTROL

You are in control of your emotions and your body.

No one can make you feel or do anything you do not want to do or feel.

People may say or do things to you to try to upset you. But you are in control of how you feel and what you do about your feelings.

Remember, no one can make you feel or do anything you do not want to feel or do.

IT IS VERY IMPORTANT THAT YOU **BELIEVE** YOU ARE IN CONTROL OF YOUR EMOTIONS.

DIRECTIONS: Say the following statements aloud. Check (✔) each statement as you say it.

_____ 1. I am in control of my emotions and my body.

_____ 2. I can choose how I want to feel.

_____ 3. I am in control of my emotions and my body.

_____ 4. I can choose how I want to feel.

_____ 5. I am in control of my emotions and my body.

_____ 6. I can choose how I want to feel.

_____ 7. I am in control of my emotions and my body.

DIRECTIONS: Think the following statements to yourself. Check (✔) each statement as you think it.

_____ 1. I am in control of my emotions and my body.

_____ 2. I can choose how I want to feel.

_____ 3. I am in control of my emotions and my body.

_____ 4. I can choose how I want to feel.

_____ 5. I am in control of my emotions and my body.

_____ 6. I can choose how I want to feel.

_____ 7. I am in control of my emotions and my body.

ANGER REDUCERS

There are different degrees of anger. Sometimes you are angry, but you are in control. Other times, you are so angry that you feel like you're going to lose control (or you do lose control). The anger control strategies listed below will help you calm down before you lose control. Some strategies work best when you are really upset. Other strategies work best before you get to the point of almost losing control. Each person is different and needs to find the strategy (or strategies) that work best.

---

1. **DEEP BREATHING:** Take a few deep, slow breaths. Try to slow down your breathing.

2. **CONSEQUENCES:** Think of what may happen if you lose control.

---

3. **SELF-TALK:** Tell yourself to *calm down and relax*. Tell yourself to *ignore it*. Say anything to yourself that will help you stay in control.

4. **COUNT:** Count to ten or more before you say or do anything. This will give you the extra time you may need to get back under control.

©1989 THINKING PUBLICATIONS

SSS: Social Skill Strategies (Book B)

5. **REMOVE YOURSELF:** If you are afraid you're losing control and may hurt someone, it's a good idea to walk away from the person or situation. It is also helpful not to look at the person you are angry with. This strategy may get you in trouble in some situations (e.g., if you're in the principal's office and he's talking to you and you walk out before he's finished). Of course, it's better to walk away from the principal than it is to hurt the principal.

6. **VISUAL IMAGERY:** When you're upset about something and you can't stop thinking about it, try using visual imagery. Visual imagery means that you picture something in your mind. It is best to picture a calm, relaxing thought, such as a favorite place you may have. Visualization helps to take your mind off your anger.

7. **PLAN AHEAD:** If you know there is a certain situation or person that may trigger your anger, plan ahead to avoid the situation or practice control strategies you can use while you're in the situation.

8. **YOUR OWN STRATEGY:** If you have your own strategy to help you control your anger, describe it/draw it in this space.

Name:_____

Practicing Anger Control Strategies

DIRECTIONS: 1) Work with a partner.
2) Role play the situations below three or four times each. (You may write your own situations in place of the ones below.)
3) Each time you do a role play, use a different strategy to help you remain in control.
4) Make your role play realistic. Pretend you are really angry and have to calm yourself.
5) Check off each anger control strategy you practice.

Situation #1

Your teacher tells you that you have to stay in for lunch to finish your math.

Situation #2

Your mother tells you that you cannot go to the concert all your friends are going to attend.

Situation #3

Your boss tells you that you cannot have a week of vacation in July (the week your family is going on a big trip).

Situation #4 (Optional)

_____

_____

_____

Situation #5 (Optional)

_____

_____

_____

_____	Deep breathing
_____	Think of the consequences
_____	Self-talk
_____	Remove yourself
_____	Count
_____	Visual imagery
_____	Plan ahead

EDUCATOR PAGE: DO NOT DUPLICATE FOR STUDENTS

DESCRIPTION: Goldstein and Glick (1987) advocate the use of role playing to teach anger control strategies. Below is a list of role plays for the educator and another adult to perform for the students. (The educator may perform the role plays with a student if a second adult is not available.) The students should watch the role plays and complete the following page. They will need to identify the following in each of the role plays:

1) trigger(s)
2) body cues
3) anger reducer(s)

The role plays below have been provided for the educator's use. The educator may wish to develop role plays which are specific to the anger control problems that students in the class are experiencing.

When performing the role plays, the educator should be sure to make the trigger(s), body cues, and anger reducer(s) observable for the students.

Role plays:

1. A student is teasing you in the lunchroom.

2. Your mother tells you she is taking you for counseling and you don't want to go.

3. A person where you work has been spreading rumors about you.

4. A teacher accuses you of doing something you didn't do just because you have a bad reputation.

5. Your brother ruins one of your cassette tapes.

6. You don't get hired for a job you really wanted.

7. You failed a test in school.

8. The principal hears you swearing in the hall and punishes you.

9. Your parents ground you for talking back to them.

10. You return a wallet you found and you get accused of stealing it.

11. Someone is picking on your little sister.

12. Your sister loans something of yours to her friend without asking you.

13. You return something to a store and the clerk is very rude to you.

14. The person sitting behind you in class keeps kicking your desk.

15. Your mother takes your younger brother's side even though he started the fight.

Name:_____

Role Plays

DIRECTIONS: 1) Watch the role plays that others perform for you.
2) For each role play, write the trigger(s), the body cues, and the anger reducer(s) used.

Role Play	Trigger(s)	Body Cues	Anger Reducer(s)
1			
2			
3			
4			

©1989 THINKING PUBLICATIONS   SSS: Social Skill Strategies (Book B)

Name:_____

Anger Control QUIZ

1. What are *triggers*?

_____

_____

2. Explain the difference between *internal* and *external triggers*.

_____

_____

_____

3. Define the term *body cues*.

_____

_____

4. Give four examples of body cues.

a. _____

b. _____

c. _____

d. _____

5. List six of the seven anger reducers and describe each one.

a. _____

_____

b. _____

_____

c. _____

_____

d. _____

_____

e. _____

_____

f. _____

Name:_____

Self-Evaluation

The most IMPORTANT step in using anger control strategies is SELF-EVALUATION. This is the step most people forget to do. **Self-evaluation** means *that you judge how well the anger control strategy worked*. ANGER CONTROL STRATEGIES WILL NOT ALWAYS WORK! That's why it's important to assess what may have gone wrong. It's also important to "pat yourself on the back" when the strategy works well.

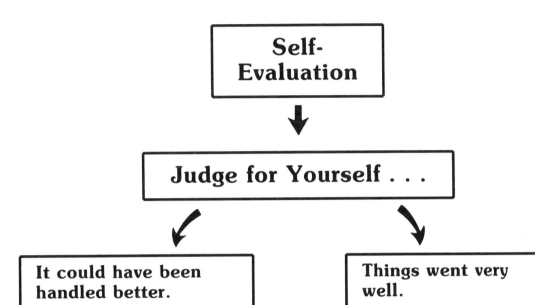

Ask yourself these questions:

• What went wrong?

• Did I forget to use a control strategy?

• Could I have started trying to control my anger sooner?

• What was I saying to myself at the time?

• Was I saying things to myself to make me get angrier?

• Would it have been better for me to use a different control strategy (e.g., leaving the situation)?

• What will I do differently the next time I'm in a similar situation?

Say these things to yourself:

• I really am in control.

• Good thing I didn't lose it!

• I handled that pretty well.

• Way to go!

• Wow, I didn't lose my temper!

• This anger control stuff really works.

• I sure kept my cool that time.

• Great, I stayed out of trouble!

• I did a good job.

Name:_____

Self - Evaluate

DIRECTIONS: Write down a situation in which you tried using anger control strategies, but things didn't go well.

_____
_____
_____
_____
_____

DIRECTIONS: Write down three questions you could ask yourself about what went wrong.

1) _____
   _____
2) _____
   _____
3) _____
   _____

DIRECTIONS: Write down a situation in which you used anger control strategies, and things went well.

_____
_____
_____
_____
_____

DIRECTIONS: Write down three things you could say to yourself because you did a good job.

1) _____
   _____
2) _____
   _____
3) _____
   _____

EDUCATOR PAGE: DO NOT DUPLICATE FOR STUDENTS

DESCRIPTION: The students will attempt to complete a word search activity under stressful circumstances (e.g., time limitations, teacher pressure). The word search has several words missing from it, thus making it an impossible task. (Educators should not tell the students about the missing words.) THE PURPOSE OF THIS ACTIVITY IS TO HAVE THE STUDENTS PRACTICE THEIR ANGER CONTROL STRATEGIES IN A STRESSFUL SITUATION.

DIRECTIONS:
1. Give the word search instructions to the students (see next page).
2. While the students are attempting to complete the activity, the educator should put additional stress on the students by saying things such as "You only have three minutes left," "You'd better hurry, you're behind everyone else," "This is such a simple activity."
3. At the end of the five minutes, tell the students about the "trick" that was played on them. Discuss how the students felt when they were completing the activity. Discuss their use of anger control strategies.
4. Hold the discussion described below with the students. (Some educators may prefer to have the discussion before the students complete the activity to remind students to remain calm.)

ACTIVITY: Tell the students to listen carefully to the following instructions:
1. You will be given a word search activity to complete.
2. You will be given five minutes to complete the activity.
3. The first person to complete the word search activity will receive a reward.
4. Those students who do not complete the activity within the five-minute time limit will receive a negative consequence.
5. There is no talking during this activity.
6. This will be a stressful activity. If you feel frustrated, you should use your anger control techniques to remain calm.

DISCUSSION: Hold a discussion with your students about frustration.
1. Discuss what *frustration* is and that everyone experiences it at various times.
2. Discuss examples of times the students are frustrated.
3. Discuss how frustration can lead to anger which may lead to a loss of control.
4. Discuss how the anger control techniques can help the students deal with frustration.
5. Discuss examples of times they are frustrated in school.
6. Discuss how teachers often provide pressure which may cause students to become frustrated easily (e.g., time limits, difficult objectives).

WORD SEARCH ACTIVITY

DIRECTIONS: Complete the word search by finding the words listed at the bottom of the page. The words are printed vertically, horizontally, and diagonally.

```
D S F F E D A H O M I W E E P O L Q M S
R F R B O M J I A T A L L P C U E S R V
B R E R E V A L K I N C O N S E E X T E
S T R A L C A L P M G T R I G G X I N T
I N T E R A V I S U E V I S U A T C U P
A N G E M Q X R E L R A X A T I E C A L
W L I N J O S A B R E A T M O N R E Y U
I N T T B R E A T H I N G A N G N C A L
T T R I G G E M O I S T R A T E A M Y C
L D I M S E G R A T O F R O G N L C O W
D O G M O U S E L L T N A C A T B I R D
A N G R E S M S E L J M O A N B R E A T
Q S E Q M I S E Q U E N C L V A L U Q E
X T R Q S U E V I S U Q U M X T E R N A
C O S E Q U E N C X T E R N A V I S U A
R T R I G G M E V A L U A M A N G E M C
Y U O P R W Q N V X I M O V I X T E R N
T R I G C O N S E Q U V I S U A L C U E
A S W E Q V E X Z S O I V P X Q R X Z M
```

WORDS TO FIND:

Anger	Consequences	Evaluation	Breathing
Cues	Triggers	Visualization	External
Calm	Strategies	Relaxation	Internal

EDUCATOR PAGE: DO NOT DUPLICATE FOR STUDENTS

DIRECTIONS: Tell your students to sit in a relaxed position for this visualization activity. Read the script below to your students in a slow, relaxed manner. During the description of the student's anger, you may wish to make your voice somewhat more excited. The script is a guided visualization activity for dealing with anger.

Close your eyes if you feel like it . . . make sure you are sitting in a comfortable position . . . let yourself relax . . . On the count of three, take a very slow, deep breath. One . . . two . . . three . . . inhale slowly . . . hold it . . . now exhale very slowly. Let your entire body relax. (pause) Now, think about a time when you were very angry . . . you may have been angry at a person, or a thing or maybe even at yourself. Think about why you were so angry . . . let your body become tense as you recall the situation . . . your breathing is faster . . . your face is tensed up . . . your whole body is angry. You keep going over the problem in your head . . . (pause for 20-30 seconds)

Now, picture yourself being taken to the edge of a peaceful stream . . . the water washes up on your feet . . . it feels cool and soothing. The water puts out the anger in your feet like water putting out a fire . . . it feels so refreshing. As you sit by the stream, it begins to sprinkle . . . the water feels so good. You can feel the anger in your body go away as soon as the cool water touches it . . . It starts to sprinkle harder, but the water feels so refreshing. It feels so cool and relaxing . . . the water puts out the burning anger in your entire body.

Your mind starts to think about how good you're feeling and how happy you are . . . your whole body is relaxed and calm and content . . . (pause) The next time you are angry, you can use this same visual image to help yourself calm down. Picture the cool water putting out the anger in your body just as water puts out the flames in a fire . . . then picture your entire body relaxing and your mind feeling refreshed.

Supplemental Activity: Have the students draw a picture of their anger being put out by the water. Also encourage students to use their imagination to draw pictures or write scripts for other visual imagery that deals with anger being controlled (e.g., the warmth of the sun changing their anger to happiness; their body condensing the anger into a very small ball).

Name:_____

⬜ Take Responsibility

When you want to tell someone why you are angry, there are a few things you can do to make things go smoothly. Use the word *I* when talking with the person. One reason for using *I* is that you are in control of your emotions and no one can make you feel anything you don't choose to feel. You take responsibility for your anger rather than blaming someone else. Therefore, it's important to say "I feel" rather than "you make me feel." Another reason for using *I* is it makes the person you're talking to feel less threatened and defensive. Also, it's important to tell the person the reason you're angry (e.g., "I'm angry because you said you would come to my game and you never showed up").

DIRECTIONS: Put a check by those statements which are "I" statements. (Be careful. Just because a sentence starts with the word *I* doesn't mean the person is taking responsibility for his anger.)

_____ 1. I'm angry because I didn't study for this test and I got an "F."

_____ 2. Ms. Smith makes me so upset. She gave me an "F" on this test.

_____ 3. George is such a jerk. I can't stand him.

_____ 4. I'm angry because I'm embarrassed when I'm with George.

_____ 5. I'm angry with myself because I didn't try my hardest.

_____ 6. I'm so stupid.

_____ 7. My parents are useless.

_____ 8. I'm upset because my parents don't trust me to stay home alone.

_____ 9. Mr. Sherman is always making me get angry.

_____ 10. I'm angry because Mr. Sherman gave me a detention for hitting Jane.

Who should John be angry with? _____ Why?

''I'' Statements

DIRECTIONS:
1) Work with a partner to cut apart the situation cards below and divide them equally between the two of you.

2) Take turns reading the situation cards to one another.

3) When your partner reads a situation to you, you should respond with an "I" statement which accepts responsibility for your anger and tells why you are upset.

Your math teacher catches you cheating on a test. Talk with your mom about it and use an "I" statement about your anger.	Your friend has been talking about you behind your back. Talk to your friend and use an "I" statement about your anger.
You forgot to do your homework assignment so you received an "F." Use an "I" statement about your anger.	The principal blames you for writing on a wall and you didn't do it. Talk to your friend about it and use an "I" statement about your anger.
The girl sitting next to you calls you a mean name. Talk to the girl and use an "I" statement to let her know why you're upset.	Your mother won't let you go out this weekend because you were late two nights in a row. Talk to your sister and use an "I" statement about your anger.
You don't understand the assignment the teacher gives you. The teacher seems impatient that you're asking about it. Talk to your teacher and use an "I" statement about your anger.	Someone pushes you when you're in the hallway. Talk to that person and use an "I" statement about your anger.
Your girl/boyfriend likes someone else. Talk to another friend and use an "I" statement about your anger.	You have to watch your baby brother and you wanted to go with your friends. Use self-talk and use an "I" statement about your anger.

You get caught shoplifting in the grocery store. Talk to your mother and use an "I" statement about your anger.	Your friend asks someone else to go to the movies. Talk to your friend and use an "I" statement about your anger.
You told your mom you would clean your room and you keep putting it off. Use self-talk and use an "I" statement about being angry with yourself.	You spill ketchup on your new shirt. Talk to your friend and use an "I" statement about your anger.
You get a ticket for riding your bike where you weren't supposed to be riding it. Talk with your friend and use an "I" statement about your anger.	Someone steals your science notebook from your locker. Talk with a teacher and use an "I" statement about your anger.
You have a big fight with one of your parents about how you're doing in school. Talk with your friend and use an "I" statement about your anger.	Someone beats you up. Talk with the principal and use an "I" statement about your anger.
The teacher won't help you with your assignment. Talk with your teacher and use an "I" statement about your anger.	You lose $10.00 you had in your pocket. Talk with your brother and use an "I" statement about your anger.

DEALING WITH ANGER - DEALING WITH ANGER

1. Define the following terms:

   Triggers - _____

   Body cues - _____

   Anger reducers - _____

2. Explain the difference between *internal* and *external triggers.*

   _____

   _____

3. Describe a situation when you could use anger reducers to help you remain in control.

   _____

   _____

   _____

4. Read the following situation. Then identify the trigger(s), body cues, and anger reducer(s).

   > Andy was riding his bike when he heard someone yell, "Hey fatso." Andy felt his muscles tighten and his face get hot. He wanted to go and punch whoever yelled that at him. But instead he said to himself, "Just ignore the jerk. It's not worth it."

   Trigger(s): _____

   Body cues: _____

   Anger reducer(s): _____

5. Write a story about someone who has problems controlling his anger. Include a part in the story about a friend who gives advice to the person on how to control his anger. (Use the back of this page if you need more space.)

   _____

   _____

   _____

   _____

6. Rate yourself from zero to ten on how well you control your anger (0 = poor control, 10 = good control). Then, provide specific examples to support how you rated yourself. #_____

   _____

   _____

SKILL HOMEWORK ACTIVITY

_____
(Due Date)

Dear Parent or Guardian of: _____

This week we are learning about the social communication skill:

DEALING WITH EMBARRASSMENT

This social skill is very important in interpersonal relationships. The skill steps are:

1. Decide if you are embarrassed (think about your body cues).

2. Use one of the strategies to help yourself feel less embarrassed (see attached page).

Before the due date, please complete one of the following activities with your son or daughter: (put a check mark by your choice)

_____ A. We acted out the role play situation listed below.

_____ B. I observed my son/daughter using this social skill in a real-life situation. (I have described the situation below.)

Description of real-life observation:

Role play situation:

YOUR FRIEND COMES TO YOUR HOUSE FOR DINNER AND YOUR PARENTS START ARGUING IN FRONT OF YOU AND YOUR FRIEND. ROLE PLAY HOW YOU WOULD HANDLE THIS EMBARRASSING SITUATION.

- -

Please circle the word below which best describes how your son or daughter did while using this social skill in either the role play or real-life situation.

NEEDS MORE HELP   GOOD   EXCELLENT

It is important for you to reinforce your child's use of this social skill at home in a positive way. Encourage and praise your child when you see the skill appropriately used. Remind him/her to use the social skill when necessary.

Thank you for your assistance.

Sincerely,

* *

PARENT/GUARDIAN SIGNATURE: _____

EMBARRASSING SITUATIONS

Everyone has embarrassing things happen to them. You can probably remember several embarrassing situations you've been in.

DIRECTIONS: Make a list of embarrassing things that might happen to you, or things that might happen to someone else that would make the situation embarrassing for you. Make sure your list has at least five situations for each. You may do this activity with a partner.

_____

_____

_____

_____

_____

_____

_____

_____

_____

Knowing When You're Embarrassed

It's important to know when you are feeling embarrassed. There are some cues your body may give you to let you know you are feeling embarrassed. A few of those cues are listed below.

Your face may blush and/or feel hot.

You may get sweaty palms and/or underarms.

Your stomach might feel strange.

QUESTION:

Are there any other cues your body gives you when you're feeling embarrassed?

_____

_____

_____

In addition to the cues your body gives, you might feel silly or foolish. You may feel like crawling in a hole for the rest of your life. You may feel like you never want to show your face in public again.

DON'T WORRY. THESE ARE NATURAL FEELINGS. THESE FEELINGS WILL EVENTUALLY GO AWAY.

QUESTION:

Look at this person. Why is this person's reaction to embarrassment silly?

Dealing With Embarrassment

Here are some strategies that may help you to feel less embarrassed and forget about the embarrassing situation faster.

* SIMPLY TELL THE PEOPLE AROUND YOU THAT YOU ARE FEELING EMBARRASSED.

(You only need to say this one time. People will think you are trying to get attention if you say it more than once.)

Example: Say, "Oh, I'm so embarrassed about this."

* DON'T MAKE A BIG DEAL OUT OF THE SITUATION.

Example: Your friend notices you are wearing two different colored socks. Don't make a big deal about it and most people probably won't even notice.

* IGNORE WHAT HAPPENED.

Example: You trip while you are walking up the stairs with your friends. None of your friends seem to have noticed that you tripped so don't say anything about it.

* JOKE ABOUT WHAT HAPPENED.

Example: You are playing basketball in gym class. When it's your turn to practice shooting baskets, you don't make any of them. You're feeling kind of embarrassed so you say jokingly to your friend, "I've been thinking of trying out for a professional basketball team. What do you think of that idea?"

* USE SELF-TALK TO MAKE YOURSELF FEEL BETTER.

Example: Say things to yourself such as:
"It's not the end of the world."
"Embarrassing things happen to everyone."
"I'll probably think this is funny a few days from now."

DIRECTIONS: Tell or write a short story. The story should be about someone who is in an embarrassing situation. Have the person in the story use one of the strategies listed above to feel less embarrassed. (Write your story on the back side of this page.)

Name:_____

What Should They Do?

DIRECTIONS: Read each situation below. After each situation, tell what you think the person should do (or say) to handle the embarrassment. Remember, you've learned several strategies for dealing with embarrassment.

1. Juan was walking down the hall when Joe shouted out, "Hey Juan, don't you think you should zip your pants up?"

   _____

   _____

2. Molly was talking to a boy she liked when her friend Kris whispered to her, "Molly, you have ketchup on the side of your face."

   _____

   _____

3. The teacher held up Jeff's test for everyone in the class to see. Jeff had gotten an "F" on the test.

   _____

   _____

4. When Marta went up to give her speech to the class, she couldn't remember a thing. She had to sit back down without giving her speech.

   _____

   _____

5. Cody had just gotten eye glasses. He had never had them before and was worried about what the others at school were going to say.

   _____

   _____

6. Jesse was looking at his body in the mirror. He was trying to make himself look manly by sticking out his chest and flexing his muscles. All of a sudden, he noticed his sister standing behind him giggling.

   _____

   _____

Name:_____

DON'T BE A JERK!

When something embarrassing happens to someone you are with, don't make a big deal about it. Think about how you would feel if you were in that person's shoes.

For example: If your friend has his shirt buttoned crooked, stop and think how you would feel if it happened to you. By doing this, maybe you won't make a big deal about it.

DIRECTIONS: Work with a partner and list some reasons why you shouldn't make a big deal when something embarrassing happens to someone else.

-
-
-

DIRECTIONS: Work with a partner and make a cartoon about a person who makes a big deal and tries to embarrass another person. You may use pictures, words, or a combination of both.

1	2
3	4

DEALING WITH EMBARRASSMENT

1. Tell the skill steps for dealing with embarrassment.

   (step 1) _____

   (step 2) _____

2. Explain why it's important to be able to deal with embarrassment in an appropriate way.

   _____

   _____

   _____

3. Describe an embarrassing situation you had to deal with during the past month.

   _____

   _____

   _____

4. Read the situation below and answer the questions that follow.

   > Harold was walking past Gertrude (the girl he likes), when he accidently bumped into a teacher and spilled the teacher's coffee. Harold said, "Oh, sorry. I'd better watch where I'm going." Harold saw that Gertrude was laughing at him. He looked at her, shook his head, and started laughing also.

   What happened that was embarrassing for Harold? _____

   _____

   What did Harold do to handle his embarrassment? _____

   _____

5. Draw a cartoon that shows how a person appropriately handles embarrassment. (Use the back of this page for your cartoon.)

6. Describe a situation in which you were embarrassed. Tell how you dealt with the embarrassment and whether you feel you handled the embarrassment appropriately.

   _____

   _____

   _____

   _____

SKILL HOMEWORK ACTIVITY

_____
(Due Date)

Dear Parent or Guardian of: _____

This week we are learning about the social communication skill:

COPING WITH FEAR

This social skill is very important in interpersonal relationships and can be broken down into the following skill steps. Please watch for the steps in your role play practice or real-life observation.

1. Decide if the fear works for you or against you. (e.g., The fear of being hit by a car works for you if it makes you more careful when crossing the street. That same fear can work against you if it causes you to refuse to cross the street.)

2. If your fear works against you, then take steps to reduce the fear:
   - Talk to someone about your fear.
   - Leave the fearful situation (if appropriate).
   - Visualize yourself facing your fear and use positive self-talk.
   - Gradually face your fear.

Before the due date, please complete one of the following activities with your son or daughter: (put a check mark by your choice)

_____ A. We acted out the role play situation listed below.

_____ B. I observed my son/daughter using this social skill in a real-life situation. (I have described the situation below.)

Description of real-life observation:

Role play situation:

PRETEND YOU NEED TO GIVE A SPEECH IN ENGLISH CLASS AND YOU ARE AFRAID. DEMONSTRATE HOW YOU COULD DISCUSS YOUR FEAR WITH ONE OF YOUR PARENTS. TELL WHAT POSITIVE SELF-TALK YOU COULD USE BEFORE YOU GIVE YOUR SPEECH AND WHAT OTHER STRATEGIES YOU COULD USE TO REDUCE YOUR FEAR.

Please circle the word below which best describes how your son or daughter did while using this social skill in either the role play or real-life situation.

NEEDS MORE HELP   GOOD   EXCELLENT

It is important for you to reinforce your child's use of this social skill at home in a positive way. Encourage and praise your child when you see the skill appropriately used. Remind him/her to use the social skill when necessary.

Thank you for your assistance.

Sincerely,

* *

PARENT/GUARDIAN SIGNATURE: _____

Name:_____

For Or Against?

When you are afraid of something, it is important to determine whether your fear is realistic or unrealistic. If your fear is realistic, then it works for you to protect you. If your fear is unrealistic, then it works against you and makes your life worse than if you didn't have the fear.

The fear of gaining too much weight . . .

- works for you if it causes you to exercise regularly.

- works against you if it causes you to become anorexic.

The fear of getting hit by a car while crossing the street . . .

- works for you if it causes you to remember to look both ways before crossing.

- works against you if it causes you to refuse to ever cross a street alone.

DIRECTIONS: Read about each of the following fears. If the fear is working for the person, write **for**. If the fear is working against the person, write **against**.

_____ 1. Dan is afraid of making a fool of himself when he gives a speech in his English class. His fear causes him to spend a great deal of time writing his speech and practicing it beforehand.

_____ 2. Rhonda is afraid of giving a speech in her English class, so she refuses to talk and takes an *F*.

_____ 3. Janelle is afraid of getting mugged at night, so she never leaves her house after dark.

_____ 4. Francis is afraid of getting mugged at night, so he never walks alone after dark and only goes on well-lighted streets.

_____ 5. Pete is afraid that he will fail science, no matter how hard he studies. His fear causes him to give up and do nothing in the class.

_____ 6. Don is afraid of failing science, so he goes for extra help from the tutor.

_____ 7. Jeanne is afraid of getting hurt by the dentist, so she makes certain to ask for novocaine before having a tooth drilled.

_____ 8. Paulette is afraid of the dentist, so she never goes.

_____ 9. Malinda is afraid of getting fired from her job, so she always gets to work on time and works as hard as she can.

_____10. Luke is afraid that his boss will fire him, so he quits before the boss has a chance.

Name:_____

"The Only Thing To Fear Is Fear Itself"

If you are afraid of something, and it starts *to get the best of you*, try one of the strategies described below to help reduce your fear.

1. Talk to someone about your fear.

2. Leave the fearful situation (if appropriate).

3. Visualize yourself doing the thing you fear, and being successful.

4. Use positive self-talk.

5. Face your fears (the more you do it, the more comfortable you will become).

DIRECTIONS: List two people you could talk to about each of the fears listed below.

1. You have a fear that you are not smart enough to graduate from high school.

   a.

   b.

2. You have a fear of staying home alone at night.

   a.

   b.

DIRECTIONS: Add three more situations to this list of times when it would be appropriate to leave when you are afraid.

1. Your friends are really pressuring you to try some drugs. You are afraid that you will break down and say *yes*.

2. You are on a diet. You are in the kitchen where there are freshly baked cookies.

3.

4.

5.

DIRECTIONS: Write down what you could say to yourself to help face the following fears.

1. You are afraid of getting a shot from the nurse.

2. Your team has two outs and you are up to bat. You are afraid of striking out.

3. The class bully is standing at the corner and you need to walk by him.

4. You are in the school play and you are afraid you will forget your lines.

DIRECTIONS: Visualize yourself in each of the situations listed above. Say what you wrote down, to yourself, and then picture yourself being successful in the situation.

GROUP LEARNING ACTIVITY

DIRECTIONS:
1. You will be working in small groups. (Your teacher will assign the groups.)

2. Work cooperatively with your team members to complete the activities on the following three pages.

3. As a team, choose one of these two ways to complete the activities:

   a. Each team member completes one of the activities. Then the members exchange activities and double check each other's work.

   b. All team members complete the activities together. One team member can volunteer to do all the writing or each team member can take a turn doing the writing.

4. All team members should sign their names on each page, indicating that everyone agrees with all the answers.

5. When all the pages are completed, turn them in for a group grade.

GROUP LEARNING ACTIVITY - A
Top Five

DIRECTIONS: Write down what you think are the top five most common fears that adults have, that teen-agers have, and that children have.

ADULTS

1.

2.

3.

4.

5.

TEEN-AGERS

1.

2.

3.

4.

5.

CHILDREN

1.

2.

3.

4.

5.

©1989 THINKING PUBLICATIONS

GROUP LEARNING ACTIVITY - B
Cause and Effect

DIRECTIONS: Write down three possible causes for each fear listed below.

A fear of speaking in front of a group

1.

2.

3.

A fear of not having friends

1.

2.

3.

A fear of being overweight

1.

2.

3.

A fear of dying

1.

2.

3.

A fear of the dentist

1.

2.

3.

Group Members:_____
_____
_____
_____

GROUP LEARNING ACTIVITY - C
Fear Script

DIRECTIONS: Write a script about a teen-ager who learns to cope with a fear. The script should include at least three characters. If you need more room, continue your script on the back of this page. (You will be allowed to tape record your script instead of writing it, if your team prefers to do it that way.)

Character Description: _____

(Write the name of each   _____
character and briefly
describe him/her.)   _____

Scene Description: _____

(Describe the scene   _____
when the script
begins.)   _____

Character's   ***What The Character Says***
Name

_____: _____
_____

_____: _____
_____

_____: _____
_____

_____: _____
_____

_____: _____
_____

_____: _____
_____

COPING WITH FEAR - COPING WITH FEAR

---

1. Write the two skill steps for coping with fear.

   (step 1) _____

   _____

   (step 2) _____

   _____

2. Explain how you can determine if a fear is working for or against you.

   _____

   _____

3. Pretend you have a fear of using a garbage disposal at home. Describe how you could use that fear to work for you. Describe what could happen if you let that fear work against you.

   (for you) _____

   (against you) _____

4. Compare the following two situations. Tell one thing that each person has in common and one thing that is different for each person.

   Samantha is afraid of getting into a car accident. Because of her fear, she is a very cautious driver.

   Bradley is afraid of getting into a car accident. Because of his fear, he refuses to drive or ride in a car.

   (commonality) _____

   (difference) _____

5. Create a mnemonic device to help you remember the five strategies for reducing fear. Explain how the mnemonic device works.

   _____

   _____

   _____

   _____

6. Describe a fear you currently have or a fear you had in the past.

_____

_____

Did you or are you dealing with the fear in a good way?   YES   NO

If *yes*, tell what strategy(s) you are using to reduce the fear.

_____

If *no*, tell what strategy(s) you think you should try to reduce the fear.

_____

SKILL HOMEWORK ACTIVITY

_____
(Due Date)

Dear Parent or Guardian of: _____

This week we are learning about the social communication skill:

DEALING WITH HUMOR

This social skill is very important in interpersonal relationships.

The students have learned that there is a difference between "safe" and "unsafe" humor. Safe humor is something funny that everyone can laugh at. No one's feelings are hurt. "Safe" humor is an important aspect in everyone's life. It can reduce stress, and help make life more enjoyable.

Before the due date, please complete one of the following activities with your son or daughter: (put a check mark by your choice)

_____ A. We acted out the role play situation listed below.

_____ B. I observed my son/daughter using this social skill in a real-life situation. (I have described the situation below.)

Description of real-life observation:

Role play situation:

TELL ONE OF YOUR PARENTS A JOKE THAT USES "SAFE" HUMOR.

- -

Please circle the word below which best describes how your son or daughter did while using this social skill in either the role play or real-life situation.

NEEDS MORE HELP   GOOD   EXCELLENT

It is important for you to reinforce your child's use of this social skill at home in a positive way. Encourage and praise your child when you see the skill appropriately used. Remind him/her to use the social skill when necessary.

Thank you for your assistance.

Sincerely,

* *

PARENT/GUARDIAN SIGNATURE: _____

A 6th Sense

You've probably learned that people have five senses: a sense of sight, hearing, taste, smell, and touch. Another sense that every person should have is a **sense of humor**. A person with a good sense of humor is someone who is able to see the funny side of things and laugh!

Humor is an important aspect in our lives. Humor helps to reduce stress and makes life more enjoyable. It can help make a difficult situation easier. Read the script below, to see how Jeff uses humor to help his friends relax.

Jeff's Idea

Situation: Jeff is sitting with his friends at lunch. They are all feeling very tense, because they have English next period and they have to give speeches.

Eddie: I wish we didn't have to give our speeches today. I hate giving speeches.

Will: I don't even want to talk about it. Just thinking about it makes me feel worse.

Jeff: Oh, come on you guys, what's the worst thing that could happen?

Eddie: The worst thing that could happen is that I start shaking and I forget what I want to say. Becky is in that class, and if she sees me make a fool out of myself, she'll never go out with me.

Jeff: Hey, I've got an idea.

Will: What is it? I'm so nervous, I'll try anything.

Jeff: (In a teasing tone of voice) I'll volunteer to go first. In the middle of my speech, I'll pretend to pass out. You guys leave the room to go get help. By the time the nurse arrives, the class period will almost be over and we won't have to give our speeches.

(Everyone laughs at Jeff's joke)

Eddie: Or maybe we could each pretend that we have laryngitis!

(The three guys start to "loosen up.")

Is It Safe?

It is important to understand the difference between "safe" and "unsafe" humor. **"Safe" humor** means *saying or doing something funny that is not at anyone's expense; something that everyone can laugh at.* **"Unsafe" humor** is *humor that can hurt someone's feelings or humor that can get you into trouble.*

DIRECTIONS: Read each situation below. Decide if each is an example of safe or unsafe humor. Put an **S** for safe humor and a **U** for unsafe humor. If you mark a situation with a **U**, then explain why you think it is unsafe.

_____ 1. You pull the chair out from under the girl sitting in front of you.

_____ 2. You are imitating a blind boy in your class.

_____ 3. Your brother has a good sense of humor. You buy candles for his birthday cake. You buy the kind of candles you can't blow out.

_____ 4. You get all the kids in the class to throw spit balls at the substitute teacher.

_____ 5. You tell a joke about your friend's crooked teeth.

_____ 6. You hide your friend's books on him and don't give them to him until the next day.

_____ 7. You tell a dirty joke in the middle of class.

_____ 8. You accidently wear two different shoes to school. You poke fun at your mistake and your friends laugh along with you.

_____ 9. You tell a joke you found printed in the magazine your English class has been reading.

_____10. You shoot a rubber band at your dog's face.

DIRECTIONS: Give an example of "safe" humor you have recently experienced. Explain why it was safe.

Give an example of "unsafe" humor you have recently experienced. Explain why it was unsafe.

Name:_____

PERSONAL DIFFERENCES

When it comes to humor, people are very different! Not everybody finds the same things to be funny. This is especially important to remember when it comes to teasing. Sometimes, it is difficult to know if your teasing will be safe or unsafe. The two cartoons below will help to illustrate just how different someone can react.

In this first cartoon, Carla is not at all sensitive about her handwriting, so she finds the teasing to be funny and laughs along.

In this second cartoon, Carla is very sensitive about her handwriting abilities. She doesn't think the teasing is funny at all and feels hurt.

If you tease someone and he starts to laugh, you may think he doesn't mind being teased. However, it is possible that he is just pretending that the teasing doesn't bother him. Maybe deep down inside he is feeling hurt by your teasing. You can never be 100% certain that your teasing will be "safe."

DIRECTIONS: Write down something that you are NOT very sensitive about and that people can tease you about. Write down something that you ARE sensitive about that you don't like people teasing you about.

I am not sensitive about: _____

I am sensitive about: _____

©1989 THINKING PUBLICATIONS

SSS: Social Skill Strategies (Book B)

Name:_____

Attention-Seekers (Funny or Sad?)

It is true that most people enjoy others who have a good sense of humor. Unfortunately, some people think they will be well-liked by others if they are funny all the time, so they go overboard and are hardly ever serious. A person like this is called an "attention-seeker." The picture below shows a "class clown." (A "class clown" is an example of an attention-seeker.)

Attention-seekers are people who will do anything to get attention. They try to get others to laugh by doing all types of inappropriate things, or by using humor at inappropriate times. Attention-seekers don't feel very good about themselves. They think that other people will like them more if they act silly and try to be humorous all the time.

DIRECTIONS: Answer the following questions about "attention-seekers."

1. Write down the first name of a person you know who is an "attention-seeker."

2. How do you feel when you are with this person?

3. Evaluate your own sense of humor. Put an **X** in the circle that best describes your sense of humor at this point in your life.

I never try to be funny, I don't think very many things in life are humorous.

I do try to be funny, but not all the time. I know there are times when I should be serious, also.

I try to be funny all the time, because I think people will like me more if I can make them laugh.

HUMOR: **Time and Place**

There is a time and a place for everything, including humor. You have learned that it is important to have a sense of humor, especially in stressful situations, because humor can help to make a difficult situation easier. This is not to say that humor is appropriate in all situations.

There are times when using humor would not be appropriate. For example, if your best friend just found out that his/her dog died, you would not want to say or do something funny.

DIRECTIONS: Add to this list of situations when it would not be appropriate to use humor.

1. You just found out that a cousin was seriously hurt in a car accident.

2. Your class is in the middle of taking a test.

3.

4.

5.

6.

7.

8.

9.

10.

DIRECTIONS: Work with a partner to create a skit about someone who uses humor at a bad time. You may use one of the situations from the list above. Perform your skit for the group. Let the group discuss what was wrong with the time and place of the humor and what could be done to "fix" the skit.

Name:_____

LAUGH!

Being able to laugh at yourself is very important. If you take yourself too seriously and can't laugh at your mistakes, then people may not enjoy being around you.

DIRECTIONS: Below, you will find two notes, written to friends at school. Write **good** under the note that is written by a person who is able to laugh at herself. Write **bad** under the note that indicates that the person is not about to laugh at herself.

Maggie,
You wouldn't believe what happened to me this morning. I was talking to Ken and I noticed that the zipper on my pants was down. I started to cry and then Ken laughed at me. I told him to shut-up and stomped off.
I'll never be able to face him again.

Maggie,
You wouldn't believe what happened to me this morning. I was talking to Ken and I noticed that the zipper on my pants was down. I zipped them up and said, "See, I wondered why it was so cold." We both laughed so hard we almost cried.
See ya later.

DIRECTIONS: Work with one or more partners to plan and perform two skits for one of the situations described below. In skit one, have the main character react to the situation in a good way, showing that he is able to laugh at himself. In skit two, have the main character react to the situation in a defensive way, showing that he is not able to laugh at himself.

Situation #1: You and your friends are talking at your locker before school. Someone looks down and notices that the snap on your pants is undone. They start to laugh.

Situation #2: You and your family are celebrating your birthday. You end up getting the same gift from three different people.

Situation #3: You and your friends are walking down the hall. You decide to go into the bathroom, but you go into the wrong one. Your friends think your mistake is hysterical!

I Don't Get It!

Picture this: You and three of your friends are playing a board game at your house. One of your friends tells a joke, and everyone starts laughing. You start laughing too, but you don't understand why the joke was supposed to be funny.

If something like this happens to you in real life, don't feel stupid. Not understanding a joke is something that happens to many people!

Here are some things you can do when you do not understand a joke:

1. If you don't feel comfortable admitting that you didn't understand the joke, then laugh and pretend you understand it. Try to remember what the joke was, so you can ask someone you trust to explain it to you later.

2. If you feel comfortable with the person who told you the joke, then tell him you didn't understand and ask him to explain it to you.

Many times, humorous things will happen even when a joke is not told. If you are in a situation when something happens that makes people laugh, and you do not understand what's funny, then you should ask someone you feel comfortable with to explain it to you.

DIRECTIONS: Find at least two jokes or comic strips. You may look in a joke book, or in the comic strip section of a newspaper. If you find a joke, then write it down in the space provided below. If you find a comic strip, then cut it out and tape it below. Explain what is humorous about each one. If you want to show more than two examples, attach them to the back of this page. (Make certain that the joke or comic you share is "safe" humor.)

_____

1)

This is funny because:

_____

2)

This is funny because:

_____

Name:_____

HUMOR Quiz

DIRECTIONS: Judge whether each of the statements below is true or false. Write *T* for true and *F* for false.

_____ 1. It's OK to hurt someone's feelings when telling a joke, as long as it gets a laugh.

_____ 2. Expressing "safe" humor means saying something funny that is not at anyone's expense.

_____ 3. An example of safe humor would be pulling a chair out from under someone.

_____ 4. Attention-seekers usually don't feel very good about themselves.

_____ 5. You probably wouldn't get in trouble for telling a dirty joke during class.

_____ 6. Everyone loves a class clown.

_____ 7. Attention-seekers are usually trying to get people to like them, but they are going about it in the wrong way.

_____ 8. Making fun of a handicapped person is "unsafe" humor.

_____ 9. Humor can help to make a difficult situation easier.

_____10. It is OK to tease people about almost anything.

_____11. People respond differently when it comes to humor.

_____12. It is better to laugh at someone else, than to laugh at yourself.

Discuss as a group, how each of the false statements could be rewritten to be true statements.

HUMOR - HUMOR - HUMOR - HUMOR - HUMOR - HUMOR

1. Explain what it means *to have a good sense of humor.*

   _____

   _____

2. Explain why humor is important in a person's life.

   _____

   _____

3. Describe a situation when you may need to show that you can laugh at yourself at home.

   _____

   _____

4. Tell one way that "safe" humor and "unsafe" humor are the same, and one way they are different.

   (same) _____

   (different) _____

   _____

5. Pretend you have an assignment to design a poster to hang in your school that deals with humor. What would your poster say?

   _____

   _____

6. Read the following story about a guy named Bart, who didn't understand a joke. Evaluate whether you think Bart handled the situation in a good or bad way. Explain your answer.

   > Bart was with his friends Jay and Ron. Ron told a joke. Bart didn't understand it, but laughed anyway so they would think he did understand it. Bart never asked anyone what was funny about the joke.

   _____

   _____

   _____

Dealing With Failure - A

SKILL HOMEWORK ACTIVITY

_____
(Due Date)

Dear Parent or Guardian of: _____

This week we are learning about the social communication skill:

DEALING WITH FAILURE

This social skill is very important in interpersonal relationships.

The students have learned that everyone fails at one time or another. Unfortunately, not everyone deals with failure in a good way. The students have learned the following skill steps for this social skill:

1. Stay calm and be positive. (Avoid negative self-talk.)

2. Think about why you failed.

3. Develop a plan for being successful next time.

4. Try again.

Before the due date, please complete one of the following activities with your son or daughter: (put a check mark by your choice)

_____ A. We acted out the role play situation listed below.

_____ B. I observed my son/daughter using this social skill in a real-life situation. (I have described the situation below.)

Description of real-life observation:

Role play situation:

PRETEND THAT YOU FAILED A MATH EXAM. WHEN YOU GET HOME FROM SCHOOL, YOUR MOM ASKS HOW YOU DID ON THE TEST. DEMONSTRATE WHAT YOU COULD SAY, TO SHOW THAT YOU ARE FOLLOWING THE SKILL STEPS FOR DEALING WITH FAILURE.

Please circle the word below which best describes how your son or daughter did while using this social skill in either the role play or real-life situation.

NEEDS MORE HELP   GOOD   EXCELLENT

It is important for you to reinforce your child's use of this social skill at home in a positive way. Encourage and praise your child when you see the skill appropriately used. Remind him/her to use the social skill when necessary.

Thank you for your assistance.

Sincerely,

* *

PARENT/GUARDIAN SIGNATURE: _____

Name:_____

failure feelings

If you **fail** at something it means *you have been unsuccessful*. Almost everybody hates failing because it can bring about negative feelings.

DIRECTIONS: Write down three negative feelings you might have when you find out you have failed at something.

1.   2.   3.

Many people get negative feelings when they fail and yet, failing is something that happens to EVERYBODY! Failing is one of those things that is just a "part of life" because nobody is perfect. Nobody can achieve everything desired.

A person can:
- fail to pass a test.
- fail to get hired for a job.
- fail to be chosen for an athletic team.
- fail to be elected.

DIRECTIONS: Add to the above list by writing down three more examples of things people can fail at.

1.   2.   3.

This unit is designed to help you deal with failure. It won't help you feel happy about failing, but it will help you deal with failure more positively.

DIRECTIONS: Read each of the sayings below and tell what each one means.

1) *If at first you don't succeed, try, try again.*

(meaning) _____

2) *It is better to have tried and failed than not to have tried at all.*

(meaning) _____

3) *To err is human.*

(meaning) _____

STEP 1

When you find out you have failed at something, the first thing you should do is **STAY CALM AND BE POSITIVE**. Here is a list of four ways to help yourself stay calm:

A - Take a deep breath and let the air out slowly.

B - Count slowly to five or more before saying or doing anything.

C - Tell yourself to calm down.

D - Picture yourself staying calm.

You can help yourself to be positive by using the right kind of "self-talk." **Self-talk** is *all the things you tell yourself inside your head. Self-talk is the thoughts you have about yourself and other people.* There are two different types of self-talk: POSITIVE SELF-TALK and NEGATIVE SELF-TALK. **Negative self-talk** is *when you think bad things about yourself or other people.* **Positive self-talk** is *when you think good things about yourself or other people.* The pictures below show the difference between positive and negative self-talk.

NEGATIVE SELF-TALK   **POSITIVE SELF-TALK**

People give themselves thousands of self-talk messages every day. Some people use mostly negative self-talk, and it makes them feel bad about themselves (powerless). Some people use mostly positive self-talk, and it makes them feel good about themselves (powerful). When you fail at something, it is very important that you use the right kind of self-talk:

Positive Self-Talk

Name:_____

Change It

DIRECTIONS: The following activity will give you practice differentiating between positive and negative self-talk. Rewrite each negative self-talk comment so it is a positive comment. Rewrite each positive self-talk comment so it is a negative comment. The last row is left blank for you to create your own situation.

NEGATIVE SELF-TALK	POSITIVE SELF-TALK
	My friend decided to go out with someone else instead of me. I am a good person — that's her/his loss.
I didn't get hired for the job because I'm no good. Why would someone want to hire me anyway?	
	I failed this test, but I have passed tests before! I'll just have to study more next time. I am a smart person.
We lost the volleyball game because I blew the last serve. I'm a bad person — the team would be better off if I quit.	

Name:_____

STEP 2

Remember! When you fail at something, the first step is to stay calm and be positive. Sometimes it helps to remind yourself of something you have been successful at in the past. For example:

Step Two is to **THINK ABOUT WHY** you failed. There are many reasons why a person might fail at something. For example, if you fail a test it can be because:
- you rushed through it.
- you didn't double-check your work.
- you didn't read directions carefully.
- you didn't study for it.
- you missed many school days.

It is important to think about why you failed, so you can learn from the experience and avoid failing in the future. You must be realistic and specific when you think about why you failed. Read below about Lon, who always blames his failures on other people.

Read below about Tanya, who assumes her failures are because she is stupid, and she never looks for specific reasons for her failures.

REMEMBER! When you think about why you failed at something, you want to be realistic and specific and you don't want to blame your failures on other people.

Name:_____

The Reasons Why

DIRECTIONS: Read each of the situations below about different people who failed. Explain why you think each one failed. Be specific.

1. Darla decided to go out for the volleyball team when she was in ninth grade. She had never been on a volleyball team before, but was pretty excited to try. Most of the other girls who were going out for it had already been on a volleyball team for two years. Darla went to all the practices and really worked hard. She even practiced at home during the weekends. When the coach chose the members of the team, Darla didn't make it. The coach told her that she had really shown improvement, and that she should keep practicing and go out for volleyball again the next year.

   Why do you think Darla failed to make the team? _____

   _____

2. Gordy took a test in French class. He studied for it and felt he was well-prepared. When he got the test and saw how long it was, he was nervous that he might not finish. To save time, he skipped over the directions and didn't double-check his work. He was relieved when he finished the test before the bell rang. When Gordy got his French test back he saw that he had received an "F" on it. The teacher had written a note at the top of the test that said, "Gordy, the directions said to put each of the vocabulary words into a sentence, not to define them."

   Why do you think Gordy failed the French test? _____

   _____

DIRECTIONS: Describe two times you can remember failing at something. Tell why you think you failed.

1) What did you fail at? _____

   _____

   Why did you fail? _____

   _____

2) What did you fail at? _____

   _____

   Why did you fail? _____

   _____

Name:_____

STEP 3

Do you remember the first two skill steps for dealing with failure?

(step one) _____

(step two) _____

Step Three is to **DEVELOP A PLAN** for being successful next time. If you want to avoid failing again, it is very important to decide what you will do differently the next time you try.

DIRECTIONS:
1. Read what Mark said to his friend George while they were talking on the phone.

2. Draw a circle around the words Mark used when he talked about staying calm and positive.

3. Draw a rectangle around the words Mark used when he talked about the reason why he failed.

4. Draw a line under the words Mark used when he developed a plan for being successful the next time he tries.

Name:_____

Developing Plans...

DIRECTIONS: 1. Read each situation below about people who failed and the reasons why they failed.

2. Work with a partner to develop a plan for each person to follow to be more successful in the future.

3. When everyone is finished, compare the plans you developed with the plans the others have developed.

Situation 1: Trudy did not get a date for the dance and wished that she had. Everyone thinks of her as the "class clown" because she is always doing stupid things during class to get a laugh. It's hard for any of the guys to take her seriously.

Plan: _____

_____

Situation 2: Manwell failed his science test. He had wanted to study, but there were always other things that would come up. He never sat down to study until 10:30 p.m. and by that time he was too tired to concentrate. Manwell wished he wasn't such a procrastinator.

Plan: _____

_____

Situation 3: Paul didn't get hired for the summer job he wanted. He was so nervous during the interview that he couldn't look at the boss. He stared at the floor or his hands most of the time and spoke too quietly.

Plan: _____

_____

Situation 4: Nancy got cut from the basketball team and was pretty upset about it. She really tried hard during practice, but every time she made a mistake, she would get embarrassed and laugh. Laughing made her look like she wasn't taking the game seriously.

Plan: _____

_____

Name:_____

STEP 4

DIRECTIONS: Write down the first three skill steps for dealing with failure.

(step one) _____

(step two) _____

(step three)_____

Step Four is to **TRY AGAIN**! The worst thing you can do when you fail at something is to give up. Unfortunately, "Give-Up Gail" isn't very good at Step Four. Read some of the things "Give-Up Gail" says during the school day below.

Unless she changes, "Give-Up Gail" probably won't accomplish much because she gives up too easily.

When you talk to people who are very successful at something, such as professional athletes, you will find they were not born champions. They had to work hard and face many failures to get where they are.

DIRECTIONS: Think of a person whom you consider to be successful at something (e.g., successful in sports, successful at a job). Interview that person by asking the questions listed below, to find out feelings about failure. Take notes on what the person says.

1. Were you always as good at _____ as you are now, or did it take a lot of practice?

2. Did you have any failures along the way that you can remember?

3. How do you deal with failure?

4. Do you believe in the saying, "If at first you don't succeed, try, try again"?

5. To what do you owe your success?

EDUCATOR PAGE: DO NOT DUPLICATE FOR STUDENTS

DIRECTIONS: 1) Cut apart the cards on the third page of this activity. Place them face down in a stack.

2) Choose four students in your group to play the parts of skill steps 1, 2, 3, and 4 (hereafter referred to as person one, person two, person three and person four). Choose a fifth person to play the part of someone who has failed at something (hereafter referred to as contestant). If you have fewer than five students in your group, then have the students play the parts for more than one skill step.

3) Have the students who are "playing the parts" of the skill steps stand or sit in a row. Cut apart the cue cards below. Give cue card one to person one, cue card two to person two, and so on.

#1	#2
SKILL STEP 1: **STAY CALM AND BE POSITIVE** "Stay calm! Take a deep breath and slowly count to five. Tell yourself to stay calm and picture yourself that way. What could you say to yourself that would be positive self-talk?"	**SKILL STEP 2:** **THINK ABOUT WHY YOU FAILED** "Why do you think you failed in this situation?"
#3	#4
SKILL STEP 3: **DEVELOP A PLAN FOR BEING SUCCESSFUL NEXT TIME** "Exactly what will you do differently so you can be successful next time?"	**SKILL STEP 4:** **TRY AGAIN!** "'If at first you don't succeed, try, try again.' Will you try again?"

4) The person chosen to be the contestant should go to the stack of cards, draw the card on top, and read aloud what it says. The card will tell what the person failed at and the reason for the failure.

5) Next, the contestant should walk over to person one. Person one should ask the contestant the question written on his/her cue card. The contestant should answer the question correctly, and then walk over to person two. Play should continue in this fashion, until the contestant has gone through all four skill steps.

6) If the contestant is unable to answer one of the questions, other members of the group may offer help/suggestions. The contestant must, however, put the answer in his/her own words before advancing to the next skill step.

7) After the contestant walks to all four persons' skill steps, and correctly answers all questions, he/she should receive some type of reward (e.g., a badge, a certificate, points, candy).

8) Continue the activity until everyone in your group has had a chance to "play the parts" of the contestant and all four skill steps. (You may want to rotate every student through this activity over a period of several class periods.)

You took last place in the 220 yard dash at the track meet. Your tried your best and practiced hard, but everyone else was better than you.	You failed your math quiz. The teacher put the problems on the blackboard and you couldn't see them because you refuse to wear your glasses.
You failed your English worksheet because you didn't follow the directions.	You failed to get a part in the school play you tried out for because everyone else trying out was more experienced than you were.
You didn't get elected to be on the student council because you didn't have any publicity to let people know you were running.	You failed to get invited to the party you were hoping you could go to. You weren't invited because you've been a real gossip lately.
You failed the driver education written test because you didn't memorize any of the information in the manual.	You failed your science test because you have "test anxiety." Whenever you take a big test, you get so nervous that you can't think.
You didn't get hired for the part-time job you wanted because you looked sloppy at the interview.	You didn't get the raise you were hoping for at work because you don't work very hard when you are at your job.

©1989 THINKING PUBLICATIONS

SSS: Social Skill Strategies (Book B)

Name:_____

DEALING WITH FAILURE - DEALING WITH FAILURE

1. Define *failure* and write down the four skill steps for dealing with failure in a good way.

   (failure) _____

   (step 1) _____

   (step 2) _____

   (step 3) _____

   (step 4) _____

2. Decide if the following statement is true or false and explain why.

   If a person really tries hard, it is possible to avoid ever failing at anything again.
   TRUE   FALSE

   (reason)_____

   _____

3. Describe a situation at home, at school, and in the community when you might fail at something.

   (home) _____

   (school) _____

   (community) _____

4. Compare yourself to "Give-Up Gail." Are you similar to her or different from her?
   _____ Explain your answer.

   _____

   _____

5. Think of a strategy to help you remember the four skill steps for dealing with failure.

   _____

   _____

6. Evaluate one of the members of your family. Does he/she usually deal with failure in a good way or a bad way? Explain your answer.

   _____

   _____

   _____

SKILL HOMEWORK ACTIVITY

_____
(Due Date)

Dear Parent or Guardian of: _____

This week we are learning about the social communication skill:

EXPRESSING AFFECTION

This social skill is very important in interpersonal relationships.

The students have learned the following skill steps for this social skill:

1. Decide if you have a feeling of attachment or caring for another person.

2. Decide if you would like to express your affection.

   If *YES*

3. Choose a good time, place, and way to express your affection.

Before the due date, please complete one of the following activities with your son or daughter: (put a check mark by your choice)

_____ A. We acted out the role play situation listed below.

_____ B. I observed my son/daughter using this social skill in a real-life situation. (I have described the situation below.)

Description of real-life observation:

Role play situation:

PRETEND YOUR SISTER HAS BEEN REALLY NICE TO YOU LATELY. DEMONSTRATE WHAT YOU COULD DO AND/OR SAY TO EXPRESS YOUR AFFECTION TO HER.

- -

Please circle the word below which best describes how your son or daughter did while using this social skill in either the role play or real-life situation.

NEEDS MORE HELP   GOOD   EXCELLENT

It is important for you to reinforce your child's use of this social skill at home in a positive way. Encourage and praise your child when you see the skill appropriately used. Remind him/her to use the social skill when necessary.

Thank you for your assistance.

Sincerely,

* *

PARENT/GUARDIAN SIGNATURE: _____

Name:_____

Affection Doesn't Have To Be Romance

Affection means *a feeling of attachment and caring one person has for another.*

Feelings of affection can include romantic feelings you have for a member of the opposite sex — the way a boy feels about his girlfriend or the way a woman feels about her husband.

Feelings of affection do not have to be romantic feelings, however. A person can feel affection or love for a parent, but those feelings are not romantic feelings.

DIRECTIONS: Add to the list below, other people you can feel affection towards.

1. *Brother*
2. *Friend*
3.
4.
5.
6.
7.
8.
9.
10.

Name:_____

Why Bother?

If you feel affection for another person, it is a good idea to express your feelings to him/her because:

1. You shouldn't assume people know how you feel. Sometimes people don't know exactly how you feel unless you tell them.

2. You feel good when you express your affection for another person.

3. Expressing your affection may help to improve your relationship with the person.

4. Expressing your affection can make the person you care about feel good.

Can you think of any other positive benefits of expressing affection?

Can you think of any situations when you may NOT want to express your affection to another person?

DIRECTIONS: Read the script below and discuss it as a group. It is a conversation between Luke and his guidance counselor, Mrs. Ernst. Luke's father died about three years ago. He has been feeling bad about something ever since, and he is talking about his feelings.

Mrs. Ernst: It sounds as though you really admired your father.

Luke: I sure did! I really miss him.

Mrs. Ernst: You said you've been feeling bad about something. Do you want to share your feelings with me?

Luke: I guess I feel guilty because I never told him how I felt about him.

Mrs. Ernst: I'm sure your father knew how you felt.

Luke: Maybe not! I can't remember ever telling him that I loved him. Now I'll never get a chance.

Mrs. Ernst: Luke, there are many ways to express your affection to someone. You can express your affection in words or through your actions. I know there were many things you did that let your father know you loved him.

Luke: I guess so. But still, I'd feel better if I had told him.

(Luke and Mrs. Ernst continue their conversation)

Name:_____

Words ╬ Actions!

There are many ways you can express your affection for another person, and those ways can be put into two categories: **WORDS** and **ACTIONS**.

DIRECTIONS: Work as a group to complete the table below. The first two rows have been completed as examples.

THE PERSON YOU FEEL AFFECTION FOR	WHAT YOU COULD DO TO EXPRESS YOUR AFFECTION THROUGH YOUR *ACTIONS*	WHAT YOU COULD SAY TO EXPRESS YOUR AFFECTION THROUGH YOUR *WORDS*
Your mother	Buy her flowers on Mother's Day.	Say, "You know what? You're a pretty cool mom!"
Your favorite teacher	Give him/her a birthday card.	Say, "I've really enjoyed having you for a teacher."
Your pet		
Your boy/girl friend		
Your sister		
Your best friend		

EXAMPLES ➤ ➤

3 Things To Remember

The social skill of expressing affection can be broken down into the following three skill steps:

---

1. Decide if you have a feeling of attachment or caring for another person.

2. Decide if you would like to express your affection.

If *YES*

3. Choose a good time, place, and way to express your affection.

DIRECTIONS: As a group, brainstorm responses to the following problems.

1. Think of times and places when it would not be appropriate to express affection to your parents.

2. Think of times and places when it would be appropriate to express affection to your boss.

3. Think of times and places when it would not be appropriate to express affection to a teacher.

4. Think of some inappropriate things people sometimes do when they do not know how to express affection appropriately.

EDUCATOR PAGE: DO NOT DUPLICATE FOR STUDENTS

PURPOSE: Some of your students may have a difficult time expressing affection to their parents or other significant adults in their lives. This activity is designed to promote positive expression of affection between your students and the adults who are most important to them.

DISCUSSION: Ask your students to think about the last time they expressed affection to one of their parents or some other significant adult in their lives.

Ask your students to think about the last time one of their parents (or some other significant adult) expressed affection to them.

Ask your students to brainstorm reasons why it may have been a long time since either of the above has happened.

ACTIVITY: 1. Ask your students to write or tape a message to one of their parents (or both) or to some other significant adult. Their message should include an expression of their affection or a positive comment. If your students have a difficult time creating their own message, try one of the following:

   • Have a private discussion with the student and ask the student to share things he likes about the selected adult while you write the comments made.

   • Have the student pick out a greeting card that expresses positive feelings, and have the student sign it.

2. Encourage your students to deliver their message to the person it was created for, but do not make it mandatory.

EDUCATOR PAGE: DO NOT DUPLICATE FOR STUDENTS

Chances are great that you have students who are similar to those described below:

1. Tami chases after boys during lunch recess. If she catches a boy, she kisses him. The kids at school avoid Tami because she expresses romantic affection in such an inappropriate way.

2. Jason is a passive, withdrawn boy who likes girls but is afraid to even talk to members of the opposite sex.

3. Whenever Jamie feels romantic affection for a girl, he starts acting strange around her. His actions either make the girl think he doesn't like her or they result in her feeling angry.

4. Trudy leads you to believe that she is sexually active and openly discusses her activities with people at school.

The students described above have not yet learned to express romantic affection in an appropriate manner. Since vast differences exist within your students, this social skill unit has been designed to focus on nonromantic affection.

The educator is, however, encouraged to meet the *individual* needs for each of their students in the area of expressing romantic affection. There are numerous resources available which can help the educator deal with the topic of romantic affection and/or sexuality. A few are listed below.

Resource Agency

Alan Guttmacher Institute (AGI)
A220 19th Street, N.W. Suite 305
Washington, D.C. 20036

Curriculum

Human Sexuality: Values & Choices
By: John Forliti, Lucy Kapp, Sandy Naughton, Lynn Youna
Search Institute
122 West Franklin Avenue
Minneapolis, Minnesota 55404

Teen Journals

Choices - A Teen Woman's Journal For Self-Awareness And Personal Planning
Challenges - A Teen Man's Journal For Self-Awareness And Personal Planning
By: Mindy Bingham, Judy Edmondson, and Sandy Stryker
Advocacy Press
P.O. Box 236
Santa Barbara, California 93102

Video Tapes

Choices: The Mating Game
Ounce of Prevention Fund
188 West Randolph, Suite 2200
Chicago, Illinois 60601

The Subject Is AIDS
(Edited version of: *Sex, Drugs, AIDS*)
ODN Productions
74 Verick South
New York, NY 10013

It Only Takes Once
(Produced by Pacific Northwest Bell and Leadership Tomorrow)
Inter-Media
1600 Dexter North
Seattle, WA 98109

The educator may want to consider describing the four students listed above to his/her students. Discussion should then focus on **why** the students described are not expressing romantic affection appropriately.

EXPRESSING AFFECTION - EXPRESSING AFFECTION

1. Define the social skill of expressing affection and tell the three skill steps.

   (definition) _____

   _____

   (step 1) _____

   (step 2) _____

   (step 3) _____

2. Explain why it is important to express affection.

   _____

   _____

3. Describe a situation when you may want to express affection at school and at home.

   (school) _____

   (home) _____

4. Explain the difference between romantic affection and nonromantic affection.

   _____

   _____

5. List two reasons why it may be difficult for someone to express affection.

   a. _____

   b. _____

6. Think about either your mom or dad. Does she/he more often express affection through actions, words, or both? Explain your answer.

   _____

   _____

SKILL HOMEWORK ACTIVITY

_____
(Due Date)

Dear Parent or Guardian of: _____

This week we are learning about the social communication skill:

DEALING WITH DISAPPOINTMENT

This social skill is very important in interpersonal relationships.

Disappointment is the negative feeling you get when something doesn't work out as planned or when you feel someone has let you down. This social skill can be broken down into the following skill steps:

1. Decide why you are disappointed.

2. Plan a way to ease your disappointment (e.g., talk to someone about your feeling, make different plans).

Before the due date, please complete one of the following activities with your son or daughter: (put a check mark by your choice)

_____ A. We acted out the role play situation listed below.

_____ B. I observed my son/daughter using this social skill in a real-life situation. (I have described the situation below.)

Description of real-life observation:

Role play situation:

PRETEND YOU ARE VERY EXCITED BECAUSE YOU ARE GOING CAMPING WITH YOUR FRIEND'S FAMILY THIS WEEKEND. YOU HAVE BEEN LOOKING FORWARD TO IT FOR WEEKS. WHEN YOU GET HOME FROM SCHOOL, ONE OF YOUR PARENTS TELLS YOU THE TRIP HAS BEEN CANCELLED BECAUSE YOUR FRIEND'S DAD IS SICK. DEMONSTRATE WHAT YOU COULD DO OR SAY TO DEAL WITH YOUR DISAPPOINTMENT IN A GOOD WAY.

Please circle the word below which best describes how your son or daughter did while using this social skill in either the role play or real-life situation.

NEEDS MORE HELP   GOOD   EXCELLENT

It is important for you to reinforce your child's use of this social skill at home in a positive way. Encourage and praise your child when you see the skill appropriately used. Remind him/her to use the social skill when necessary.

Thank you for your assistance.

Sincerely,

* *

PARENT/GUARDIAN SIGNATURE: _____

It's Disappointing

Disappointment is *the negative feeling you get when something doesn't work out as planned, or when you feel someone has let you down.* For example, pretend that your aunt has been telling you all month about how much you are going to love the birthday present she got for you. You have been very eager for your birthday so you can see what her gift is. Your birthday finally arrives. When you open the box from your aunt, you see a very outdated pair of pants that you would be embarrassed to wear to school. Of course, you wouldn't want to let your aunt know, but the feeling you have inside is disappointment and it doesn't feel very good.

DIRECTIONS: Read or listen to the story below, about Will and his disappointment. Answer the questions at the end of the story.

> Ever since the first day of school, when Will first saw Annette, he had been trying to work up the courage to talk to her. Will had Annette in two of his classes. Every day he would look over at her and think about talking to her, but he never could seem to do it.
>
> One day, his friend Adam asked Will if he wanted to come to a hayride he was having at his farm that weekend. Adam said he was inviting a bunch of friends from school and that they could roast hotdogs and marshmallows afterwards. When Will found out that Annette was going to be there, he thought to himself, "This will be my chance to talk to her."
>
> Will was so excited to go on the hayride, that he bought a new pair of pants to wear. He even planned what he would say when he talked to Annette during the ride.
>
> The day of the hayride finally arrived. When Will got to Adam's farm, he didn't see Annette anywhere. He asked Adam where she was and he said, "She called to say she couldn't come because she has the flu."

QUESTIONS:

1. What do you think Will felt like when he found out Annette wasn't coming?

2. What do you think Will's body language looked like when he found out Annette wasn't coming?

Everyone is disappointed from time to time. This unit will help you learn how to deal with disappointment when it happens to you.

Name:_____

Causes For Disappointment

The disappointments that you will face in your life can be grouped into three categories. You can be disappointed in yourself, you can be disappointed in other people, or you can be disappointed in an object or thing.

DIRECTIONS: Add three more examples to each column in the following table.

	SITUATIONS WHEN YOU ARE DISAPPOINTED IN YOURSELF	SITUATIONS WHEN YOU ARE DISAPPOINTED IN SOMEONE ELSE	SITUATIONS WHEN YOU ARE DISAPPOINTED IN AN OBJECT OR THING
EXAMPLES →	You are disappointed because you did not do well on your book report.	You are disappointed in a friend because she broke a promise to you.	You are disappointed in a movie because you did not think it was very good.
→	You are disappointed because you forgot to do something important.	You are disappointed in your older brother because he got stopped by the police for drunk driving.	You are disappointed in the meal you ordered at a restaurant because you did not like how it tasted.

DUMP Your Disappointment

The social skill of dealing with disappointment can be broken down into two skill steps:

1) Decide why you are disappointed.
2) Plan a way to ease your disappointment.

Skill step two is especially important, because when you are disappointed, you do not want to sit around and think about how bad you feel. If you do that, you will just make yourself feel worse. Sometimes you can ease your disappointment by talking to someone about it, or by planning something fun to do.

DIRECTIONS: Read the comments below to find out what other people do to ease their disappointment.

Write down two things you could do to deal with the disappointment in each of the following situations.

1. You are planning to do something fun outside, but it starts raining.

    (1) _____

    (2) _____

2. Your friend was supposed to go shopping with you, but forgot all about it.

    (1) _____

    (2) _____

3. You really wanted to win the basketball game, but your team didn't play very well.

    (1) _____

    (2) _____

EDUCATOR PAGE: DO NOT DUPLICATE FOR STUDENTS

DIRECTIONS: Give a piece of unlined paper to each of your students. Make certain that each has something to draw with. Ask your students to sit comfortably in their chairs, with their spines straight but relaxed, their feet flat on the floor, and their hands in a resting position. You may want to turn off some or all of the lights in the room to make it a more peaceful environment. Read the script below to your students, in a relaxed and slow manner. The script is a guided visualization/imagery session for dealing with disappointment.

Close your eyes and on the count of three take a very slow, deep breath. One . . . two . . . three . . . inhale slowly . . . hold it . . . and now exhale slowly. Let all the air out. As you do this, you should feel your body relaxing. Take another slow, deep breath . . . only this time imagine that you are breathing in very clean, cool, relaxed air and that you are breathing out all the tension and tiredness you have in your muscles. Ready? One . . . two . . . three . . . take a slow . . . deep breath . . . hold it . . . and now exhale slowly. Remember to imagine that you are breathing in relaxed, clean air . . . and that when you exhale . . . you are letting go of all the tiredness and tension in your body . . . Take a minute to concentrate on your deep, slow breathing (pause) . . . Now, you are going to imagine yourself traveling back to a time when you were very disappointed. It may have been a time when you were feeling very disappointed in yourself, or disappointed in someone else. Maybe it was a time when you were disappointed because things did not work out the way you had expected them to . . . Try to relive this experience with all your feelings and senses . . . Try to imagine the person or people you were with . . . or maybe you were alone . . . Try to imagine what your disappointment felt like (pause) . . . Now, travel throughout your entire body collecting those feelings of disappointment . . . start pressing those negative feelings into a small ball . . . As you continue traveling through your body, and you find more feelings of disappointment, add them to the ball you are forming . . . Now take a minute to complete your journey so that you are holding all the disappointment you could find in the ball in your hands . . . Now take the ball of disappointment and imagine yourself throwing it far, far away . . . Concentrate on how your body feels, now that all the disappointment has been taken away . . . Do you feel happy? . . . Relaxed? . . . Are the sights and sounds around you comfortable? . . . Now prepare yourself to return to the classroom . . . On the count of three you will open your eyes and you will be able to draw a picture of the ball of disappointment traveling through the air to a far away place . . . One . . . two . . . three . . . Open your eyes and begin to draw your picture. Remember to try to make your picture as detailed as possible. If you want to add words to your picture you may do so.

DIRECTIONS: Encourage your students to use this visualization technique on their own when they are feeling disappointed.

DEALING WITH DISAPPOINTMENT

1. Explain what *disappointment* means, and write down the two skill steps for dealing with disappointment in an appropriate way.

   (definition) _____

   _____

   (step 1) _____

   _____

   (step 2) _____

2. Explain why it is not a good idea to sit and think about how miserable you feel when you are disappointed.

   _____

   _____

3. Describe a situation at home, at school, and in the community when you might feel disappointed.

   (home) _____

   (school) _____

   (community) _____

4. Explain how being disappointed in yourself is different from being disappointed in the weather.

   _____

   _____

5. Create a list of three things you could do to ease your disappointment if you were planning to sleep over at a friend's house, but your friend got sick.

   (1) _____

   (2) _____

   (3) _____

6. On a scale of 1 to 10 (one being poor and 10 being good), rate your ability to deal with disappointment appropriately. _____ Explain your answer.

   (explanation) _____

   _____

   _____

SKILL HOMEWORK ACTIVITY

_____
(Due Date)

Dear Parent or Guardian of: _____

This week we are learning about the social communication skill:

UNDERSTANDING THE FEELINGS OF OTHERS

This social skill is very important in interpersonal relationships.

The students have learned that it is very important to recognize and understand the feelings of others. They will get along better with people when they learn to do this, because they will say the right thing at the right time and place.

Before the due date, please complete one of the following activities with your son or daughter: (put a check mark by your choice)

_____ A. We acted out the role play situation listed below.

_____ B. I observed my son/daughter using this social skill in a real-life situation. (I have described the situation below.)

Description of real-life observation:

Role play situation:

YOUR MOTHER HAS JUST ARRIVED HOME FROM WORK. SHE LOOKS VERY TIRED AND UPSET. SHE TELLS YOU THAT SHE WAS FIRED FROM HER JOB TODAY. DEMONSTRATE WHAT YOU WILL SAY TO HER.

- -

Please circle the word below which best describes how your son or daughter did while using this social skill in either the role play or real-life situation.

NEEDS MORE HELP   GOOD   EXCELLENT

It is important for you to reinforce your child's use of this social skill at home in a positive way. Encourage and praise your child when you see the skill appropriately used. Remind him/her to use the social skill when necessary.

Thank you for your assistance.

Sincerely,

* *

PARENT/GUARDIAN SIGNATURE: _____

Understanding Others' Feelings

DIRECTIONS: 1. Read the information below about understanding the feelings of others.
2. Copy the information into your notebook the way it appears on this page. Think about each part of it as your write it.

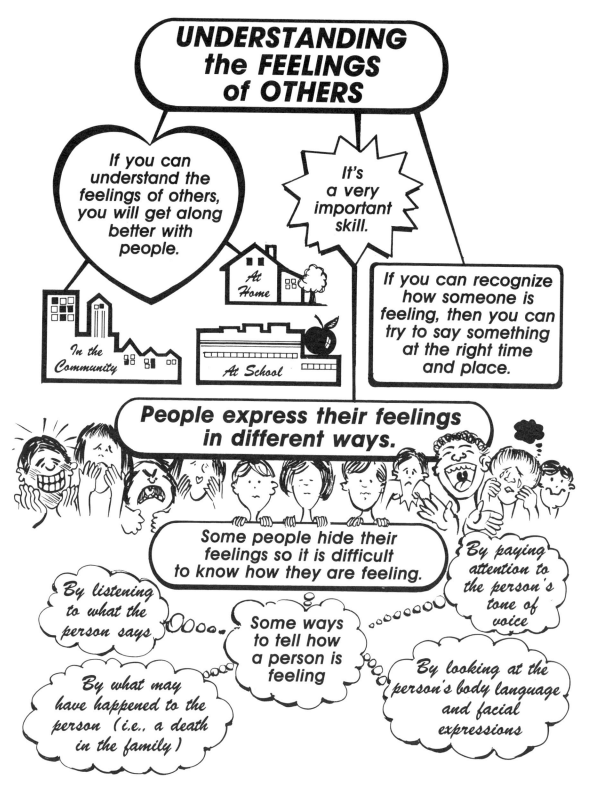

UNDERSTANDING the FEELINGS of OTHERS

If you can understand the feelings of others, you will get along better with people.

It's a very important skill.

If you can recognize how someone is feeling, then you can try to say something at the right time and place.

At Home

In the Community

At School

People express their feelings in different ways.

Some people hide their feelings so it is difficult to know how they are feeling.

By listening to what the person says

Some ways to tell how a person is feeling

By paying attention to the person's tone of voice

By what may have happened to the person (i.e., a death in the family)

By looking at the person's body language and facial expressions

OTHERS' FEELINGS

DIRECTIONS: Look at each picture. Describe how you think the person in each picture is feeling.

How do you think Ben is feeling?
Why?

How do you think Dana is feeling?
Why?

How do you think Maria is feeling?
Why?

How do you think Mr. Link is feeling?
Why?

Name:_____

PEOPLE OBSERVATION

DIRECTIONS: Observe various people for the next few days. Try to determine how they are feeling by the body language they use and by their tone of voice. Complete the chart below.

EXAMPLE →

PERSON OBSERVED	BODY LANGUAGE OBSERVED	TONE OF VOICE	HOW THE PERSON SEEMED TO BE FEELING
Science teacher	Big smile "Bouncy"	Sounded higher and happier than usual.	In a really good mood.

Name:_____

Situation Cards

DIRECTIONS: These cards may be used in any manner the educator and students desire:

Renaldo just got his report card and he received three *F*'s on it. Renaldo is feeling very worried and upset. Demonstrate what Renaldo's body language would look like and what he might say to his mother.	Patty just found out that she got the part in the play she had tried out for. She is very excited. Demonstrate what Patty's body language would look like and what she might say to her friend.
Mrs. Martin is trying to teach an important lesson, but two students in the class keep fooling around. Mrs. Martin is feeling frustrated. Demonstrate what Mrs. Martin's body language would look like and what she might say to the students.	Jay just found out his parents are getting a divorce. Jay is very upset. Demonstrate what Jay's body language would look like and what Jay might say to his friend.
Tanya was just in a big fight with her boyfriend. She thinks he likes someone else. Demonstrate what Tanya's body language would look like and what she might say to her sister.	Mr. Morris just found out that he is being laid off from his job. He does not know when or if he will be called back to work again. Mr. Morris is very worried. Demonstrate what Mr. Morris' body language would look like and what he might say to his family.
Joey does not understand the math assignment he is supposed to be working on. He is feeling very stupid and frustrated. Demonstrate what Joey's body language would look like and what he might say to the teacher.	Jill just got an *A* on her science test. She is proud of herself, but she is worried that the other kids will tease her about being a "teacher's pet." Demonstrate what Jill's body language would look like and what she might say to her friend.
Mr. Toma's mother died yesterday. He is feeling very sad. Demonstrate what Mr. Toma's body language would look like and what he might say to his boss.	Julio is overweight and often gets teased by the other students. Julio just tripped in the hallway. Julio is feeling very embarrassed. Demonstrate what Julio's body language would look like and what he might say to the students around him.
Mrs. Blair just found some drugs in her daughter's bedroom. Mrs. Blair is feeling very scared and upset. Demonstrate what Mrs. Blair's body language would look like and what she might say to her daughter.	Kelly's best friend just moved to another town. Kelly is feeling very sad and lonely. Demonstrate what Kelly's body language would look like and what she might say to her brother.

WRONG, WRONG, WRONG

DIRECTIONS: Read each situation below about Oscar Oddball. In each situation, Oscar fails to recognize/understand how other people are feeling. For each situation, tell what you think Oscar SHOULD have said or done and WHY.

1. It was almost time for math class to start. Oscar was waiting for the teacher to get to class. The teacher came rushing into class just as the bell rang. She looked upset. She quickly went to her desk and began searching for something. Oscar walked up to the teacher and said, "I don't think it was fair that you only gave me a *D* on my project."

   _____

   _____

   _____

2. Oscar was walking home with his friend Glen. Some older boys rode past them and shouted, "Glen, you big fat slob!" Glen looked really upset. Oscar said, "You really should go on a diet, Glen."

   _____

   _____

   _____

3. Oscar walked into his house. His mom was sitting at the table. She looked very happy and excited when she said, "Oscar, guess what? I just got hired as a waitress at Big John's Restaurant. I get to start work tomorrow. Isn't it great?" Oscar just shrugged his shoulders and walked out of the room.

   _____

   _____

   _____

4. Oscar was walking down the hall when he saw his friend Lisa crying. Oscar asked, "What's the matter, Lisa? Did your boyfriend finally dump you?"

   _____

   _____

   _____

5. Oscar's younger brother, Ollie, told Oscar that he had accidently broken Oscar's new cassette tape. Ollie apologized and told Oscar he would pay for it. Ollie looked like he really felt bad. Oscar said, "You big jerk! You're so careless. You break everything you touch. I'll never let you use my things again."

_____

_____

_____

6. Oscar was standing with some of his friends before school. Two of his friends, Tim and Tom, were in a big argument. Oscar stepped in between them and said, "You both think you are so tough! I could take on either one of you."

_____

_____

_____

7. Oscar was sitting at lunch with his friend Heather. Heather told Oscar that she thought her parents were going to get a divorce. She looked very upset. Oscar asked Heather if she had ever heard the joke about the man and the cow.

_____

_____

_____

8. Oscar was walking down the hallway. He saw a girl he knew trip and fall on the stairs. She looked around to see who had seen her fall. She looked very embarrassed. Oscar started to laugh and said, "Wait until I tell everyone how funny you looked."

_____

_____

_____

How Are You Feeling?

DIRECTIONS: Choose one of the projects below to do. Ask your teacher for help if you do not understand what to do.

The project I chose is: (✔ one)	Projects
	Project A - Write a poem(s) about how people feel.
	Project B - Write out the words to a song that describes how someone is feeling. Then explain in your own words how the person in the song is feeling.
	Project C - Watch a television show. Choose one of the characters in the show. Throughout the show, describe the different ways the character is feeling and tell why you think he or she is feeling that way.
	Project D - Choose a character from a story or book you have recently read. Choose one of the characters and describe the different ways that character feels throughout the story.
	Project E - Design your own project that deals with how people feel. Be sure to get it approved by your teacher before you begin.

UNDERSTANDING THE FEELINGS OF OTHERS

1. Write three things that can help you to recognize how a person is feeling.

   (#1) _____

   (#2) _____

   (#3) _____

2. Explain why it's important to recognize and understand the feelings of others.

   _____

   _____

   _____

3. Give an example from the past week of a time when you understood how someone was feeling.

   _____

   _____

4. Compare the way two different people you know express anger.

   (person #1) _____

   _____

   (person #2) _____

   _____

5. Write a short story about a person who didn't recognize how another person was feeling and ended up saying or doing the wrong thing. (Use the back of this page if you need more space.)

   _____

   _____

   _____

   _____

6. Tell how good you think you are at recognizing the feelings of others. Explain your answer and describe some ways you can improve your understanding of the feelings of others.

   _____

   _____

   _____

   _____

APPENDICES

Social Communication Skills Rating Scale

(Adult Form)

Name of student: _____ Grade:_____

Age:_____ Date rating scale completed: _____

Name of person completing rating scale: _____

Relationship with student (e.g., parent, case-
manager, regular education teacher): _____

_____

DIRECTIONS: Rate this student on how well he/she uses the following social skills. Circle:
1 - If the skill is NEVER used correctly.
2 - If the skill is SELDOM used correctly.
3 - If the skill is SOMETIMES used correctly.
4 - If the skill is OFTEN used correctly.
5 - If the skill is ALWAYS used correctly.

For example: A student who **usually** speaks too loudly would be rated as follows:

VOLUME - Speaks at a volume that is   1 (2) 3 4 5
appropriate to the situation.

Please give examples/comments when appropriate (e.g., if you give a low rating for volume, you should explain if the student speaks too softly, or too loudly).

_____

Social Communication Skill   **Rating**

Social Communication Skill	Never	Seldom	Sometimes	Often	Always
A-1. EYE CONTACT - Looks at the person he/she is speaking with when appropriate.	1	2	3	4	5
A-2. MANNERS - Uses manners, such as saying "please" and "thank you" in social situations.	1	2	3	4	5
A-3. VOLUME - Speaks at a volume that is appropriate to the situation. (Speaks with a normal volume, softer volume, and louder volume when necessary.)	1	2	3	4	5
A-4. TIME AND PLACE - Chooses a good time and place before beginning a conversation with another person.	1	2	3	4	5

			Never	Seldom	Sometimes	Often	Always

A-5. TONE OF VOICE - Uses a tone of voice which is pleasant. Is not sarcastic or disrespectful.   1 2 3 4 5

A-6. GETTING TO THE POINT - Does not "beat around the bush." Brings up the main point of his/her conversations when appropriate.   1 2 3 4 5

A-7. STAYING ON TOPIC AND SWITCHING TOPICS - Sticks to the topic of conversation or prepares the listener for a topic shift.   1 2 3 4 5

A-8. LISTENING - Gives his/her full attention to a speaker in order to understand the meaning of the message.   1 2 3 4 5

A-9. STARTING AND ENDING A CONVERSATION - Takes the initiative to start a conversation. Begins with a greeting and name. Ends a conversation smoothly and with a farewell.   1 2 3 4 5

A-10. PROXIMITY - Stands at a proper distance (not too close and not too far) while talking to a person.   1 2 3 4 5

A-11. BODY LANGUAGE - Uses body language (expression of feelings with body parts) which is appropriate to the situation.   1 2 3 4 5

A-12. MAKING A GOOD IMPRESSION - His/her actions, appearance, and personal qualities make other people think favorably about him/her.   1 2 3 4 5

A-13. FORMAL/INFORMAL LANGUAGE - Talks in a more "traditional" way and uses the longer forms of words when speaking to people in respected positions. Talks in a more "relaxed" way, by using shorter forms of words and slang, when speaking to peers and adults he/she feels close to.   1 2 3 4 5

A-14. GIVING REASONS - Gives reasons which are specific and relevant when answering questions.   1 2 3 4 5

A-15. PLANNING WHAT TO SAY - Thinks about what he/she will say before speaking.   1 2 3 4 5

A-16. INTERRUPTING - Interrupts in an appropriate way and only when necessary.   1 2 3 4 5

A-17. GIVING A COMPLIMENT - Remembers to compliment others, and is honest when doing so.   1 2 3 4 5

A-18. ACCEPTING A COMPLIMENT - Accepts compliments by saying "thank you."   1 2 3 4 5

A-19. SAYING *THANK YOU* - Expresses appreciation when someone has done something nice.   1 2 3 4 5

©1989 THINKING PUBLICATIONS
Duplication allowed for educational use only.

SSS: SOCIAL SKILL STRATEGIES (Book B)

		Never	Seldom	Sometimes	Often	Always

A-20. INTRODUCING YOURSELF - Introduces him/herself to a new person. Remembers to give his/her name when doing so. 1 2 3 4 5

A-21. INTRODUCING TWO PEOPLE TO EACH OTHER - Helps two people who do not know each other to learn each other's name. (Makes the introduction reciprocal. For example, "Steve, meet Beth. Beth, meet Steve.") 1 2 3 4 5

A-22. MAKING A REQUEST - Remembers to ask instead of demand when he/she wants something. 1 2 3 4 5

A-23. OFFERING HELP - Offers help to people in need. Remembers to ask first instead of just "taking over." 1 2 3 4 5

A-24. ASKING FOR HELP - Asks for help when needed, but attempts something on his/her own first. 1 2 3 4 5

A-25. ASKING PERMISSION - Asks for permission from authority figures. 1 2 3 4 5

A-26. ACCEPTING NO - Responds appropriately when told no by an authority figure. 1 2 3 4 5

A-27. MAKING AN APOLOGY - Says he/she is sorry when appropriate. 1 2 3 4 5

A-28. STATING AN OPINION - Does not try to pass his/her opinion off as a fact. 1 2 3 4 5

A-29. AGREEING/DISAGREEING - Disagrees without putting down the other person's idea/opinion. Doesn't get angry when someone disagrees with him/her. 1 2 3 4 5

A-30. CONVINCING OTHERS - Provides good reasons when trying to convince others. 1 2 3 4 5

A-31. GIVING INFORMATION - Is precise and easy to understand when giving information (e.g., explaining a problem, giving directions). 1 2 3 4 5

A-32. DEALING WITH CONTRADICTIONS - Knows when he/she is receiving messages which are unclear or opposite in meaning and asks for clarification. 1 2 3 4 5

A-33. BEING HONEST - Is honest and understands the consequences of losing someone's trust. 1 2 3 4 5

A-34. BEING OPTIMISTIC - Looks on the "bright side." Expects good things to happen. Has a positive attitude. 1 2 3 4 5

B-1. REPUTATION - Has a "good" reputation in the home, school, and community. 1 2 3 4 5

B-2.   STARTING A FRIENDSHIP - Is able to start new friendships with people based on common interests.   1 2 3 4 5

B-3.   MAINTAINING A FRIENDSHIP - Is able to treat a friend appropriately in order to maintain the relationship.   1 2 3 4 5

B-4.   GIVING EMOTIONAL SUPPORT - Listens and provides encouragement to a friend who is making a difficult decision, or who is feeling depressed.   1 2 3 4 5

B-5.   GIVING ADVICE - Gives advice only when asked, and only in areas he/she is competent in.   1 2 3 4 5

B-6.   IGNORING - Ignores disruptions and negative behaviors of other people.   1 2 3 4 5

B-7.   RESPONDING TO TEASING - Responds appropriately to "friendly" teasing and ignores "unfriendly" teasing.   1 2 3 4 5

B-8.   PEER PRESSURE - Says *no* to negative peer pressure.   1 2 3 4 5

B-9.   JOINING IN - Joins into an activity or a conversation without disrupting those involved.   1 2 3 4 5

B-10.   BEING LEFT OUT - Copes with being left out of an activity or conversation.   1 2 3 4 5

B-11.   TATTLING - Does not tattle in front of his/her peers.   1 2 3 4 5

B-12.   BEING ASSERTIVE - Can make comments in a confident and firm way, without making threats.   1 2 3 4 5

B-13.   MAKING A COMPLAINT - Makes a complaint to the correct person in a nonaggressive manner.   1 2 3 4 5

B-14.   RECEIVING A COMPLAINT - Suggests a solution when he/she is responsible for a complaint received.   1 2 3 4 5

B-15.   GIVING CONSTRUCTIVE CRITICISM - Is specific about behaviors he/she would like to see improved without making personal insults.   1 2 3 4 5

B-16.   ACCEPTING CONSTRUCTIVE CRITICISM - Accepts constructive criticism without getting defensive.   1 2 3 4 5

B-17.   MAKING AN ACCUSATION - Seeks proof before accusing someone.   1 2 3 4 5

B-18.   DEALING WITH A FALSE ACCUSATION - When falsely accused, he/she offers proof and/or offers another explanation without getting angry.   1 2 3 4 5

	Never	Seldom	Sometimes	Often	Always

B-19. COMPROMISING/NEGOTIATING - Meets a person "half-way" when working to solve a problem.   1 2 3 4 5

B-20. ACCEPTING CONSEQUENCES - Accepts negative consequences of his/her behavior.   1 2 3 4 5

B-21. EXPRESSING FEELINGS - Expresses his/her feelings instead of holding them inside.   1 2 3 4 5

B-22. DEALING WITH ANGER - Expresses his/her anger without acting impulsively.   1 2 3 4 5

B-23. DEALING WITH EMBARRASSMENT - Reacts appropriately when something makes him/her feel uncomfortable/self-conscious.   1 2 3 4 5

B-24. COPING WITH FEAR - Takes steps to reduce unrealistic fears.   1 2 3 4 5

B-25. DEALING WITH HUMOR - Enjoys "safe" humor and avoids "unsafe" humor (i.e., humor that hurts or upsets others).   1 2 3 4 5

B-26. DEALING WITH FAILURE - Deals with failure appropriately and does not let it get him/her "down."   1 2 3 4 5

B-27. EXPRESSING AFFECTION - Lets other people know about his/her positive feelings in an appropriate way.   1 2 3 4 5

B-28. DEALING WITH DISAPPOINTMENT - Handles disappointment without getting impulsive.   1 2 3 4 5

B-29. UNDERSTANDING THE FEELINGS OF OTHERS - Is perceptive to the way other people are feeling.   1 2 3 4 5

Write down the five social skills you believe this student needs to work on improving the most.

1.

2.

3.

4.

5.

©1989 THINKING PUBLICATIONS
Duplication allowed for educational use only.

SSS: SOCIAL SKILL STRATEGIES (Book B)

STUDENT SOCIAL SKILL SUMMARY FORM

STUDENT'S NAME:	Identified as Being Problematic	Demonstrated Comprehension of Skill in Class	Demonstrated Correct Use of Skill in Class	Reported/Observed Use of Skill Outside of Class	GRADE: _____ YEAR: _____	Identified as Being Problematic	Demonstrated Comprehension of Skill in Class	Demonstrated Correct Use of Skill in Class	Reported/Observed Use of Skill Outside of Class
A-1. Eye Contact					B-1. Reputation				
A-2. Manners					B-2. Starting A Friendship				
A-3. Volume					B-3. Maintaining a Friendship				
A-4. Time And Place					B-4. Giving Emotional Support				
A-5. Tone Of Voice					B-5. Giving Advice				
A-6. Getting To The Point					B-6. Ignoring				
A-7. Staying On Topic And Switching Topics					B-7. Responding To Teasing				
A-8. Listening					B-8. Peer Pressure				
A-9. Starting, Maintaining, And Ending A Conversation					B-9. Joining In				
A-10. Proximity					B-10. Being Left Out				
A-11. Body Language					B-11. Tattling				
A-12. Making A Good Impression					B-12. Being Assertive				
A-13. Formal/Informal Language					B-13. Making A Complaint				
A-14. Giving Reasons					B-14. Receiving A Complaint				
A-15. Planning What To Say					B-15. Giving Constructive Criticism				
A-16. Interrupting					B-16. Accepting Constructive Criticism				
A-17. Giving A Compliment					B-17. Making An Accusation				
A-18. Accepting A Compliment					B-18. Dealing With A False Accusation				
A-19. Saying Thank You					B-19. Compromising/Negotiating				
A-20. Introducing Yourself					B-20. Accepting Consequences				
A-21. Introducing Two People To Each Other					B-21 Expressing Feelings				
A-22. Making A Request					B-22. Dealing With Anger				
A-23. Offering Help					B-23. Dealing With Embarrassment				
A-24. Asking For Help					B-24. Coping With Fear				
A-25. Asking Permission					B-25. Dealing With Humor				
A-26. Accepting NO					B-26 Dealing With Failure				
A-27. Making An Apology					B-27. Expressing Affection				
A-28. Stating An Opinion					B-28. Dealing With Disappointment				
A-29. Agreeing/Disagreeing					B-29. Understanding The Feelings Of Others				
A-30. Convincing Others					NOTES:				
A-31. Giving Information									
A-32. Dealing With Contradictions									
A-33. Being Honest									
A-34. Being Optimistic									

Social Communication Skills Rating Scale

(Student Form)

Name: _____ Grade:_____

Age:_____   Date: _____

_____

DIRECTIONS: Rate yourself on how well you use the following social skills. Please be honest.

Circle:

1 - If you NEVER use the skill correctly.
2 - If you SELDOM use the skill correctly.
3 - If you SOMETIMES use the skill correctly.
4 - If you OFTEN use the skill correctly.
5 - If you ALWAYS use the skill correctly.

For example: If you **usually** speak in a volume which is too loud, you would rate yourself on skill number three in this way:

A-3. VOLUME - I use correct volume.   1 ② 3   4   5

Please give examples/comments when necessary (e.g., If you give yourself a low rating of "1" or "2" on volume, you should explain if you speak too softly or too loudly).

_____

Social Communication Skill   **Rating**

Social Communication Skill	Never	Seldom	Sometimes	Often	Always
A-1. EYE CONTACT - I am good at looking at a person during a conversation.	1	2	3	4	5
A-2. MANNERS - I use good manners (e.g., saying "please" and "thank you," and using good table manners).	1	2	3	4	5
A-3. VOLUME - I use correct volume.	1	2	3	4	5
A-4. TIME AND PLACE - I choose a good time and place to talk to someone.	1	2	3	4	5

	Never	Seldom	Sometimes	Often	Always

A-5.   TONE OF VOICE - I use a pleasant tone of voice. I do not sound sarcastic or "snotty." 1 2 3 4 5

A-6.   GETTING TO THE POINT - I bring up the main point of my conversation at the correct time. I do not "beat around the bush" or "put off" saying something. 1 2 3 4 5

A-7.   STAYING ON TOPIC AND SWITCHING TOPICS - My comments deal with the main topic when I have a conversation. I warn the listener before I switch topics. 1 2 3 4 5

A-8.   LISTENING - When someone is talking to me, I give that person my full attention, so I can understand him/her. 1 2 3 4 5

A-9.   STARTING AND ENDING A CONVERSATION - I feel comfortable starting conversations. I begin with a greeting and name. I end conversations smoothly and I say "good-bye." 1 2 3 4 5

A-10. PROXIMITY - I stand at a good distance while talking to a person. I don't stand too close or too far away. 1 2 3 4 5

A-11. BODY LANGUAGE - I know which body actions and facial expressions to use to show my feelings. 1 2 3 4 5

A-12. MAKING A GOOD IMPRESSION - I try to make a good impression by how I look and by what I say and do. 1 2 3 4 5

A-13. FORMAL/INFORMAL LANGUAGE - When I speak to people in respected positions, I talk in a more "traditional" way. I use longer forms of words (e.g., "Thank you very much."). When I speak to people my own age or adults I feel close to, I talk in a more "relaxed" way. I use shorter forms of words and slang (e.g., "Thanks a lot."). 1 2 3 4 5

A-14. GIVING REASONS - When someone asks me to explain something, I give reasons that are specific and relevant. 1 2 3 4 5

A-15. PLANNING WHAT TO SAY - I think about what I am going to say before I speak, so it comes out sounding right. 1 2 3 4 5

A-16. INTERRUPTING - I only interrupt people when it is necessary. I interrupt in a good way. 1 2 3 4 5

A-17. GIVING A COMPLIMENT - I give people compliments about the way they look, the things they have, and what they say and do. 1 2 3 4 5

A-18. ACCEPTING A COMPLIMENT - When someone gives me a compliment, I say "Thank you." 1 2 3 4 5

©1989 THINKING PUBLICATIONS
Duplication allowed for educational use only.

SSS: SOCIAL SKILL STRATEGIES (Book B)

	Never	Seldom	Sometimes	Often	Always

A-19. SAYING *THANK YOU* - I thank people when they do something nice for me.   1 2 3 4 5

A-20. INTRODUCING YOURSELF - I introduce myself to people I don't know. I remember to tell my full name.   1 2 3 4 5

A-21. INTRODUCING TWO PEOPLE TO EACH OTHER - I introduce two people when they do not know each other. (For example, "Steve, meet Beth. Beth, meet Steve.")   1 2 3 4 5

A-22. MAKING A REQUEST - When I want something, I ask for it in a polite way. I do not demand it.   1 2 3 4 5

A-23. OFFERING HELP - I offer help to people in need. I ask first, instead of just "taking over."   1 2 3 4 5

A-24. ASKING FOR HELP - I try things on my own first. If I can't do something, then I ask for help.   1 2 3 4 5

A-25. ASKING PERMISSION - I ask for permission from authority figures whenever I should.   1 2 3 4 5

A-26. ACCEPTING *NO* - When I am told that I can't do something, I can accept it in a calm way.   1 2 3 4 5

A-27. MAKING AN APOLOGY - I say "I am sorry" when I have done something wrong.   1 2 3 4 5

A-28. STATING AN OPINION - When I say something that is just my opinion and can't be proven as a fact, I remember to begin with "I think . . ." or "In my opinion . . ."   1 2 3 4 5

A-29. AGREEING/DISAGREEING - When I disagree with someone, I do not put down his idea or opinion. I do not get angry when someone disagrees with me.   1 2 3 4 5

A-30. CONVINCING OTHERS - I give good reasons when I try to convince someone to believe the same way I do.   1 2 3 4 5

A-31. GIVING INFORMATION - I express myself clearly when I give information (e.g., give directions, explain a problem).   1 2 3 4 5

A-32. DEALING WITH CONTRADICTIONS - When someone contradicts himself (says something that is unclear and opposite in meaning), I ask what he means.   1 2 3 4 5

A-33. BEING HONEST - I am honest, even when I have done something wrong. I don't want to lose people's trust in me.   1 2 3 4 5

©1989 THINKING PUBLICATIONS
Duplication allowed for educational use only.

SSS: SOCIAL SKILL STRATEGIES (Book B)

| | | Never | Seldom | Sometimes | Often | Always |

A-34. BEING OPTIMISTIC - I try to have a positive attitude. I expect good things to happen. I look on the "bright side" when something goes wrong.   1 2 3 4 5

B-1. REPUTATION - I have a "good" reputation at home, at school, and in the community.   1 2 3 4 5

B-2. STARTING A FRIENDSHIP - I am good at starting new friendships with people.   1 2 3 4 5

B-3. MAINTAINING A FRIENDSHIP - I keep my friends because I treat them well.   1 2 3 4 5

B-4. GIVING EMOTIONAL SUPPORT - When one of my friends is feeling depressed or is having a problem, I listen and give encouragement.   1 2 3 4 5

B-5. GIVING ADVICE - I only give advice when someone asks me for it. I avoid giving advice about things I don't know much about.   1 2 3 4 5

B-6. IGNORING - I am able to ignore disruptions. I ignore kids when they try to get my attention in a negative way.   1 2 3 4 5

B-7. RESPONDING TO TEASING - I laugh when people tease me in a nice way. I ignore people when they tease me in a mean way. (I don't let them get me upset.)   1 2 3 4 5

B-8. PEER PRESSURE - I say *no* when kids try to pressure me into doing things I don't feel comfortable doing.   1 2 3 4 5

B-9. JOINING IN - I join conversations and activities after they have already begun, in a way that is not a disruption.   1 2 3 4 5

B-10. BEING LEFT OUT - When I am left out of an activity or a conversation, I try to determine if it happened by mistake or on purpose.   1 2 3 4 5

B-11. TATTLING - I am not a "tattletale."   1 2 3 4 5

B-12. BEING ASSERTIVE - When someone goes against my rights, I tell the person how I feel and what I want. I do not make threats and get aggressive.   1 2 3 4 5

B-13. MAKING A COMPLAINT - When I complain to a person about something he is doing wrong, I correct the person without getting angry/upset.   1 2 3 4 5

Never Seldom Sometimes Often Always

B-14. RECEIVING A COMPLAINT - When someone complains to me 1 2 3 4 5
and I know I am responsible, I apologize and offer a solution.

B-15. GIVING CONSTRUCTIVE CRITICISM - When I criticize 1 2 3 4 5
someone, I tell exactly what I think should be improved. I do not
personally insult the person. I try to say something positive about
the person first.

B-16. ACCEPTING CONSTRUCTIVE CRITICISM - I can handle it 1 2 3 4 5
when someone tells me I need to improve on something. I don't
get defensive.

B-17. MAKING AN ACCUSATION - I make sure I have proof, before 1 2 3 4 5
I accuse someone of doing something wrong.

B-18. DEALING WITH A FALSE ACCUSATION - When someone 1 2 3 4 5
accuses me of doing something and he is wrong, I stay calm. I
offer proof that I am innocent or try to offer another explanation.

B-19. COMPROMISING/NEGOTIATING - I am willing to give in a 1 2 3 4 5
little to help solve a disagreement. I don't always have to have
things my way.

B-20. ACCEPTING CONSEQUENCES - When I know I have done 1 2 3 4 5
something wrong, I am willing to pay the consequences.

B-21. EXPRESSING FEELINGS - I talk about my feelings. I do not 1 2 3 4 5
hold them all inside.

B-22. DEALING WITH ANGER - When I get angry, I can control 1 2 3 4 5
myself. I don't lose control.

B-23. DEALING WITH EMBARRASSMENT - I handle myself well 1 2 3 4 5
when I get embarrassed. I don't fall apart.

B-24. COPING WITH FEAR - When I am afraid of something, I don't 1 2 3 4 5
let it get the best of me. I face my fears and try to reduce them.

B-25. DEALING WITH HUMOR - I only use humor that is "friendly" 1 2 3 4 5
and will not upset or hurt anyone. I avoid "unfriendly" humor.

B-26. DEALING WITH FAILURE - I don't let myself get "down" when 1 2 3 4 5
I fail at something. I just try to do better the next time.

©1989 THINKING PUBLICATIONS
Duplication allowed for educational use only.

B-27. EXPRESSING AFFECTION - I let other people know that I have   1 2 3 4 5
positive feelings about them in an appropriate way.

B-28. DEALING WITH DISAPPOINTMENT - When I am disappointed   1 2 3 4 5
because someone or something lets me down, I stay in control.

B-29. UNDERSTANDING THE FEELINGS OF OTHERS - I am   1 2 3 4 5
sensitive to the way other people are feeling.

Write down the three social skills you think you should work on the most.

1.

2.

3.

CLASS SUMMARY FORM
BOOK A
(Mark the social skills which are problematic for each student.)

											STUDENTS' NAMES / SOCIAL SKILLS
											A-1. Eye Contact
											A-2. Manners
											A-3. Volume
											A-4. Time And Place
											A-5. Tone Of Voice
											A-6. Getting To The Point
											A-7. Staying On Topic And Switching Topics
											A-8. Listening
											A-9. Starting, Maintaining, And Ending A Conversation
											A-10. Proximity
											A-11. Body Language
											A-12. Making A Good Impression
											A-13. Formal/Informal Language
											A-14. Giving Reasons
											A-15. Planning What To Say
											A-16. Interrupting
											A-17. Giving A Compliment
											A-18. Accepting A Compliment
											A-19. Saying Thank You
											A-20. Introducing Yourself
											A-21. Introducing Two People To Each Other
											A-22. Making A Request
											A-23. Offering Help
											A-24. Asking For Help
											A-25. Asking Permission
											A-26. Accepting NO
											A-27. Making An Apology
											A-28. Stating An Opinion
											A-29. Agreeing/Disagreeing
											A-30. Convincing Others
											A-31. Giving Information
											A-32. Dealing With Contradictions
											A-33. Being Honest
											A-34. Being Optimistic

CLASS SUMMARY FORM
BOOK B

(Mark the social skills which are problematic for each student.)

SOCIAL SKILLS	STUDENTS' NAMES										
B-1. Reputation											
B-2. Starting A Friendship											
B-3. Maintaining A Friendship											
B-4. Giving Emotional Support											
B-5. Giving Advice											
B-6. Ignoring											
B-7. Responding To Teasing											
B-8. Peer Pressure											
B-9. Joining In											
B-10. Being Left Out											
B-11. Tattling											
B-12. Being Assertive											
B-13. Making A Complaint											
B-14. Receiving A Complaint											
B-15. Giving Constructive Criticism											
B-16. Accepting Constructive Criticism											
B-17. Making An Accusation											
B-18. Dealing With A False Accusation											
B-19. Compromising/Negotiating											
B-20. Accepting Consequences											
B-21. Expressing Feelings											
B-22. Dealing With Anger											
B-23. Dealing With Embarrassment											
B-24. Coping With Fear											
B-25. Dealing With Humor											
B-26. Dealing With Failure											
B-27. Expressing Affection											
B-28. Dealing With Disappointment											
B-29. Understanding The Feelings Of Others											

Dear_____:

As you know, your child will be participating in a social skills class. The purpose of the class is to teach children social skills which will help them to get along better with people and to feel better about themselves. A list of social skills taught during the class is attached.

Each social skill taught is broken down into small steps to make it easier to learn. For example, the social skill of "Asking For Help" is divided into the following skill steps:

1. Try to do it on your own first.

   If you can't,
2. Ask for help (explain yourself clearly).
3. Pay attention when the person helps you.
4. Thank the person for helping you.

Your child will have several homework activities during each social skill unit. One assignment, entitled the **SKILL HOMEWORK ACTIVITY**, should be completed together by you and your child. The activity sheet includes information about how the social skill was taught in class. You are asked either to complete a given role play situation with your child or to describe a real-life situation in which you have observed your child using the skill.

The major goal of the class is to get students to transfer what they learn in class to other settings (e.g., other classes, home, and the community). You can assist your son/daughter in becoming more socially appropriate in other environments by completing the **SKILL HOMEWORK ACTIVITY** with your child. You can also help your child by giving praise when you observe him/her using a social skill appropriately (e.g., "John, you really did a good job of asking for help.").

I look forward to working together with you to improve your child's skills for getting along with others. If you would like further information about the class, please contact me at any time. In addition, if you have any questions, concerns, or suggestions, I will be glad to discuss these with you.

Sincerely,

Dear_____:

As you know, many students have a difficult time getting along with their peers and/or adults. Some are too aggressive, while others are extremely withdrawn. These students lack the social skills necessary to get along with people.

We assume that all students have learned appropriate social skills in their early years. Many have not, and thus need to have these skills taught directly to them. Research has indicated that students can learn social skills through modeling, role playing, and other activities. Therefore, instruction in appropriate social skills will be provided through my social skills class.

The following student(s) will be participating in the social skills class which meets

_____:

Since you have contact with the above mentioned student(s), I would like to provide you with some information about social skill instruction. A list of the social skills taught in the class is attached. Throughout the school year, you will receive further information about specific social skills as they are taught.

A major goal of the class is to get students to transfer what they learn in class to other settings (e.g., other classes, home, and community). You can assist the students to transfer their use of social skills by positively reinforcing them when you observe correct use of a skill (e.g., "You accepted your consequence in a mature manner.").

I look forward to working together with you to improve our students' skills for getting along with others. If you would like further information about the class, please contact me at any time. In addition, if you have any questions, concerns, or suggestions, I will be glad to discuss these with you.

Sincerely,

©1989 THINKING PUBLICATIONS
Duplication allowed for educational use only.

SSS: SOCIAL SKILL STRATEGIES (Book B)

Independent Activity #1   Name:_____

DIRECTIONS: Work on your own to complete the activities on this page. Do both activities. You will earn extra credit points from your teacher for:
- working without asking for help
- working without distracting other students
- working and ignoring other students

ACTIVITY A   How Social Are You?

1. Get a large piece of construction paper.
2. Write your name in large letters across the page. Use stencils if you wish.
3. Draw a large oval on the paper.
4. Think of ten words that describe what you are like when you are around other people. Here is a list of words to help you, but you may think of words on your own.

shy	out-going	bashful	passive
loud	aggressive	assertive	a good listener
funny	serious	a complainer	talkative
friendly	honest	a liar	exciting
boring	scared	a tattler	a troublemaker
a bully	a leader	concerned	quiet
helpful	humorous	caring	a know-it-all

5. Look in a magazine or newspaper to find the ten words you have chosen. You may have to cut out individual letters to make the words.
6. Glue the words inside the oval.
7. Decorate the paper using markers.
8. Write your full name on the back of the paper.

ACTIVITY B   Getting Social

1. Get a piece of lined paper.
2. Write a 7-8 sentence paragraph about how you think this class can help you (or is helping you) get more friends and get along better with people.
3. Remember to indent, use good punctuation/capitalization, and write in complete sentences.
4. Proofread your paragraph when you are finished.

IF YOU FINISH BEFORE CLASS IS OVER, FIND SOMETHING TO DO QUIETLY!

DIRECTIONS: Work on your own to complete the activities on this page. Do both activities. You will earn extra credit points from your teacher for:
- working without asking for help
- working without distracting other students
- working and ignoring other students

ACTIVITY A   **Communicating!**

1. Get a piece of lined paper.
2. Make a list of 30 situations when you communicate with other people. Here are some examples: when you talk to your teacher
    when you tell someone you're sorry
    when you ask your brother for something
3. Write your situations on the lined paper.
4. Make sure your name is on the paper.

ACTIVITY B   **Positive Poster**

1. Get a large piece of construction paper and a piece of typing paper.
2. Think up a positive saying or choose one from below.
3. Design a "positive poster." Use pencil and draw a sketch of your poster on a piece of typing paper. Put your saying on the paper. Add things such as a rainbow, a sun, flowers, a tree, a butterfly, clouds, stars, etc. These items will add interest to the poster.
4. After you have drawn your design on typing paper, use your pencil to draw it on the larger piece of construction paper.
5. Color your poster with magic markers.
6. Put your name on the back of your poster.
7. Turn in both your sketch and your poster to the teacher at the end of the class.

POSITIVE SAYINGS

You are responsible for your day!
Have a good day!
I feel happy around you!
Friends are forever!
You are human, you have dignity!
May your accomplishments be many!
People like you make the world much brighter!
Communicate! Try it, you'll like it!
I like you just the way you are!
Friendship keeps hearts in touch!
Friends are always in our hearts!
Life is outstanding!
Tell your face you're happy!
People make the world go 'round!
There's no problem so great it cannot be solved!

Keep smiling!
You're the greatest!
Today's your lucky day!
Friends are special!
You're so special!
May life bring you joy!
You brighten my day!
Friends mean so much!
You're the best!
You're lookin' good!
Today is a great day!
Everyone is important!
You can do it!
It's a super day!

IF YOU FINISH BEFORE CLASS IS OVER, FIND SOMETHING TO DO QUIETLY!

©1989 THINKING PUBLICATIONS
Duplication allowed for educational use only.   314   SSS: SOCIAL SKILL STRATEGIES (Book B)

DIRECTIONS: Work on your own to complete the activities on this page and the
next. Do both activities. You will earn extra credit points from your
teacher for:
- working without asking for help
- working without distracting other students
- working and ignoring other students

ACTIVITY A   Find the Social Words

Complete the following word search puzzle, which is filled with "social skill" words.
The words you need to find are listed below for you. The words run vertically ↓ or
horizontally → with the puzzle. Leave out the spaces when you are looking for phrases.
Systematically search through each row of letters to find the words.

```
D I S A P P O I N T M E N T T E A T H J O P R Q S T
C N G Q A E R E A A D M I L B E I N G L E F T O U T
O T R S E A R E D N E G O T I A T E T I F R E I D O
N R B O D Y L A N G U A G E E G U G R S U I A O P F
T O M E I N B O P E G U A G E R D I S T B O S B O F
R D T H S E A T R R W E A D R E W A N E K L I Q W E
A U B O A C C U S A T I O N E E I K F N F O N C E R
D C B E G M Y O U R S M A C C I E P T I A C G G R I
I E L F R I E N D S H I P E I N O P O N Q W E R E N
C B E I E N G C O M O F F E R G C O M G G I V G I G
T M A N E N E C O M P L I M E N T E R S L I S T E H
I E W X I M I J K O C O M P L A I N T Q U A R S M E
O T H R N E N I M C O M A G G R O F H F E O F F A L
N T E A G S T E A M I K L O P F R I U E F R E I N P
S A C C E P T I N G N O L E R O V E M R S T U V N H
A Z C A R T E A S N G C O P T O N E O F V O I C E Q
N L C O M P R O M I S E D O G T E A R S A T E L R B
G I V I N G R E A S O N S F R E D W R I T E N S S S
```

FIND THESE WORDS AND PHRASES:

		introduce	contradictions
manners	compliment	friendship	negotiate
tone of voice	offering help	teasing	anger
listening	accepting NO	being left out	humor
body language	agreeing	complaint	disappointment
giving reasons	disagreeing	accusation	compromise

ACTIVITY B   **TV Social Skills**

1. Think of one of your favorite TV characters.
2. Write down the character's name, and the title of the show he/she appears in.
3. List three social skills the character has. Then write a sentence for each, explaining why he/she is good at the skills.
4. List three social skills the character lacks. Then write a sentence for each, explaining why he/she is not good at the skill.
5. Look at the list of social skills in your journal if you need help thinking of different skills.

IF YOU FINISH BEFORE CLASS IS OVER, FIND SOMETHING TO DO QUIETLY!

Independent Activity #4   Name:_____

DIRECTIONS: Work on your own to complete the activities on this page. Do both
activities. You will earn extra credit points from your teacher for:
- working without asking for help
- working without distracting other students
- working and ignoring other students

ACTIVITY A **Picture/Emotion**

1. Get some magazines, to cut pictures from, and five pieces of typing paper.
2. Choose 5 feelings from this list:

happy	relaxed
angry	sorry
tired	excited
scared	confused
bashful	embarrassed

3. For each feeling word, find a picture of a person in a magazine who looks like he/she is expressing that feeling.
4. Cut out the picture and glue it to a piece of typing paper.
5. Write the feeling word under the picture. Describe the main cue you used to decide how the person in the picture was feeling (e.g., TIRED - the person was yawning).
6. Do the same for the other four feeling words you chose.
7. Staple the five pieces of typing paper together to make a booklet.

ACTIVITY B **School and Social Skills**

1. Get a piece of lined paper.
2. Make a list of ten situations in school when you would have to use social skills. Here are some examples:
   - I have to control my temper when someone makes fun of me at lunch.
   - I should compliment my friend when she gets an "A" on a test.
   - I have to listen to the teacher when he's giving a lecture.
3. Use a complete sentence when you write down each situation.
4. Make sure your name is on the paper.

**IF YOU FINISH BEFORE CLASS IS OVER, FIND SOMETHING TO DO
QUIETLY!**

DIRECTIONS: Work on your own to complete the activities on this page and the next. Do both activities. You will earn extra credit points from your teacher for:
- working without asking for help
- working without distracting other students
- working and ignoring other students

ACTIVITY A   A Story

1. Choose one of the topics below.
2. Write a story about the topic you choose. The story should be 1-2 pages long.
3. Write neatly and use good punctuation/capitalization. Write in complete sentences and give your story a title.

Topics: Write a story about . . .

- a teen-ager who has a hard time resisting peer pressure.
- a teen-ager who is very bashful and doesn't have conversations with people.
- a teen-ager who is really well-liked and has many friends.
- a teen-ager who does something wrong and has to apologize for it.
- a teen-ager who uses good manners.
- a teen-ager who doesn't know how to make friends.
- a teen-ager who gets accused of something she didn't do.
- a teen-ager who doesn't know how to express his anger.
- a teen-ager who is good at resisting peer pressure.
- a teen-ager who is good at listening.

ACTIVITY B   You Are a Star

1. Read the directions on the attached "I'm a Star" page.
2. Complete the page.

IF YOU FINISH BEFORE CLASS IS OVER, FIND SOMETHING TO DO QUIETLY!

You are a Star!

DIRECTIONS: You are a STAR! There are many good things about you. In each star below, write something that's good about yourself.

I'm . . .

I'm good at . . .

I'm . . .

I'm . . .

I have . . .

Duplication allowed for educational use only.

DIRECTIONS: Work on your own to complete the activities on this page and the next. Do both activities. You will earn extra credit points from your teacher for:
- working without asking for help
- working without distracting other students
- working and ignoring other students

ACTIVITY A   Social Word Search

Complete the following word search puzzle, which is filled with "social skill" words. The words you need to find are listed below for you. The words run vertically ↓ and horizontally→within the puzzle. Leave out the spaces when you are looking for phrases. Systematically search through each row of letters to find the words.

```
I M C O N S T R U C T I V E C R I T I C I S M P E E
N B O M E I N F O R M A T I O N A P S O A P R E E M
F I N U M M A R P E A P I J I O F R L P I M S E F O
O R S E A R S T I F O R N A L E T O P I C Y O R F T
R W E T I M E A N D P L A C E P E X S C M I N P O I
M Z Q C E R E B I F X E W L K H N I G M V V U R R O
A D U E R A W C O F O I F W V U A M R A T F I E M N
L R E Q U E S T N A S T F S S E R I I V E P R S A A
L S N T U V O R E N B R A S S E R T I V E F L S L L
A P C R M I S S I O N A I R E A T Y O C K H I U L S
N P E R M I S S I O N A L N O U J L A S J P O R A U
G W S E R F R E A M I N U T I N T E R R U P T E N P
U I N P E R R U P V L O R R E Y E C O N T A C T G P
A O P T I M I S T I C C E E O I U T H A N K Y O U O
G P T I E M I S T L C B E F E E L I N G S A S T A R
E M B A R R A S S M E N T E L L I R G Z A R T E G T
J X N O B G R L A Z P M I C H U K E Y Q F T D V E W
```

FIND THESE WORDS AND PHRASES:

			consequences
eye contact	interrupt	optimistic	embarrassment
time and place	thank you	emotional support	failure
topic	request	peer pressure	feelings
proximity	permission	assertive	informal language
formal language	opinion	constructive criticism	information

©1989 THINKING PUBLICATIONS
Duplication allowed for educational use only.   320   SSS: SOCIAL SKILL STRATEGIES (Book B)

ACTIVITY B　　**Analyze Someone You Know**

1. Think of a person you know well (e.g., a family member, teacher, friend).
2. Write down the person's name on a piece of paper. Tell the person's role in your life (e.g., parent, teacher, friend, brother, sister).
3. List three social skills the person is good at. Then write a sentence for each, explaining why he/she is good at that skill.
4. List three social skills you think the person lacks. Then write a sentence for each, explaining why he/she isn't good at that skill.
5. Be honest! The person you choose will not see your list.
6. Look at the list of social skills in your journal if you need help thinking of different skills.

IF YOU FINISH BEFORE CLASS IS OVER, FIND SOMETHING TO DO QUIETLY!

DIRECTIONS: Work on your own to complete the activities on this page. Do both activities. You will earn extra credit points from your teacher for:
- working without asking for help
- working without distracting other students
- working and ignoring other students

ACTIVITY A   How Great I Am . . .

1. Get a lined piece of paper.
2. Write a paragraph about all of your good qualities. Tell all of the nice things you can think of about yourself.
3. Your paragraph should be at least 7-8 sentences long.
4. Make sure your name is on your paper.

ACTIVITY B   My Collage

1. Get a large piece of construction paper.
2. Get magazines and newspapers you can cut from.
3. Make a collage on construction paper that represents YOU. Find pictures/words that show things you like to do. Find pictures/words that represent what your personality is like. You can put anything on the collage that is about you.
4. If you would like, you can draw the pictures rather than cutting them from a magazine.
5. Make sure your name is somewhere on the front of the collage.

IF YOU FINISH BEFORE CLASS IS OVER, FIND SOMETHING TO DO QUIETLY!

DIRECTIONS: Work on your own to complete the activities on this page. Do both activities. You will earn extra credit points from your teacher for:
- working without asking for help
- working without distracting other students
- working and ignoring other students

EXAMPLE

ACTIVITY A **The People You Know**

Write the names of seven people you know in the left hand column of the table below. Think of a compliment you could give to each person about a social skill they are good at. Write the compliments in the column on the right. An example has been provided. Look at your list of social skills in your journal if you need ideas.

NAME	COMPLIMENT
→ *Bill (my dad)*	*Dad, you are really good at listening.*

ACTIVITY B **Hand It To Yourself**

1. Draw an outline of each of your hands on a piece of typing paper.
2. Write different social skills you are good at, inside each finger on the left hand. (There will be five skills in all.)
3. Write different social skills you need to improve on, inside each finger on the right hand. (There will be five skills in all.)

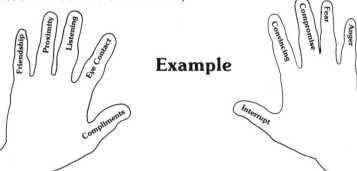

Example

IF YOU FINISH BEFORE CLASS IS OVER, FIND SOMETHING TO DO QUIETLY!

Independent Activity #9   Name:_____

DIRECTIONS: Work on your own to complete the activities on this page and the
next. Do both activities. You will earn extra credit points from your
teacher for:
- working without asking for help
- working without distracting other students
- working and ignoring other students

ACTIVITY A   # Where Are the Social Words?

Complete the following word search puzzle, which is filled with "social skill" words.
The words you need to find are listed below for you. The words run vertically ↓ and
horizontally→within the puzzle. Leave out the spaces when you are looking for phrases.
Systematically search through each row of letters to find the words.

```
O V T X U S U R F P W U X A A G A E C C O H C T S A
A G E T T I N G T O T H E P O I N T V O L U M E X A
C O N V I N C E R S L Y O N U P L A N N I N G A F
A O A D I Y Q F O F V I C L T I C R Q V E E A L R F
P D K M A I H O V R A G B O K I O G H E L P D L B E
P I F N C G E I Q I A H L G N G L D O R B J F E M C
R M J E F P H O N E S T Y I U N D E R S T A N D N T
E P A K J B F C E N V M J Z K O G P E A H G L P C I
C R L D M H I O A D V I C E N R G R A T I T U D E O
I E K F E A R L P L H G D O F I X J O I N I N G I N
A S E G U M E N K Y O L P B Q N R J Q O T F R Q P L
T S B I L D C A G Q J I M R H G A E I N M C R O D I
I I O S I N T R O D U C E S F C O M P L I M E N T O
O O I R Q K B E A T I N G A R O U N D T H E B U S H
N N S B O P I E X P R E S S I N G F E E L I N G S N
```

FIND THESE WORDS AND PHRASES:

volume	getting to the point	planning	ignoring	appreciation
fear	beating around the bush	compliment	joining in	gratitude
help	good impression	introduce	affection	convince
advice	expressing feelings	apologize	understand	honesty
friendly	conversation			

ACTIVITY B   # Design a Social Skill Poster

1. Pick one social skill listed in your journal to create a poster.
2. Write the name of the skill at the top of a piece of construction paper.
3. Create your poster by doing one or more of the following:
   - Draw a person who is using the skill correctly.
   - Draw a person who is using the skill incorrectly.
   - Write the skill steps or important tips for the skill.
   - Find pictures from magazines of people who are using the skill.
   - Draw a cartoon about the skill.
4. Put your name on the back of the poster when it is complete.

IF YOU FINISH BEFORE CLASS IS OVER, FIND SOMETHING TO DO QUIETLY!

Independent Activity #10   Name:_____

DIRECTIONS: Work on your own to complete the activities on this page. Do both
activities. You will earn extra credit points from your teacher for:
- working without asking for help
- working without distracting other students
- working and ignoring other students

ACTIVITY A   # Write a Story About . . .

1. Choose one of the topics below.
2. Write a story about the topic you choose. The story should be 1-2 pages long.
3. Write neatly and use good punctuation/capitalization. Write in complete sentences
   and give your story a title.

   Topics: Write a story about . . .
   - a teen-ager who has a difficult time looking at people while talking.
   - a teen-ager who always seems to choose a bad time and place to talk.
   - a teen-ager who has a problem with switching topics.
   - a teen-ager who is good at offering help to others.
   - a teen-ager who is good at introducing himself to new people.
   - a teen-ager who has a problem because he holds all his feelings inside.
   - a teen-ager who is a poor sport when he loses.
   - a teen-ager who gives advice appropriately.
   - a teen-ager who has a habit of spreading rumors.
   - a teen-ager who remembers to think about the consequences of his actions.

ACTIVITY B   # Facial Expressions

Each of these face outlines has a feeling word written below it. Draw the mouth, eyes,
eyebrows, nose, and forehead inside each outline, so that the facial expression represents
the feeling word. If you need help, look through books and magazines to find people
who look like they have the feelings listed below.

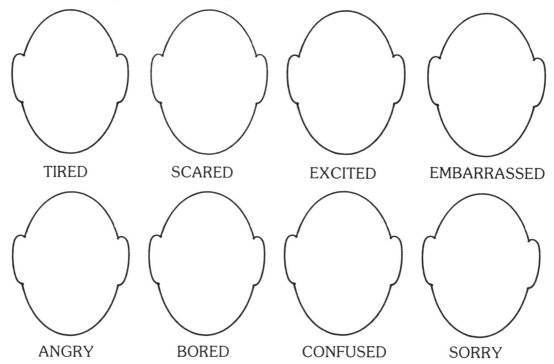

TIRED   SCARED   EXCITED   EMBARRASSED

ANGRY   BORED   CONFUSED   SORRY

Pair Practice Record

Name:_____

Skills to Practice

Date												
_____ (Skill)												
Initials												
Date												
_____ (Skill)												
Initials												
Date												
_____ (Skill)												
Initials												
Date												
_____ (Skill)												
Initials												

©1989 THINKING PUBLICATIONS

Duplication allowed for educational use only.

QUESTION REVIEW

B-1. REPUTATION

1. Define the word *reputation*. (How other people view you)

2. Tell the important tips to remember about reputations. (1. Some reputations are the truth about people while other reputations are not really what the person is like. 2. Reputations can be changed, but it is not easy to do.)

3. Last year, Phil made several mistakes with his teachers and his friends. Almost everyone at school started thinking of Phil as being a "trouble-maker." Phil doesn't think it makes any difference what others think of him and he doesn't plan to do anything differently this year. What social skill does Phil need to improve? (Reputations)

4. Explain why some reputations are the truth about people while other reputations are not.

5. Tell two negative consequences of having a *bad* reputation with adults.

6. Tell two positive consequences of having a *good* reputation with adults.

B-2. STARTING A FRIENDSHIP

1. Define the social skill of starting a friendship. (Beginning a relationship with another person in which that person becomes your companion)

2. Tell six tips for starting a friendship. (1. Like yourself first. 2. Be where the people are. 3. Have things in common. 4. Talk to people. 5. Don't be pushy. 6. Try the "out" crowd.)

3. Nancy wishes she had some people her own age that she could do things with. She usually stays at home and doesn't get involved in any activities. She doesn't talk to other students very much at school. What social skill does Nancy need to improve? (Starting a friendship)

4. Tell what a *dneirf* is.

5. Explain why starting a new friendship can feel uncomfortable sometimes.

6. Complete the following sentence: It is important for people to know how to start friendships because . . .

B-3. MAINTAINING A FRIENDSHIP

1. Tell what *maintaining a friendship* means. (Keeping a friendship going once it has started)

2. Tell eleven good tips for keeping a friendship going. (1. Communicate with your friend. 2. Be honest. 3. Be loyal. 4. Keep secrets unless your friend is in danger. 5. Be supportive. 6. Try to be fun and optimistic. 7. Remember that neither one of you is perfect. 8. Expect that your friend will sometimes disagree with you. 9. Do nice things for your friend. 10. Remind your friend every once in a while how important the friendship is to you. 11. Share your friend.)

3. Barb made a new friend named Arlene. Unfortunately, Barb wasn't very good at keeping secrets Arlene told her and whenever Arlene did anything with someone else, Barb got mad. Pretty soon, Arlene gave Barb the brush off. What social skill does Barb need to improve? (Maintaining a friendship)

4. Name some characteristics of a friendship that isn't worth maintaining.

5. Describe a situation when you should not keep a secret that your friend told you to keep.

6. True or false? There isn't anything special a person should do to keep a friendship going. (False)

B-4. GIVING EMOTIONAL SUPPORT

1. Define the social skill of giving emotional support. (Recognizing how people are feeling and letting them know you are thinking about them; supporting people when they need you)

2. Tell two specific things you can do to give emotional support. (e.g., listen to the person, tell the person you care, congratulate the person, send a card or flowers, spend extra time with the person)

3. Rudy recognized that his friend Steve was depressed. Rudy thought, "I better just ignore him until he is over this thing." What social skill does Rudy need to improve? (Giving emotional support)

4. Complete this sentence: If you feel that a person is severely depressed, you should . . .

5. Give an example of a time when you would need to give one of your parents emotional support.

6. True or false? You may need to offer support several times to help a friend through a problem. (True)

B-5. GIVING ADVICE

1. Tell what *giving advice* means. (Giving someone a recommendation or suggestion for what you think he/she should do)

2. List the three skill steps for giving advice. (1. Decide whether the person asked for your advice. 2. Find out as many facts as you can before giving advice. 3. Try not to sound bossy when you give the advice.)

3. Ben asked his friend Craig what was wrong. Craig said, "I got a detention in science class because of something I didn't do." Ben said, "Oh, come on! You ought to be smart enough to figure this one out! Go talk to the principal about it. That's what I'd do." What social skill does Ben need to improve? (Giving advice)

4. Tell when you should not give advice to someone, even when asked.

5. Tell what a *know-it-all* is. Is it good or bad to be a *know-it-all*?

6. Explain the difference between giving advice about simple and difficult topics.

B-6. IGNORING

1. Tell what *ignoring* means. (Choosing not to pay attention to another person)

2. Tell two good reasons why you should ignore inappropriate behaviors from others. (1. So you don't get into trouble. 2. So you can show that you have good self-control.)

3. Jancy doesn't have much self-control. Whenever someone in class does something inappropriate, she turns around and laughs. What social skill does Jancy need to improve? (Ignoring)

4. Describe exactly what you should and should not do when you are ignoring someone's inappropriate behavior.

5. Tell the difference between *good* ignoring and *mean* ignoring.

6. Describe a situation when you should ignore someone at school.

B-7. RESPONDING TO TEASING

1. Define *friendly teasing* and *mean teasing*. (Friendly teasing - When someone gives you a hard time about something, but they do it in a nice way to make you laugh. Mean teasing - When someone gives you a hard time about something and they want to hurt your feelings.)

2. List the skill steps for responding to teasing. (1. Decide if the person is teasing you in a *friendly* way or a *mean* way. 2. If the teasing is *friendly*, you have a choice to laugh along or tease back in a friendly way. 3. If the teasing is *mean*, you have a choice to ignore or be assertive.)

3. Some people were giving JoAnne a hard time about her acne. They wanted to hurt her feelings. JoAnne started kicking them and then started to cry. What social skill does JoAnne need to improve? (Responding to teasing)

4. True or false?   A person who teases others in a mean way doesn't feel very good about himself. (True)

5. Explain why what feels like *friendly* teasing to you may not feel friendly to someone else.

6. Explain why it is important not to take yourself too seriously and to be able to handle *friendly* teasing.

B-8. PEER PRESSURE

1. Tell what *negative peer pressure* is. (People in your age group trying to convince you to do something you do not want to do)

2. List six good ways to say NO to peer pressure. (1. Keep repeating your NO statement. 2. Say something that will put some pressure back on the other person. 3. Give another idea that you both can live with. 4. Don't discuss it any further. 4. Say something funny. 6. Tell the reason why you won't.)

3. Dean is the only one who knows Joel was late for work again. Joel said, "Dean, you have to cover for me and tell the boss I was on time. Come on Buddy, will you do it for me?" Dean said, "Well, I don't know about this. I've already covered for you three times." "Give me a break! If you were cool, you'd do this for me," said Joel. Dean didn't want to look like a wimp, so he lied for Joel again. What social skill does Dean need to improve? (Peer pressure)

4. Explain the difference between positive and negative peer pressure.

5. Why is it so difficult to say NO to negative peer pressure?

6. Explain why a person might pressure another person in a negative way.

B-9. JOINING IN

1. Tell what *joining in* means. (Finding a way of entering into an activity or conversation without disrupting those already involved)

2. Tell the three skill steps of joining in. (1. Decide if you would like to join in an activity. 2. Decide what you should do to join in. 3. Try to join in before an activity starts or during a break, if possible.)

3. Kari really wants to help paint banners for spirit week at school. Every night after school, she hangs around and watches from a distance as others paint them. She hopes they will see her and ask her to help. They wonder why she just stands around and doesn't offer to help. What social skill does Kari need to improve? (Joining in)

4. Explain the difference between *joining in* and *butting in*.

5. Why is it important to try to join in an activity before it begins, or during a break in the activity?

6. Describe the difference between joining in when you want to and joining in when you should.

B-10. BEING LEFT OUT

1. Tell what *being left out* means. (When people do not include you in an activity and your feelings are hurt)

2. Tell the skill steps for being left out. (1. Try to determine if you were left out on purpose or by mistake. 2. If a mistake was made, talk to the person who forgot you, or just ignore it. 3. If you were left out on purpose, choose a strategy to make yourself feel better.)

3. Mike found out all his friends went swimming together, and no one asked him. He had been getting along great with all of his friends and couldn't remember doing anything to make them upset. Mike got very depressed, and refused to go to school. What social skill does Mike need to improve? (Dealing with being left out)

4. Tell what a *clique* is and how the term relates to the social skill of being left out.

5. Tell two specific things you can do or think about to make yourself feel better when you are left out on purpose.

6. Tell the difference between being left out by mistake and being left out on purpose.

B-11. TATTLING

1. Tell what *tattling* means. (Telling what someone else has done or is going to do)

2. Tell the two skill steps for the social skill of tattling. (1. Ask yourself, "Is what happened important enough for me to tell someone?" 2. If it is, decide whom you should tell and choose a good time and place.)

3. When the teacher came back into the classroom, Marty said, "While you were gone, Ben got out of his seat three times, Colline passed a note to Julie, and Rob threw a piece of paper at the trashcan. He missed and didn't pick it up." What social skill does Marty need to improve? (Tattling)

4. Explain why it is bad to have a reputation of being a tattletale.

5. True or false? A person should never tell on another person. (False) Explain your answer.

6. Describe two situations when it would be appropriate to tattle.

B-12. BEING ASSERTIVE

1. Tell what *being assertive* means. (Making your feelings known in a firm and confident way without making threats)

2. Tell the three skill steps for the social skill of being assertive. (1. Decide if your rights have been violated. 2. State your feelings in a firm/confident way, without making threats. 3. Listen to what the other person says.)

3. Olly bought a new tape. The first time he played it, he discovered it was defective. When Olly tried to return it, the sales clerk said, "You teen-agers are all alike! You don't take care of your things and when you break something, you try to blame the stores." Olly said nothing and left the store. What social skill does Olly need to improve? (Being assertive)

4. Define the words *passive* and *aggressive*. (*Passive* - Not standing up for your rights at all. *Aggressive* - Making threats.)

5. What is the importance of knowing how and when to be assertive?

6. Describe a situation when a person should be assertive.

B-13. MAKING A COMPLAINT

1. Tell what *making a complaint* means. (Protesting against something you feel is wrong or unfair)

2. Tell the three steps for making a complaint. (1. Decide if you have a reason to make a complaint. 2. Make the complaint in an assertive manner. 3. Tell what you want to happen.)

3. Robby was sick in bed. His sister turned on the stereo full blast and Robby decided to protest. He got out of bed, grabbed his sister by the neck and said, "If you don't turn down the stereo, I'm going to hurt you." What social skill does Robby need to improve? (Making a complaint)

4. Tell the acronym you learned to help you remember the skill steps for making a complaint and how the acronym works. (RAT - Reason, Assertive, Tell)

5. Tell something that would be fair to complain about and something that would not be fair to complain about.

6. True or false? People who make complaints are all loudmouths. (False)

B-14. RECEIVING A COMPLAINT

1. Tell what it means to receive a complaint. (When you receive a protest from someone against something you have done or are doing)

2. Tell the five skill steps for receiving a complaint. (1. Listen carefully to the complaint. 2. Decide if you are responsible for what the person is complaining about. 3. If you are responsible, then apologize. 4. Tell what you will do about the complaint. [OR] 5. Ask the person to suggest what to do about the complaint.)

3. Thelma had not done any of her house chores in a long time. When her father expressed his concern, Thelma got defensive and said, "Give me a break! How come I'm the only one you pick on around here? It's not fair." What social skill does Thelma need to improve? (Receiving a complaint)

4. Explain what *making a million excuses* means, and why it is not a good way to receive a complaint.

5. What should you do if you receive a complaint but you are not to blame?

6. Why is it important for everyone to know how to receive a complaint correctly?

B-15. GIVING CONSTRUCTIVE CRITICISM

1. Tell what *giving constructive criticism* means. (Telling a person something that will lead to improvement)

2. Tell the two skill steps for giving constructive criticism. (1. Tell what behavior you want to see improved. 2. Say something positive.)

3. After hearing her sister practice her speech, Violet said, "You look disgusting when you rock back and forth on your feet. Don't do that." What social skill does Violet need to improve? (Giving constructive criticism)

4. Explain the difference between giving constructive criticism and personally insulting someone.

5. Why does it help to say something positive when you give constructive criticism?

6. Give an example of a situation when you might give constructive criticism to a friend.

B-16. ACCEPTING CONSTRUCTIVE CRITICISM

1. Tell what *accepting constructive criticism* means. (Responding appropriately when someone suggests a way for you to improve)

2. Tell the four skill steps for accepting constructive criticism. (1. Stay calm. 2. Listen carefully. 3. Thank the person for the suggestion. 4. Follow the suggestion for improvement.)

3. William's mom pointed out that when he ran, he moved his arm incorrectly and she suggested a way for William to improve. William got angry and said he could run any way he wanted to. What social skill does William need to improve? (Accepting constructive criticism)

4. Tell the difference between receiving a complaint and receiving constructive criticism.

5. Why is it difficult for some people to accept constructive criticism correctly?

6. Complete the following sentence: It is important to be able to accept constructive criticism because . . .

B-17. MAKING AN ACCUSATION

1. Tell what it means to make an accusation. (Blaming someone for doing something wrong)

2. Tell the four skill steps for making an accusation. (1. Decide if you should gather more information before making the accusation. 2. Decide whom you will make the accusation to. 3. Choose the best time and place to make the accusation. 4. Decide what you will say.)

3. Allison jumps to conclusions and blames people for doing things wrong before she has adequate proof. What social skill does Allison need to improve? (Making an accusation)

4. Tell what *jumping to conclusions* means. (Making your decision about a situation before you have all the facts)

5. When you actually accuse someone, what two things should you do? (Tell what you are accusing the person of doing wrong and what proof you have.)

6. Is it better to make an accusation or give someone the "cold shoulder" when the person has done something wrong? Explain your answer.

B-18. DEALING WITH A FALSE ACCUSATION

1. Tell what *being falsely accused* means. (You are blamed for doing something wrong that you have not done)

2. Tell the five skill steps for dealing with a false accusation. (1. Decide if you are guilty of doing what the person is accusing you of doing. 2. If not, then judge whether the accuser is in or out of control. 3. Think about why the person might be falsely accusing you. 4. Think about what you will say or ask to help clear things up. 5. Communicate with the person in a calm manner.)

3. The principal accused Bart of smoking in the school bathroom. Bart did not do it. Bart said sarcastically, "Well, if you think I did it, then I guess I did." What social skill does Bart need to improve? (Dealing with a false accusation)

4. Tell at least two reasons why a person may falsely accuse another person.

5. Complete the following sentence: It is important to stay calm when you are falsely accused because . . .

6. Explain why a person who has lost credibility may be more likely to be falsely accused than someone who is a credible person.

B-19. COMPROMISING/NEGOTIATING

1. Define the words *negotiate* and *compromise*. (Negotiate - Have a discussion with the person you are disagreeing with, to see if you can both come to an agreement. Compromise - Come to an agreement that is acceptable to both people, by each "giving in" a little.)

2. Tell the five skill steps for the social skill of compromising/negotiating. (1. Decide if you and someone else are having a conflict or disagreement. 2. Remind yourself to be flexible and calm. 3. Suggest a solution that might be acceptable to both of you. 4. Find out if your suggestion is acceptable to the other person. 5. If it is not acceptable, then continue to compromise and negotiate until an agreement is made.)

3. Cathy wanted to go to one restaurant and her sister wanted to go to a different restaurant. Cathy said, "If we don't go to the one I want, then I'm not going at all." What social skill does Cathy need to improve? (Compromising/Negotiating)

4. Describe the difference between solving a conflict situation in a win-win way, a win-lose way, and a lose-lose way.

5. True or false? It is possible to negotiate with another person and still not come to an agreement through compromise. (True)

6. Tell what a mediator is and how a mediator can be helpful when there is conflict between two people.

B-20. ACCEPTING CONSEQUENCES

1. Define the word *consequence*. (The result of an action)

2. Tell the two skill steps for accepting consequences. (1. Accept the consequence without arguing or making excuses. 2. Be responsible and follow the consequence.)

3. Duane knew what the fine was for speeding, but he drove fast anyway. When he got stopped and fined by a police officer, Duane argued and said the police officer was being unfair. Duane ended up getting another ticket because he argued. What social skill does Duane need to improve? (Accepting consequences)

4. Describe an action that would have a positive consequence and an action that would bring a negative consequence.

5. What could happen if you do not accept a negative consequence in a mature way?

6. Explain why two people may receive different consequences for doing the same thing.

B-21. EXPRESSING FEELINGS

1. Define the social skill of expressing feelings. (Letting others know the emotions you are experiencing in an appropriate manner)

2. Tell the important tip to remember about expressing feelings. (Don't hide your feelings by keeping them inside.)

3. Whenever Evelyne feels frustrated, embarrassed, afraid, or disappointed, she never tells anyone about it. What social skill does Evelyne need to improve? (Expressing feelings)

4. List six emotions a person can experience.

5. True or false? We are not in control of what we feel. Other people are in control of our emotions. (False)

6. Explain what an "I" statement is.

B-22. DEALING WITH ANGER

1. Define the social skill of dealing with anger. (Recognizing that you are feeling upset and dealing with those feelings in a way that respects the rights of others)

2. Tell the four skill steps for dealing with anger. (1. Be aware of what triggered your anger. 2. Notice your body cues. 3. Use an anger control strategy. 4. Evaluate how well your anger control strategy worked.)

3. Fritz and Glenn both have a problem. When Fritz becomes upset, he usually blows up and gets into trouble. When Glenn becomes upset, he holds his feelings inside. Glenn has developed an ulcer. What social skill do they need to improve? (Dealing with anger)

4. List four body cues that let people know you are feeling angry.

5. Tell what an *anger trigger* is and describe the difference between internal and external triggers.

6. List four anger control strategies.

B-23. DEALING WITH EMBARRASSMENT

1. Define the social skill of dealing with embarrassment. (Feeling uncomfortable or self-conscious and handling those feelings in an appropriate way)

2. List the two skill steps for dealing with embarrassment. (1. Decide if you are embarrassed. 2. Use one of the strategies to help yourself feel less embarrassed.)

3. Helen went to work with a big rip in her pants. Most of the employees laughed at her. She went home and never came back to work that day. What social skill does Helen need to improve? (Dealing with embarrassment)

4. True or false? If you are smart and very careful you can avoid having embarrassing things happen to you. (False)

5. List two body cues that let you know you are feeling embarrassed.

6. List five strategies for reducing embarrassment.

B-24. COPING WITH FEAR

1. Tell what *coping with fear* means. (Recognizing unrealistic fears and working to reduce those fears)

2. Tell the two skill steps for coping with fear. (1. Decide if the fear works for you or against you. 2. If the fear works against you, then take steps to reduce the fear.)

3. Trudy was afraid to give speeches, so she refused to try to give one. What social skill does Trudy need to improve? (Coping with fear)

4. Explain how a fear can work for or against you.

5. Tell five strategies for reducing fears.

6. List three common fears that parents have.

B-25. DEALING WITH HUMOR

1. Define *safe humor* and *unsafe humor*. (Safe humor - Saying or doing something funny that is not at anyone's expense. Unsafe humor - Humor that can hurt someone's feelings or humor that can get you into trouble.)

2. Tell the important tip to remember about safe humor. (Humor is an important aspect in our lives. It helps to reduce stress and makes life more enjoyable.)

3. When Inez first met Gary and found out he was Mexican, she told him a Mexican joke. What social skill does Inez need to improve? (Dealing with humor)

4. Tell what an *attention seeker* is.

5. Give an example of a situation when it would not be appropriate to use humor.

6. Tell two things you can do if you don't understand a joke.

B-26. DEALING WITH FAILURE

1. Define the word *fail*. (Being unsuccessful)

2. Tell the four skill steps for the social skill of dealing with failure. (1. Stay calm and be positive. 2. Think about why you failed. 3. Develop a plan for being successful next time. 4. Try again.)

3. Jesse got an "F" on his civics exam. He got upset and decided never to bother studying for a civics test again. What social skill does Jesse need to improve? (Dealing with failure)

4. Complete the following sentence: Everyone needs to deal with failure because . . .

5. Explain how positive self-talk can be helpful when dealing with failure.

6. Tell three reasons why people fail.

B-27. EXPRESSING AFFECTION

1. Define the word *affection*. (A feeling of attachment or caring one person has for another)

2. Tell the three skill steps for expressing affection. (1. Decide if you care about another person. 2. Decide if you would like to express your affection. 3. Choose a good time, place, and way to express your affection.)

3. Whenever Marty likes a girl, he starts throwing things at her during study hall, and sometimes the girl ends up getting into trouble with the teacher because of it. What social skill does Marty need to improve? (Expressing affection)

4. True or false? Affection means having romantic feelings about a member of the opposite sex. (False)

5. Fill in the blanks. A person can express affection through_____ or_____. (Actions, words)

6. List two benefits of expressing your affection to another person.

B-28. DEALING WITH DISAPPOINTMENT

1. Define the word *disappointment*. (The negative feelings you get when something doesn't work out as planned or when you feel someone has let you down)

2. Tell the two skill steps for the social skill of dealing with disappointment. (1. Decide why you are disappointed. 2. Plan a way to ease your disappointment.)

3. Alexis was looking forward to going shopping with her mom after school. When she got home, her mom called and said she couldn't go shopping because she had to work late. Alexis sat in her dark bedroom for two hours and thought about how miserable she felt. What social skill does Alexis need to improve? (Dealing with disappointment)

4. Explain the difference between being disappointed in yourself and being disappointed in someone else.

5. Tell two things you can do to lessen your feelings of disappointment.

6. True or false? It is not a good idea to sit around and think about how miserable you feel when you are disappointed. (True)

B-29. UNDERSTANDING THE FEELINGS OF OTHERS

1. Tell what *understanding the feelings of others* means. (Recognizing the emotions that other people are experiencing)

2. Tell an important tip to remember about understanding the feelings of others. (People express their feelings in many different ways.)

3. Zach is so into himself that he hardly ever notices when his friends are feeling embarrassed, frustrated, or depressed. What social skill does Zach need to improve? (Understanding the feelings of others)

4. Name three things you can pay attention to if you want to figure out how another person is feeling.

5. Explain why it is important to be able to recognize how others are feeling.

6. Complete the following sentence: People who think only of themselves, and never recognize how others are feeling . . .

POSITIVE COMMENTS

- **I am a good person.**

- **I am a friendly person.**

- **When I use my social skills, I get along better with people.**

Personal Page

Date:_____

Today's class was about the social skill of_____

_____

I will be able to use what I learned today during_____

_____

_____

Today, class was _____

_____

_____

Date:_____

Today's class was about the social skill of_____

_____

I will be able to use what I learned today during_____

_____

_____

Today, class was _____

_____

_____

ATTENDANCE AND DAILY PARTICIPATION POINTS

Date:_____

Students' Names	Attendance (50%)	60%	70%	80%	90%	100%	Total Participation

Comments:

Role Play Critique Sheet

Name of person doing role play: _____

Name of person completing this sheet: _____

---

1. List two positive things you saw in this role play situation.

   -

   -

2. Did the person use all the skill steps (or tips) correctly?   YES   NO
   If not, what skill steps did the person forget to do or have problems with?

3. What did the partner do to help in the role play situation?

4. Could this role play situation really happen?   YES   NO
   Explain your answer.

Student Evaluation Form

Name of Social Skill Unit: _____

	Strongly Agree	Agree	Undecided	Disagree	Strongly Disagree
I understand the skill steps of this social skill.	1	2	3	4	5
It was helpful to role play in class.	1	2	3	4	5
I practiced this social skill enough in class.	1	2	3	4	5
The activity pages were helpful.	1	2	3	4	5
Reading the scripts helped me to understand the skill better.	1	2	3	4	5
The filmstrips/videos (if any) were helpful.	1	2	3	4	5
I know when I should use this social skill.	1	2	3	4	5
I will be able to use this skill correctly outside of class.	1	2	3	4	5
This unit was interesting.	1	2	3	4	5

I liked this unit because _____

_____

_____

The thing I liked least about this unit was_____

_____

If I were the teacher, I would include a section in this unit about _____

_____

_____

_____

An interesting thing for students to do in this unit would be_____

_____

_____

©1989 THINKING PUBLICATIONS
Duplication allowed for educational use only.

SSS: SOCIAL SKILL STRATEGIES (Book B)

Student Name *John D.*

Date _____

A = Acceptable
U = Unacceptable
NA = Not Applicable

	Reading (M-F)	Math (M-F)	History (M-F)	English (M-F)	Social Skills (T-Th)	Physical Education (M-F)	Science (M-W-F)	Drafting (M-S)	At home
Goal #1: Used a tone of voice appropriate to the situation (was not sarcastic).	A U	A U	A U	A U	A U	A U	A U	A U	A U
Goal #2: Made a good impression based on his actions and appearance.	A U NA	A U NA	A U NA	A U NA	A U NA	A U NA	A U NA	A U NA	A U NA
Goal #3: Remembered to ask/request instead of demand/tell when he wanted something.	A U NA	A U NA	A U NA	A U NA	A U NA	A U NA	A U NA	A U NA	A U NA

SIGNATURE & COMMENTS:

NEXT ASSIGNMENT:

WHEN DUE:

PARENT/GUARDIAN SIGNATURE:

Duplication allowed for educational use only.

COOPERATIVE LEARNING ASPECTS

The following eighteen aspects should be considered when planning a cooperative learning lesson (Johnson and Johnson, 1984). Cooperative learning is discussed in Chapter One, pages 4-5 and Chapter Two, page 24.

THE TEACHER'S ROLE IN COOPERATION

Objectives

Specifying Academic and Collaborative Objectives. These need to be specified before the lesson begins.

Decisions

Deciding on the Size of the Group. Once the objectives are clear, the teacher must decide which size of learning group is optimal. Cooperative learning groups tend to range in size from two to six.

Assigning Students to Groups. Questions asked include the following: Homogeneous or heterogeneous in ability? Non-task-oriented and task-oriented students together or separated? Should students select the group or teacher assign? How long should groups stay together?

Arranging the Room. This will be a symbolic message of what is appropriate behavior, and can facilitate the learning groups within the classroom. Members should sit in a circle and be close enough to communicate without disrupting the other learning groups.

Planning Materials. Teachers may wish to distribute materials in carefully planned ways to communicate that the assignment is to be a joint effort.

Assigning Roles. Cooperative interdependence may also be arranged through the assignment of complementary and interconnected roles to group members.

Task, Goal Structure, Learning Activity

Explaining the Academic Task. Several aspects should be considered: Setting the task so that students are clear about assignment; explaining the objectives of the lesson and relating the concepts; defining relevant concepts, explaining procedures, and giving examples; and asking specific questions to check students' understanding of the assignment.

Structuring Positive Goal Interdependence. Communicate to students that they have a group goal and must work collaboratively.

Structuring Individual Accountability. A learning group is not truly cooperative if individual members let others do all the work. In order to ensure that all members learn and that groups know which members to provide with encouragement and help, teachers will need to assess frequently the level of performance of each group member.

Cooperative Learning Aspects (Con't)

Structuring Intergroup Cooperation. Positive outcomes found within a cooperative learning group can be extended throughout a whole class by structuring intergroup cooperation other than through tournament format.

Explaining Criteria for Success. Evaluation within cooperatively structured lessons needs to be based on criteria established for acceptable work. At the beginning of the lesson, teachers should clearly explain the criteria by which the students' work will be evaluated.

Specifying Desired Behaviors. Teachers need to define _cooperation_ operationally by specifying the behaviors that are appropriate and desirable within the learning groups.

Monitoring and Intervening

Monitoring Students' Behavior. Much of the teacher's time after the groups start working should be spent in observing group members in order to see what problems they are having in completing the assignment and in working collaboratively.

Providing Task Assistance. In monitoring the groups as they work, teachers will wish to clarify instructions, review important procedures and strategies for completing the assignment, answer questions, and teach task skills as necessary.

Intervening to Teach Collaborative Skills. While monitoring the learning groups, teachers sometimes find students without the necessary collaborative skills and groups with problems in collaborating. In these cases, the teacher may intervene to suggest more effective procedures for working together and more effective behaviors for students to engage in.

Providing Closure to the Lesson. To reinforce student learning, teachers may wish to summarize the major points in the lesson, ask students to recall ideas or give samples, and answer any final questions they may have.

Evaluating and Processing

Evaluating the Quality and Quantity of Students' Learning. Whatever the product of the lesson, student learning needs to be evaluated by a criteria-referenced system. Group members should also receive feedback on how effectively they collaborated.

Assessing How Well the Group Functioned. Even if class time is limited, some time should be spent talking about how well the groups functioned today, what things were done well, and what things could be improved.

Reprinted with permission